May God's riches
blessings be upon you.

David K. Webb

May you be blessed
by this book!

Christine Henruil

THE WISDOM OF LIFE

THE WISDOM OF LIFE

Letters from Dad

LETTERS FROM
DAVID K. WEBB
COMPILED BY CHRISTINE HENRICHS

Pleasant Word (a division of WinePress Publishing, PO Box 428, Enumclaw, WA 98022) functions only as book publisher. As such, the ultimate design, content, editorial accuracy, and views expressed or implied in this work are those of the author.

Unless otherwise noted, all Scriptures are taken from the Holy Bible, New International Version, Copyright © 1973, 1978, 1984 by the International Bible Society. Used by permission of Zondervan Publishing House. The "NIV" and "New International Version" trademarks are registered in the United States Patent and Trademark Office by International Bible Society.

Scripture references marked KJV are taken from the King James Version of the Bible.

Scripture references marked NASB are taken from the New American Standard Bible, © 1960, 1963, 1968, 1971, 1972, 1973, 1975, 1977 by The Lockman Foundation. Used by permission.

ISBN 13: 978-1-4141-0886-5
ISBN 10: 1-4141-0886-9
Library of Congress Catalog Card Number: 2006937733

TABLE OF CONTENTS

AUTHOR'S NOTE

I want to share my reasons for creating this book.

1. To bring glory to God–the ultimate Father
2. To honor my earthly father–the godliest man I know
3. To preserve these letters for my family to enjoy for generations to come
4. To allow others to also be blessed by the wisdom found in these letters

I want to thank my dad–for the letters, for his wisdom, and for his love. I want to also thank him for allowing something so personal to be made public. I want to thank my mom, my husband, and Heidi Landes for all their help during this project.

Christine Henrichs

INTRODUCTION

Dear Christine,

This will be the final letter I will write before you leave home for college. I plan to write you very often and continue to be a father to you and point you through life and toward becoming a godly woman. For your mother and me, your leaving for college brings bittersweet emotions. We believe you are prepared and well equipped for this step and that you have matured to exactly the right point to now begin the "uncleaving" process. This is a giant step from childhood to adulthood—but one we believe is right, proper, and well timed. We stand behind you every step of the way. We love you and are ready to give counsel, share your feelings and trials, and continue to build our friendship. Yet we will miss you being here and being the child-daughter. We remember well the many experiences and times we have spent as your parents raising you from a mere "Pixie" baby. So if we shed a tear or two, understand that they are shed with joy and sadness together. One of my favorite psalms is Psalm 91. I would like you to read this often while away and trust fully in its promises. I have long planned for this to be your psalm on this occasion.

Psalm 91 speaks of God being your true mother and father—always with you and always protecting, guiding, and giving comfort and refuge. God, the Father, is always there for you and is a real and present Father—this I cannot be since I am only your earthly father. Your mother and I have always prayed even before you were born, the essence of verse 11: "He shall give His angels charge over thee, to keep thee in all thy ways."

We will continue to give you to the Lord and pray that His angels will keep you—protect, guide, mold, and develop you. Please be assured that we will continually and daily pray for you that God's angels will keep you.

We look forward to the excitement of the years to come as we relate more and more as peers and friends. Yet we will always be your parents and covet any and all opportunities to share your life and give you the counsel that comes from life's experiences. Not only because we have had more life experiences, but because of our deep and eternal love for you and because God has ordained and blessed the relationship between us, your parents, and you, our daughter.

1992 — FRESHMAN
YEAR OF COLLEGE
OXFORD, OHIO

Dear Christine,

I so enjoy hearing from you and all that is happening at college–your new friends, the academic challenges, the opportunities for the development of your gifts, and the exciting spiritual environment you can be a part of!

I will be writing about the book of Proverbs, and making it relevant to your time now and in the future. Chapters 1-4 were the basis of the prose I wrote on the "graduation poem" given to you last May.

Our dear firstborn daughter, of whom we are so proud, we write to you of the four essentials to unlock a godly, satisfying, and productive life.

The first, and cornerstone of all the rest, begins with the "fear of the Lord" (Prov. 1:7). Such a fear flows out of reverence and respect for God's lordship and headship in your life. This fear brings His child to awe when confronted with the caring and disciplining love of the Father. Quickly such fear and awe yield praise for the Lord and move the beloved to offer her life to His service.

The second essential conveys a warning for His child. Do not be enticed by the shallowness and deception of the world and the self-centered sinfulness of the humanist. Many will be the opportunities awaiting you, beckoning you to walk in the way of the world. Look with God's wisdom beyond these seductive cries and deep into the hearts of those who urge you. "These men (and women) be in wait for their own blood; they waylay only themselves!" (Prov. 1:18).

The third essential reveals God to you, His child, as He pours out His heart and makes His thoughts known to you. Knowledge from God is information of sound character, trustworthy, everlastingly true and beneficial. Wisdom is seen in the life of the one who walks with God into her daily life. "Accept God's word (revealed through the Scripture) and store up His commands within you" (Prov. 2:1). His Word and command will forever light your way and will never betray you. They will bring you love, joy, and peace—forever elusive to those who turn from His Word. Seek God's knowledge and wisdom as a lamp to your path!

The fourth, and last, essential directs God's child away from a life of folly and frivolity and toward a life of diligence and carefulness. God loves and blesses a disciplined, patient, and industrious worker. Seek His vision and make it your own, persevere toward its achievement. God hates "haughty eyes, a lying tongue, a heart that deceives, feet that are quick to rush into evil, a false witness and a man (or woman) who stirs up dissention" (Prov. 6:17-19). Even as God's Word is a lamp to your path, still you must move with determination down the lighted path.

These four essentials will lead to a life glorifying to God and personalize in your life His promise: "He holds victory in store for the upright, He is a shield to those whose walk is blameless, for He guards the course of the just and protects the way of His faithful ones" (Prov. 2:7-8).

You will experience ups and downs during the next four years but it can be one of the most extraordinary times of growth in your life. Your choices are the key.

Proverbs 5

Let's now look at chapter 5 of Proverbs. Verses 1-6, first of all, ask us to "pay attention"–this is important stuff! The writer is talking to us on two levels–first at the level of the personal flesh (sexual sin) and second at the level of the spiritual being (turning away from God/Christ). He points out that the deceiver or "adulteress" is very alluring and can easily pull us away if we aren't careful. However, it is all "window dressing" and later after the alluring surface wears off, we will be hurt.

In verses 7-14, we are encouraged not even to be in the vicinity ("keep to a path far from her") of the deceiver. God is afraid we will be enticed and we will choose wrongly. This would lead to regret, grief, and sorrow. Often (verses 12-13) we become proud, cocky, and not teachable–we feel we know it all and don't submit ourselves to those people who point us in the right direction.

Verses 15-20 talk about fidelity–being faithful and true to one person (physically, emotionally) and to God and His ways. It speaks of the beautiful and wonderful satisfaction and abundance that come from this choice. It is a mystery but an absolute fact that the physical/sexual relationship between a husband and a wife is so magnified and enriched by waiting until marriage and, of course, faithfulness after. You will be blessed manyfold if you remain faithful to God and His teaching. Verse 20 asks the question: Given such blessing for faithfulness, why choose anything else?

Verses 21-23 tell us that God knows all of our actions and thoughts. Even though your thoughts at times go astray, do not act on them–for it is your deeds that will trap you and lead you in the wrong direction. Sin is sin, in thought or deed, and God will forgive us for our sin if we confess it. But the deeds will lead us closer to the tempter and make us more likely to sin further.

We have just come home from church and several people asked me to send you their greeting. I hope you had a great time of worship and Scripture study; God is really blessing me through the Matthew study.

Proverbs 6

I want to discuss Proverbs 6 with you today. I hope you will have some time to read this letter with your Bible open so you can look at the actual words and text. Verses 1-5 instruct us what to do if we find we have undertaken more than is wise to do. We are to go to the people we need to break our commitment with in humility and confess our problems and ask that they relieve us of our responsibilities. Most of the time, overcommitment occurs when we, in pride, think too highly of our ability or time availability. At other times we have not learned well our limitations or cannot say "no" without feeling less of ourselves. The Scripture asks us to get out of this "trap."

Verses 6-11 warn against laziness and slothfulness. We are to use our time well and efficiently–working daily and not sitting back for long periods of time sleeping and resting. We are to plan ahead and provide when able for the times when we are unable. We have to become a "self starter" and be our own "overseer," and produce for self and family. We can appreciate these wise instructions in physical/material ways, but also relative to interpersonal and spiritual levels. That is, we need to relate to those we love and are entrusted to care for, daily and regularly–not putting it off or missing opportunities. Also our spiritual growth–learning about and relating to God–should not be neglected but regularly participated in.

Verses 12-15 basically show that a person can use all parts of his or her body (that is, can find all kinds of ways and methods) to stir up conflict and disunity. Be careful of that person who always seems to be in the center of conflict and controversy; the Scripture calls him a scoundrel and a villain.

Verses 16-19 list seven things God hates:

1. Pride and self-centeredness
2. Untruthfulness with intent to stir up others; intentionally deceive to cause problems

3. People who kill or physically hurt others–especially without just cause
4. A planner who devises evil plans in his heart
5. People who quickly and willfully desire to do wrong
6. People who gossip and tell lies or slander others
7. People who cause conflict and disunity; some people continually seem to cause problems between others

Verses 20-23 encourage us to never forsake what we learned in a godly home or from godly parents–let these things guide and continually instruct you.

Verses 24-29 again instruct the reader to be careful and stay away from sensual, worldly people and ways. Our senses can betray us and usually our will cannot resist that which our senses desire. Therefore, the Bible tells us not to get too close to the seductive, immoral parts of life. If you don't resist, you will be hurt and your actions will be punished.

The last verses (30-35) contrast the sin of adultery (or unfaithfulness) to other sins. The other sins can be forgiven but there is a significant price required of those caught. But unfaithfulness can never be amended and the wounds can never fully heal. This is very true as I have seen many times in my practice, and a marriage will never be the same when this trust and commitment are betrayed. Likewise, in a spiritual sense, we should never be unfaithful to God; rejecting Him for the world or our own ego needs will result in a major breach in our relationship and trustworthiness in God's eyes. We are still saved, but our usefulness in His kingdom will be forever reduced.

In college, indeed in all of life, we are presented with many opportunities and choices; be careful to choose to stay away from the temptress in body, mind, and spirit. Look deeply into and beyond the things presented to you. Be sure they will bring God glory and that He could dwell in them or their presence. If asked to do something or believe a particular way, ask yourself the question: "Would God be able to be there with me?" If the answer is no, then don't choose that.

Thanks for your recent letter; we really enjoy keeping up with all that is going on now in your life. Your interest in Campus Crusade for Christ and the dorm floor Bible study is particularly exciting to me. I am so excited that you are surrounding yourself with godly, Christian people. But always be cautious and hold all people and things up to the test of Scripture.

Proverbs 7

Proverbs 7 is in most part an allegory. It describes a young man being seduced by a prostitute but really is showing us how the sensual world distracts us from a true walk with God. The young man is described as a "youth who lacked judgment." He is led by his heart and emotional needs and not by the true wisdom that comes from studying and knowing God's heart. The prostitute is described as "loud" and "defiant." In other words, she is demanding, stubborn, and always present. She is movable and seeks out those who would not seek her–she will penetrate our world even when not sought out by us. In verses 14-17 she puts on a religious front that is crafty and designed to entice us away from God. Verses 21-23 show how seductive evil around us can be; however, we also see that the result of giving in to this evil is death. Unfortunately, man sometimes finds out too late that the path of sin leads to death and is denied heaven and fellowship with God.

I've thought of you often this week–I've been praying for your Campus Crusade for Christ retreat. I've also been praying that God would give you courage and discernment as you are presented with "humanism" and the world (as in your English class). We enjoyed having you and Andrea visit last weekend. I thank God that you have found Christian brothers and sisters there at Miami. God promises that for Christians, their true family are those who "do His will"; that is so comforting for me, to realize you have a part of God's family there as well as here. You also, therefore, have a responsibility to be a sister to other Christians there at Miami.

Proverbs 8

I want to call your attention to Proverbs chapter 8. This chapter talks about "wisdom;" this in general refers to God's wisdom that is personified in Christ. When you think about it, Christ is the ultimate expression of God's wisdom (and His love) and it is because of Christ that the Holy Spirit has been able to continue to reveal true wisdom to those who open their hearts to Him. When you read this chapter think of wisdom as being centered in and emanating from Christ.

Verses 1-11 express that God's true wisdom seeks us and pursues us. God really desires His creation to go from "simple" to "prudent" and from "foolishness" to "understanding." In other words He wants us to switch from the world's perspective to His perspective and from that which causes destruction to that which is right and brings about life. Everything God speaks or reveals is true but this truth is only fully revealed to those who are able to recognize Him. Our eyes and heart must be open in order to see and hear this wisdom. This wisdom is greater than anything the world has to offer.

Verse 13 shows us that those with true wisdom grow to hate evil, pride, arrogance, bad behavior, and perverse speech. Verses 14-16 tell us that all power and just behavior come through Him. No person will hold power long in this world except as is permitted by true wisdom. Through Christ and true wisdom come enduring wealth and prosperity. God rewards all who seek Him (verses 17-19).

The relationship between Christ and true wisdom is more direct and explicitly presented from verse 22 on. In verses 22-31 you see the inseparable nature of Christ and God. Verse 31 emphasizes Christ's focus and love–mankind.

The last verses (32-36) show how the person who listens to God, who watches daily to see Him work and who keeps His ways is blessed. Verse 35 promises that whoever finds Him, finds life. It will seem like foolishness to all who have never experienced Him, but to be fully alive is only available to those who allow God's wisdom to govern their lives.

We just returned from "Mr. Steak"–Alice took us out to celebrate my birthday. I had a great time with my family and Alice but I missed having my oldest daughter at the table. Thank you for my card–the words you wrote made my birthday special. As I get older, I've come to value the giving of "the self" by one person to another as the best gift of love. I will treasure your words as a gift of love.

Proverbs 9

Chapter 9 of Proverbs is the last teaching that contrasts wisdom with folly. Remember that Christ is the personification of God's wisdom. Verses 1 and 2 tell us that Christ has prepared the house (heavenly home with God our Father), set the table (remember the banquet table that we as Christians in heaven will share with God/Christ) and prepared the meal (God's sustenance that will be eternal and always refreshing and filling). In verse 3 the maids are Christians who serve as evangelists–seeking out those who would become fellow believers. Verses 4-6 emphasize that those who are yet to come to Christ lack character and judgment. But if they come to Him, eat His food (His Word), and drink His wine (the Holy Spirit), then they will "live and walk in the way of understanding." That is, they will know true life and understand the things of God's world. This is in contrast to man's wisdom–false understanding and life that doesn't give lasting joy or peace.

Verses 7-9 tell us that trying to witness to a "mocker or wicked man" (one who is cold to God and refuses to see the possibility of Christ as God's Son and our Savior) brings pain and abuse to the Christian. But instructing and disciplining a wise man (one who is positive and open to the salvation message) will cause him to appreciate you and grow further in the Lord. There are many people who are stone cold to spiritual things and, as the Pharisees, cannot be reached. We need to allow the Holy Spirit to help us discern who is cold and who is open.

Verse 10 repeats a truth that we have discussed before. To gain understanding of true wisdom, we must have an awesome respect for the Lord. Verses 11 and 12 tell us that there is a reward for becoming wise. Generally, we will live longer and suffer less. We will be filled with joy and peace. To reject God and His wisdom will cause he who rejects to be the loser.

Folly and the result of seeking her are described in verses 13-18. Folly in the preceding chapters of Proverbs is seen as a prostitute or harlot. Here folly is summarized: folly, or the world's way, is "undisciplined" (wild and reckless) and "without knowledge" (accepts no truth to direct its actions). The world sits and waits for man to walk by so she can try to seduce him to her ways. She attracts the "simple" (poor or lacking in good character) and those "who lack judgment" (unable to know right from wrong). Wicked ways have temporary and fleeting sweetness but ultimately lead to fellowshipping with the "dead" (in Christ). These verses summarize the conflict presented to each of us: life (God's way) or eventual death (man's/Satan's way).

Thanks for your recent letter–I enjoy being kept updated on your life. Did you talk with your calculus teacher? The course, or the way it is being taught, seems to be more difficult or unconventional than you had imagined. I urge you not to be discouraged about calculus or your academic ability simply based on this course and its teacher. Persevere and spend the time needed.

Proverbs 10

Proverbs 10 begins the larger part of this book. It is full of wisdom. We will need to move slower and think carefully. Let us start with verse 1 of chapter 10. How do we, as sons or daughters, bring joy or grief to our parents and to God, our perfect spiritual parent? First Chronicles 22:12 says we bring joy when we seek "discretion and understanding" and when we "keep the law of the Lord." First Chronicles 1:9-12 gives us an example of a wise son (Solomon) who sought wisdom by seeking God's heart and mind instead of wealth and honor. Therefore, seeking God's perspective is of eternal value, makes one wise, and brings joy to God. In Genesis 26:34-35 and 27:46 we see what brings grief to God (and the human parent)–marriage of our children to ungodly, humanistic ideals and goals. The Hittites were a living symbol of all that is against the God of Israel. For our children to embrace the world and forsake godly principles brings the parent sorrow and grief.

I've thought of you often this weekend–your concert and your church solo. I have prayed they both went well and that you grew musically and as a maturing servant of God. Mom read your letter today in church concerning your experience with the All-State choir and conductor. You should know that you were a real blessing to many this morning.

I'd like to share with you some thoughts on Proverbs 10:2 and 3. "Ill-gotten treasures are of no value, but righteousness delivers from death." A parallel Old Testament scripture is Jeremiah 17:11–the man who gains riches by unjust means will find they will soon be depleted and in the end he will have deep regrets and grieve deeply (be a fool). A good example of people who demonstrate this point is found in the book of Esther. Haman is a good portrait of one who has obtained treasures wrongly. Mordecai, on the other hand, shows us the result of right living (righteousness). A person (such as Haman) who connives, plots, and climbs over other people for self-glory and material gain might seem for a while to be succeeding. However, sooner or later (even if it is as late as the time of judgment for all people), this person's motives and his low character will be made visible. His treasures then (if any still exist) will have no value to save him from death and destruction. Alternatively, the righteous person (one with godly values, morals, and selflessness) like Mordecai will, because of his character, ultimately be delivered from eternal damnation and be rewarded for his godly service. Many times, but not always, this righteousness will also prevent us from deep grief, regrets, and unhappiness in this life.

In verse 3, Solomon again contrasts the righteous with the wicked. Despite famine or lack of abundance, the Lord will give strength and joy to those who trust Him. Habakkuk 3:17-19 is a vivid illustration of this promise. God provides materially, emotionally, and spiritually for His children. Contrast this with the "rich man" in Luke 12:16-21 who was only concerned with material gain. Jesus calls this man a fool–for he worked all his life for this. What a waste! We are not in charge in God's world, and our standards will never bring long lasting and eternally valuable rewards unless they conform to those of God.

I'm sure you are hard at work preparing for all the pre-Christmas deadlines. Thanks for calling when you arrived at Miami. I guess it is natural for a dad to worry about his daughter when she is driving alone. Again, sorry I missed your choral concert. Your mom and I had to split up so we could be a part of all our wonderful daughters' events.

Let's look at Proverbs 10:4 and 5 today. These verses can be taken literally as they apply to our daily life and spiritually as they apply to our walk with God. Literally, verse 4 emphasizes that to be wealthy we must not be lazy. It is true that in this world a person is judged by his or her effectiveness. Please read 2 Thessalonians 3:7-12. However, it is also very true that diligence and discipline in learning about God pay off in the wealth of God's blessings. For example, laboring in Scripture provides knowledge of God along with joy, peace, and real excitement. Ruth chapters 2-4 present how material and spiritual wealth are linked to hard work, diligence, and obedience.

Verse 5 reminds us that we should never lose opportunities. The word "gather" means to capture the moment and use it effectively, while the word "sleep" indicates inactivity and rejecting opportunity. To succeed in life you must identify and act on opportunities. Spiritually, this principle applies as well. God gives us opportunities to know and serve Him. The diligent disciple must be constantly alert to these and not hesitate in taking full advantage of them.

I've been thinking about you often in the last two days—wondering how the new semester is going. I sure enjoyed having you home over Christmas. I am impressed with your continued growth and maturity in all areas of your life. I continue to pray for you daily.

Proverbs 10:6-7 contrasts the righteous and the wicked. The righteous are those who seek to do what is pleasing to God. The wicked use others wrongly and distort truth in order to please themselves. Proverbs tells us that the righteous will be blessed. Be careful that we don't interpret blessings as external good things or happenings; although, I feel these do increase for the righteous. Blessedness for the Christian is guaranteed inner peace and joy if we stay in a vital relationship to God. One of the most exciting and fulfilling aspects of my life is the joy, peace, and wealth I feel after I study the Word of God. The wicked heart is consumed with hurting others and being hurt while often such a person is hypocritically pleasant on the surface. In verse 7 we see that even after the person is gone, the memory of the righteous person will minister and give positive influence to others, but the memory of the wicked will be either forgotten or will continue to negatively influence and hurt people.

Verse 8 contrasts the "wise in heart" and a "chattering fool." This verse tells us that the wise person can accept authority and be taught by those placed above him by God, but the fool doesn't accept teaching and stubbornly continues to reject authority. The fool, therefore, never learns and must be oppressed (controlled by force). Daniel 5:18-23 shows Nebuchadnezzar, who was once wise but became a fool—we see his ruin.

How's everything there in Oxford? I have had a number of opportunities to pray with patients these last several weeks. I've been learning a lot about "having in mind the things of God, not of man" (Matt. 16:23). If you are led into medicine please be aware of the awesome privilege you will have to touch people for God and to participate in the building of His kingdom.

Let's look at Proverbs 10:9-10 today. Verse 9 tells us that the person who has integrity will walk above reproach. He will not be able to be criticized relative to his character. People may not agree with him but they will not be able to attack his honesty or reliability. In contrast, the person who "takes crooked paths" or finds easy and at times dishonest ways of doing things will eventually be "found out" or seen for his poor character, thereby losing credibility.

In verse 10 Solomon instructs us in two other areas of godly wisdom. The person who "winks maliciously" says one thing but intends to do the opposite. This will cause himself and others grief. Sure, such a person may fool others for years, but he will be miserable inside—robbed of peace and joy. The "chattering fool" is the person who doesn't take time to really listen to another or to God. We need to listen to others who may need to tell us hard things in love for our growth or who may need to express a great need or deep hurt. A person who will not listen is headed for ruin because this is a sign of pride and self-centeredness.

I know that you will be coming home in a couple of days but I wanted to write you again before you arrive–I plan to leave it in your room and not send it.

Proverbs 10:11-12 are the verses we will study now. In verse 11 Solomon is teaching that the words of righteous people will be a blessing and refreshment to others. God loves His creation and wants to minister to it in times of need. His children should and can give life and vitality to others. The wicked, however, will communicate destruction, negativism, hostility, contempt, and hatred. This will not build up another but will tear him down in a merciless manner.

In verse 12 Solomon teaches us that "hatred" will create and accentuate disunity, causing gossip, slander, and cruelty to another. Or looking at this verse in reverse, where we see disruption of unity or people relating cruelly to one another, we will find people who desire to see another harmed, broken, or estranged. See 1 John 3:15. In contrast, love will overlook a person's errors, shortcomings, and faults. It is this attitude that leads to true friendships and healthy marriages. God looked beyond our faults and in love sought to restore us to Him through sacrificing His own Son.

We just arrived home from Miami. I was very proud of you–your character and your hard work and talent. God has a great vision and love for you. Work hard on zoology; don't be discouraged, you will get it. Erin had a great time–thanks for being a good big sister.

Proverbs 10:13 discusses wisdom–where it can be found and the results of godly versus ungodly wisdom. Wisdom (truth applied correctly) is always from God, because God is light (a biblical term for absolute truth). A discerning person is the one who distinguishes God's true wisdom from the relative, situational, self-centered, self-righteous opinion of man. Discernment can only be available to the person who has a vital, dynamic personal relationship with God and has an active, trusting prayer and study life. Solomon is an excellent example of a man who is discerning and thereby possesses God's wisdom (1 Kings 3:5-28). In contrast, King Rehoboam (1 Kings 12:8-19) is a man who heeds the advice of his worldly, ungodly friend over the advice of godly men of counsel. He exemplifies what Proverbs 10:13 calls "him who lacks judgment"–that is a person who judges wrongly and turns away from God. The result is self-destruction over time, or overt pain inflicted upon him by the same world that gave him the advice. Solomon was given more wisdom for his proper discernment as well as wealth and power, which he didn't even seek.

Verse 14 continues the contrast. The wise man is willing to learn and accumulate knowledge (God's truth). Second Timothy 3:14-15 is a truly great reference to this teaching. In contrast, the fool will by his statements bring himself to ruin. He will lack peace and joy and will be betrayed by the world and ultimately fall into despair. Acts 13:6-11: Elymas is a good example of such a fool and his fate.

Please enjoy your trip next weekend, but be careful and use good judgment. Consider having a time each day during spring break when you and your friends can spend time together with the Lord.

Proverbs 10:15 states the world's standards for success and wealth. Wealth here is a term relative to a person's possessions ("fortified city"), with poverty being a lack of possessions ("ruin"). In contrast is Jesus' story of the rich man and Lazarus in Luke 16:19-31. Here we see the way it will be in eternity and we see that the values and standards for success will be opposite to those of the world. The scheming and striving for wealth in this world often causes one to forget compassion and spiritual growth. This will lead to grieving and regret in eternity. This doesn't mean that wealth and success in this world automatically lead to this situation, but great caution should be exercised, and one must always be ready to put his or her own needs and desires aside. Never sacrifice spiritual wealth for worldly wealth.

Proverbs 10:16 states that the labor ("wages") of the person walking rightly with God will bring him life. This is both eternal life and the abundant life of God's Holy Spirit within His child yielding joy, peace, and love. This life cannot be bought by the money of the wicked. Instead, the production of the ungodly will yield only punishment. This is eternal punishment and present misery and loneliness. The latter is denied by this world, but is understood by the person who comes to know truth and the excitement and reward of the life of the disciple. Romans 8:6-8 is a great parallel scripture.

We are all looking forward to your dance presentation this weekend. In only a few weeks you will be home for awhile and then off to be a camp counselor for the summer. Time really seems to fly. I'm still looking at potential cars–it might be fun if you and I could look together during the month of May.

Let's continue in Proverbs 10. Verse 22 talks about how, for the person seeking to serve God, His involvement in his life will bring great "wealth." That is, through our obedience to Him as a response to His love for us, we will receive the rich and lasting joy and peace of His Holy Spirit. This is why we are wealthy. God never promises life will be free of tribulation but that stress, pain, and suffering come from the world; He is not capable of harming His loved ones.

Verse 23 declares that a "fool" finds some perverted pleasure in his evil conduct. This is contrasted with the "man of understanding" who will have "delight" as he is blessed with God's insights and perspectives on life and eternity. How sad it is for people to have to settle in life for momentary, self-centered, cruel, and self-demeaning thrills when something so much better is available.

The outcome of these two verses is seen in verse 24. What the wicked dreads will eventually happen. Calamity, misery, loneliness, and lack of true peace and love will finally overtake them and defeat them. Ultimately this will lead to death and damnation. But, for the righteous, their desire will be achieved–in this life by the abundance given via the Holy Spirit and eventually in eternal fellowship with our Creator.

This will be the last letter I will be able to write before you finish your freshman year at Miami. Needless to say, I am proud of you–proud most of all for the character qualities I've seen portrayed in your actions and choices. Godly character is much more desired and brings greater joy than any human accomplishment. It is ironic that a world so deplete of godliness still frequently admires and rewards godly characteristics. You being chosen as "Dancer of the Week" despite being far from the best dancer in the troupe (so you tell me) is proof of this statement.

Let's continue in Proverbs 10. Verse 25 summarizes the lesson of Daniel 6:4-24. When trouble enters a person's life, the person who is motivated by worldly, self-centered interests will buckle and fall. But those who walk according to God's standards will not fall but will stand forever. If we are not self-centered, then the assault to one's self will not destroy us.

Verse 26 talks about the "sluggard"–a person who is of no use to God in His kingdom's work. This person is as repulsive to God who created Him as vinegar is to our taste or smoke is to our eyes. The Christian who will not give himself to God in lordship is a sluggard. Please always ask yourself the question: "How is this decision, action, or attitude going to build up God's kingdom and make me useful to Him?" See Luke 19:20-26 as a parable example for this proverb.

Well, only one more week left of your summer camping/counseling experience. I've been praying that God has been revealing Himself and instructing you in His ways, via the various experiences you've had this summer. It is really exciting to realize that when we give ourselves to God, He is faithful and uses many different life experiences to develop us into His children.

Proverbs 10:29-30 contrasts the fate (now in this world and eternally in heaven) of God's people (those who are called and respond to Him) compared to those who reject God's way (via Christ) in favor of their own human desires/needs. In verse 29, Solomon assures us that the righteous will always find a refuge (protection, strength, time of recovery and refreshment, and nurturance) in God's ways. This may sometimes give us an emotional warmth and overt feeling of His presence; but at times it becomes a trusting reliance on His ways (versus man's ways) that in the end, or over the long term, will lead us to true life. In contrast, the wicked (not following God) will come to ruin, if not now or in the near future, certainly in judgment. Verse 30 further assures us that the righteous will never be uprooted (taken or torn away from Him and His refuge); we will abide with God/Christ now and forever. This is His promise–again not always emotionally felt but believed in trust and faith. Fortunately God rarely makes us fully rely on faith for future answers to our needs/hurts, but gives us enough (maybe not the total) of His direct and felt presence so we can believe (trust) for the rest. Perhaps the more mature in Him we are, the less we need immediate verifications. The wicked, in contrast, will have no inheritance ("remain in the land").

1993 — Sophomore Year of College

Oxford, Ohio

Dear Christine,

I pray that the persecution you face by your teacher, many other students (peers) and the "worldly pressures of a secular, humanistic university" will make you thrive and mature in your walk. As a father I find myself a bit fearful when I think of the pressures you face. I realize that these college years will be a critical time for you–to either really catch God's vision for you, or to succumb to the humanistic secular pressures. I am assured in my soul that God will hold you close to Him and you will continue to seek Him. Stay firm in your English class, be loving and kind–an attractive witness to what God can do in a person–and hold firm to your roots and your Christian commitment.

Proverbs 11

Proverbs 11:4-8 speaks to the general theme of the fate of the righteous person, compared to that of the wicked. Remember as you look at these verses that righteousness is the state we enjoy because (only because) we have sought and accepted Christ's work on the cross and now have a renewed and changed life. The wicked person is not inherently a worse person than we are, but has shunned God's offering of a new life through Christ. Verse 4 tells us that "wealth"–often the life goal of worldly (wicked) people–is worthless when we are at our final judgment (Revelation 6:12-17; 20:12-15, and the story of Noah in Genesis). But our righteousness, God's salvation accepted by us, protects us not from physical death but from eternal separation from God (eternal damnation). Verse 5 tells us that those who are right with God have a straight (unencumbered) path to endless glory, but the wicked are never to taste this because of their rejection of God ("brought down by their own wickedness"). Verse 6 tells us that it is the new heart of the one saved by God that will deliver him or her to a new life here on earth (with fruits of the Spirit–Galatians 5:22-23) and then eternal life. But the "unfaithful" (do not have a trusting belief in God's salvation) are continually enslaved ("trapped") by their evil (unregenerated) hearts. Verse 7 confirms again that the wicked person has no hope after his death at the end of this life. All his power, wealth, and expectation are valueless and "come to nothing." How sad! To deceive yourself and seek the self-centered human life for this instant of existence (this life) and give up eternity with God (infinity compared to an instant). Verse 8 tells us that this righteous person is rescued from trouble–that is, we can have deep spiritual and emotional peace and joy in this life, despite some difficult circumstances; and then unbelievable and total peace and joy forever in the next life. The troubles multiply and consume the non-Christian in this life (I see this often in my medical practice) and then forever in hell.

Thanks for going to Pittsburgh with Mom to be with your grandparents. It meant a lot to them and to us. I was interested to read of your date to the "Christian men's party." I think you're very wise in exercising prayerful caution concerning dates and social events. Be assured that God will bless you for your choices with a good Christian man as a husband.

We will begin with Proverbs 11:10-11, then add verse 14 today. Verses 10 and 11 demonstrate and speak of the moral state of the people being the determinant of national and municipal blessing. When those who are seeking to obey God ("righteous") are able to exert influence in and upon a city or nation ("prosper"), the city rejoices because it prospers, grows, knows success, and has dominance. Verse 11 continues this theme; through the right work, obedience, and God-centeredness of the leaders, the city is blessed by God and receives benefits (is "exalted"). But by the words, deeds, example, and teaching of those who are apart from God (especially if they are leaders), the city will undergo decline and eventual destruction. Verse 14 explains that a nation, city, or any organization that does not have proper godly guidance at its head will not succeed, but will fail; but when leaders receive godly advice and then obey it, that nation, city, or organization will prosper and have victory. The United States was founded and initially led by godly, righteous people who accepted godly advice; high morals and Christian values were valued and taught. The country prospered. Many grieve that this is disappearing from our country and our leadership; the ungodly (worldly) and wicked (led by Satan) have control and we see loss of God's blessing and loss of prosperity.

Grandpop is improving; the tumor was a cancer but the tissue analysis showed that it was removed fully. We need to continue praying for his healing–it really was a gift from God that it was discovered early.

Verse 16 of Proverbs 11 is a good one. The writer tells us that a "kind hearted" woman gains respect. First Samuel 25 shows us some qualities of kindheartedness in the person of Abigail. Such a person doesn't insist on her own way (even if she deserves it or has it coming rightfully), she is wise and insightful, and gives way (on nonessential or unworthy issues) to others in the short term in order to affect some change or influence another in the long term. She is humble and other-person centered. But because these traits are godly and so extraordinary, they almost always bring respect and admiration, and enhance the personal value of such a woman. The opposite (Nabal in 1 Samuel 25) of kindhearted is ruthless–the quality of self-centeredness driving a desire to have your needs met (even the ugly ones) at the expense (brutal if necessary) of others. Such a person will gain power and wealth (possibly) but at a great devaluating personal expense. Also, either in this life or surely in the next, he (she) will be seen for what he really is–he will pay dearly.

Verse 17 is a parallel one. The kind person will gain in personal benefit–how she is viewed or regarded, her attractiveness to other people, her self-image and how she is loved and cared for by people in this life, and by God in heaven. Also such a person is going to be used greatly by God here in His kingdom. The cruel man will cause his own demise (for sure)–definitely in how he is related to and regarded by others, and when he is rewarded after death.

I was honored that you called me to read the letter you wrote to Chad. I will always be available for you and to be of help in your decisions and concerns. Continue to make this issue a prayer concern and be at peace.

PS–Your mom is one of the most kindhearted people I've ever known.

Proverbs 11:18-21 discusses a common theme: the wicked versus the righteous. Remember that in Proverbs, the wicked are not in relationship with God while the righteous have a personal relationship with God via Christ. In verse 18, the rewards of the two are contrasted. The wicked person gets what he thinks is a good reward for his ungodly, self-centered loving–the world seems to reward this. But these rewards are deceptive because they actually lead to destruction and misery. The person who is right with God will reap true (lasting, satisfying, eternal) reward. More generally but also more poignantly is the description in verse 10. The righteous attain life while the person who pursues himself will go to his death. Verse 20 contrasts the two from God's perspective. He delights in "those whose ways are blameless." Surely this can't mean that we must be perfect! No, we become blameless as a result of Christ's work on the cross. Finally, verse 21 assures us that despite the affirmation given by the world to the unrighteous, ultimately the wicked will be punished. A life lived apart from God is always an unsettled, joyless pursuit of that which will bring happiness.

This past week has been a really busy one for me at the office—many needy people (physically, emotionally, spiritually, and relationally)!

I really love my work as a physician, especially when I can connect it with my love of God and the life-sustaining power of His spirit for our lives. It is amazing how people respond and are very grateful for my praying with them as they are encountering life's problems. It is so important that Christian doctors strive to see their work as their ministry also–loving our patients with God's love should be the backbone of our practice. What an opportunity physicians have!

Proverbs 11:28 speaks about this same theme. It asks the question, what are true riches and what are the consequences of the two different general types of riches? Truly rich people know the joy and peace of serving God in their lives and participating in His kingdom and being a part of His miraculous and real involvement with His creation. Such people can receive and give godly love because of their fellowship with God. The righteous person seeks to hear God speaking to him/her (not generically but specifically) and then to obey. This begins a fantastic, fulfilling, privileged adventure in life–your toil becomes work (work is taking part in God's ongoing creation activities). This then makes one feel really alive and satisfied beyond description–"thrive like a green leaf." This is how my practice of medicine can make me feel if (and when) I allow myself to serve God as a doctor!

But the person who seeks worldly riches and is disobedient to God's desire to orchestrate his/her life will fall. What does it mean to fall? To fall is to be dead–unsatisfied in the soul, to possess but want, to strive and grow weary, to settle into the monotony of life, to become disillusioned, cynical, and ungrateful, and so on. When we cut ourselves off from God and seek what the world tells us is desirable, we turn from being truly alive. God can provide the things of our heart (worldly things) as a gift and out of His love, but seeking them only will never satisfy.

I've thought of you several times today knowing you are beginning a new semester. By the time you receive this letter I will have probably called to see what classes and professors you ended up with. I have been praying about this.

Let's look at Proverbs 11:29-30. Verse 29 speaks to parents about how they live their lives in the presence of their children. Parents set the tone and direction of the family. If they choose worldly or evil standards by which to live, they will lead the whole family into trouble. Trouble can be manifested in many ways, but most importantly as estrangement between God and His children leading to deep spiritual isolation. The traits that will be learned will be fleeting and valueless like the wind. The person who society sets up to be in charge is really a fool from God's perspective. In reality that person will be a servant to the person who has God's wisdom.

Verse 30 tells us that the result of living a life in fellowship with God will be to win souls to God. The "tree of life" indicates a person who is living and growing, nourished by true living water because of his relationship to God. Therefore, a wise person is one who lives his life in such a way that others are attracted by it and can be brought to know true life because of it.

This is the coldest day and night I can ever remember experiencing. However, I'm sitting here in my library in sheer delight with my faithful collie dog beside me, a roaring fire in my fireplace, and a good cup of black coffee, writing to you from the Word of God.

Proverbs 11:31 and 12:1 are related. In 11:31 the writer is talking about "due" not in terms of positive, comfortable things, but in terms of the loving rebukes or corrections that God will give to His children. He will do this in order to have us receive His blessings and for us to serve Him in His kingdom. We live in a tough, evil-controlled world and in order for us to survive and serve Him, we must be directed, refined, and molded by God. This loving correction is nothing compared to the painful, final, and terrible judgment that those who reject God will receive.

Proverbs 12

In 12:1 the writer tells us that the Christian who accepts and positively regards God's discipline is a person who understands life from the perspective of eternity and through God's eyes. The person who resists and hates this refining is not teachable and prefers to follow his own will to that of God—how short-sighted and blind! (See 1 Peter 4:17 and 18.)

I put your nameplate on your jewelry box yesterday. I hope that you will remember us when you open the box for a pair of earrings or a necklace–remember that we love you. How are your classes? I am anxious to see, as the semester goes on, what God's reasons were for you taking these classes with these professors. I encourage you to listen for the answer.

Proverbs 12:2-3 will be the subject of today's comments. As I studied these verses, I was reminded of Psalm 1. A "good man" is contrasted to a "crafty man." A good man is one who acknowledges his status as a child of God and is therefore obedient to Him. A crafty man is self-centered and is out to manipulate the world for his own end. He is also flagrantly opposed to God having any right in his life. A good man will be blessed by God while the crafty one is condemned. Certainly this ultimately relates to eternal destiny but it also applies to this life. I am thoroughly convinced that despite outward appearances, a worldly/crafty man cannot be inwardly content or at peace. This is because he has rejected the very mold he was created in and he has tried to control a world created by God. The good man can never be brought down or defeated by life's circumstances. He will flourish because he is nourished directly by God who is his Creator and the Creator of the world we live in.

How are your classes coming? I know they are hard and that you are spending a great deal of time with them. I do hope the material is interesting to you. I have great confidence in you but realize the demand and at times emotional discomfort such a schedule brings. Don't look too far ahead, persevere, lean on God and His strength, and remember I will be praying for you all the harder.

Proverbs 12:4 is a verse about the godly wife and is greatly expanded in Proverbs 31. The godliness of this woman is not because she is a wife or mother, but because she has godly character and this godly character is manifested in her role as a wife and mother. Proverbs speaks of this woman as having "noble character" as contrasted to being "disgraceful." The woman of noble character is her husband's crown. She brings great honor and value to her husband. He will love and exalt her and proudly walk through life with her. Without her he is much less valuable, less honorable, and less influential. In contrast, the woman who brings disgrace upon her husband by her slothful, lowly, fleshly ways is like decay in his bones. That is, her behavior and heart will weaken his structure and he will collapse. His life will not be useful to God in His kingdom.

I'm still really happy for you that you will be taking chemistry from your desired professor–a real answer to prayer. I've been growing in my confidence and obedience to prayer. I'm convinced God really wants to hear from us and wants to answer our prayers to our benefit (although not always as we hope or in the time frame we desire).

Proverbs 12:5-7 seems to go together. Verse 5 discusses "plans" and "advice." The person walking in communication with God makes plans that are proper, sensitive, caring, beneficial, and honorable to God. Plans imply the inner thought process–our strategy or means to accomplish. The wicked person deceives himself and others with his advice. The Hebrew word for advice focuses again on the inner mental process. Verse 6 concentrates on the speech that emanates from the inner thoughts (plans, advice). Because the thoughts of the wicked are impure, the works cause damage and pain. But the speech of the godly person has a positive, constructive, helpful effect on others. In verse 7 we see that eventually the person whose inner thoughts and schemes are deceitful and not in harmony with God's heart will be undone and tragically "no more." However, the person whose thoughts and speech reflect God will stand firm.

We had a nice Valentine's Day celebration yesterday evening since we all are on different schedules today. I found Mom a 1930s art deco signed print at an antique shop that was dirty and in a frame that was falling apart. Erin and I bought it and we reframed it into an oval frame–it is really nice now. It has a woman holding some roses and says, "The message of Roses." I thought it had meaning for your mom and I since I enjoy giving her two roses every Friday.

Proverbs 12:8 is a worthy proverb to remember. A person is recognized as valuable and wise by both the natural man and the spiritual man. The man, however, with a warped mind (delighting on perverse, cruel, and violent misuses of the body) is regarded negatively by everyone. Ironically, the warped person seems, in our world, to get the spotlight too often, while the wise person is placed on a shelf and only taken down when one seriously wants a good example and person. I think that deep in each of us is that remnant of God that wants for our own what God wants for us–good, wholesome, high character in obedient and faithful people. Also, down deep in each is the silent recognition of the lawlessness of the overtly warped person. Please study Judges 7-9.

It was so good to have you home for a day or two–it was really great to see and hear how God has been showing His love to you. Remain steadfast in your desire for Christian character, purity, and vision. Be wise in Him and wary of Satan's temptations and traps. I have prayed many times about the concerns you shared with me before this semester began–it was, and is, great to hear of the answers God has provided.

Proverbs 12:9 exhorts us to be humble and hardworking versus having a pompous display and in reality having nothing. On the surface and to the casual observer it is better to appear to be common, having adequate goods and situations but not calling attention to yourself; while because of hard work, perseverance, and good judgment ("sober living") you really have a great deal. The person like this doesn't have a need for public approval but has a healthy self-worth that allows her to make mature, wise use of her resources–for the whole family. Opposing such a person is another who will sacrifice (unwisely) for himself (and those who depend upon him) the necessary, practical, "life-giving" things in order to gain superficial public recognition. Such a person would do anything for approval–even to the point of death (not eating). So also is the person who will trade an authentic walk with God (health and life giving) for man's praise that will in time lead only to death (spiritual death–succumb to sin and temptation of the world). Pivotal to all this is the necessity of feeling loved and valuable and then not needing this from the world.

I continue to pray for you and all your classes and the opportunities God gives you to grow as a godly Christian woman. I encourage you to practice "seeing" God's involvement and His expressed love in your daily activities. I've begun meditating on the day (late in the evening) and stretching myself to see God's hand on my life and the lives of those I love. I know He loves you and desires to be fully involved with all aspects of your daily life.

Proverbs 12:10 is interesting because it defines (in part) a righteous man as one who cares for the needs of his animal. Such a person has a character that leads him to be caring, kind, generous, and sensitive even to an animal–a beast that cannot acknowledge such caring and therefore gives very little back. The person acts not out of self-interest and "what's in it for me" motives, but because they are truly of that character. Such character is described as righteous, or as of God; therefore the ultimate one who cares is God–He gives to us unconditionally and regardless of our ability or inclination to give back. The wicked (self-centered, ego-centric) person is so motivated by wrong self-exalting motives that even if he does what seems to be kind, it really is a manipulative, misleading, and therefore "cruel" act toward another. This is not God's character, nor should it be the character we seek.

Concerning your spring break mission trip to Mexico, I appreciate having the letter you sent me, describing more details about your week. I am really excited for you because God is planning to speak to you and meet you in that place, even while you do physical work. He will expand your view of the world and God's activity in other parts of His kingdom. You will better understand the needs and circumstances of other people in more difficult settings, your strengths and weaknesses, the value and importance of faithfulness and obedience, and the need for reliance on prayer. You will discover areas of your heart you didn't even know existed and an enlarged or more detailed vision of what He wants from Christine Webb and much more. I will pray three times each day for you while you are gone.

I can't wait to hear of your trip and work in Mexico. By now you are completing your first day back from spring break and I imagine you are tired. Well, forget this line of writing; I just talked with you on the phone. I thank God that all went well and that the time was profitable. You will continue to see God's way in this adventure, and to be blessed by it, not only now but also in the months and years to come.

God doesn't make mistakes; He chose you to go there at this time in your life for His reasons as He matures you and builds His kingdom.

Proverbs 12:11 encourages us to work hard and invest ourselves in efforts that require patience, perseverance, hard work, sweat, and toil. Practically, we are encouraged that good, valuable, and abundant results are yielded only when we spend the time and effort, at times even to the point of giving up–yet persevering and reaching back for added effort, relying often on God when we are used up. This parable can be applied to God's Word–when we study God's revelation to us (via the Word and His ongoing personal relationship to us) we gain truth, wisdom, intimacy, and a wonderful feeling of being loved. On the other hand, the person that avoids hard work and study, and chases after the easy way (fantasies), believing that one can grow and know truth by shortcuts and schemes, doesn't think wisely and logically. Compare 2 Timothy 3:14-17.

Verse 12 further tells us that the righteous (those who seek often and become changed by God, more like Christ) send down roots that make them able to bear good fruit and grow strong. Roots are the source of substance and stability that allow a hardy plant that is able to withstand the elements. The person "grounded" in God and His Word will be able to stand strong in the world and yield good fruit. The wicked (those who reject God and His ways) seek to take for themselves (without earning it) the plunder (that which is ruthlessly and unethically acquired) that evil men get in this world. They focus on the world's "glitter" and even take that away from others like themselves. (See 2 Kings 5:20-27.)

As you wrestle and sweat through the tough courses and roads that lead you to become a doctor and a strong, mature Christian, remember you are "working" the land and establishing righteous "roots." Eventually you (and God through you) will flourish and yield abundant food. Stay tough but remember you aren't alone, God and His Holy Spirit are with you.

By now at least two of your tests will be completed–be assured that I have prayed frequently over this last week for your success on them. Mom said that you and your friends shared at the Crusade meeting about your Mexico trip—how was it received and how did you feel about the trip as you shared?

Proverbs 12:13-14 carries a similar theme—the effect of our speech on others. I am convinced of the underestimation of the power of the spoken word to influence good or evil. As Christians we need to respect the words we say and be sure that they reflect a recreated Christ-centered heart. An evil man is one who is not in relationship with God and therefore his heart, mind, actions, and words reflect his self-centeredness and chosen excommunication from truth and wisdom. Such a person, via his talk, will repeatedly cause himself trouble. He will leave himself open to his own selfish interests and talk in such a way as to alienate himself and bring others to wrath. Anytime you are out of God's grace, you will be vulnerable to "trapping" yourself. The righteous man, through his speech, will escape trouble and yield good things.

I'm relieved you returned safely to Miami. We were happy you were able to be with us on Easter. I'm so excited about your personal and spiritual growth—God is really doing a good work in your life and desires to use you powerfully in His kingdom. Thanks for the opportunity to make some suggestions about your Bible study.

Proverbs 12:15 is a great one to apply because it shows us the proper heart of a learner. The fool can only see and will only rely upon his own insights and decisions. He will not seek wisdom, truth, or advice from God. He is proud and self-righteous and lacks divine wisdom. Compare this to the wise man who listens to advice—not the advice of man but of God. God seeks to give instruction to those He loves and calls to Himself. This instruction comes via prayer, Scripture study, and God's body.

Verse 16 tells us that the fool also shows his annoyance at others. He is intolerant of others' faults and becomes indignant toward others due to self-centeredness. On the other hand, a prudent man overlooks a harsh word, accusation, or insult. The prudent man is willing to look for truth in the insult in order to learn and grow in godliness. He is not so self-righteous that he cannot be open to discipline or being admonished.

You will not have too many more days left in your sophomore year at Miami. Wow, how time flies! I look forward to you being home this summer. Perhaps we could do a Bible study together or I could help you work on some studies you could use for Crusade small group Bible studies next year?

Proverbs 12:17-19 talks about telling the truth versus lying. I have found true honesty a very hard virtue to have 100 percent of the time. It seems to be against human nature. The value of being honest is not just in the ethical rightness of it, but also in the fact that it brings us closer to God. Verse 17 simply states that what one says or testifies to is a reflection of the inner character and heart of that person. A person who gives false testimony reflects a person who is unloving, a coward, a manipulator, or an egotist.

Verse 18 states that words chosen carelessly, said without considering their consequence, said at the wrong time, or said in the wrong manner will bring pain and sorrow and can wreck a relationship. Words said wisely, on the other hand, will heal relationships and will build up a person's performance in God's kingdom. Be careful in how you talk to friends and family.

Verse 19 tells us that truth endures in a person's heart forever. What you say in God's wisdom and spoken with God's love will change, grow, and linger in a person forever. These words of truth will be a part of their fabric and will shape their character. However, lies and hurtful words will be rejected from a person's deep character fabric although they can continue to harm the relationship.

It's at the end of a very busy day but I want to write to you out of my love and desire to never cease helping you to become a godly woman. I'm so proud of you and am confident God will delight in blessing you and using you in His kingdom's work. Never limit God and therefore never be limited in your vision and confidence in what He will do in and through you.

Proverbs 12:20-21 compares the righteous and the wicked. Verse 20 shows us how intentional motives to harm or betray others result in people who plot to carry out evil. Evil here is destructive activities that go against what God intends. But there is joy in the hearts of those who promote peace or what God intends for His people. Joy is a deep sense that all is well and an utter gladness to be in the situation serving God. The opposite is that discomforting, painful sense we get when we are trying to serve against the Creator. It is like trying to swim upstream against rapids.

Verse 21 assures us that no harm will befall the righteous. They may have superficial and transient hurt, but nothing that is deep and eternal. However, the wicked will never know the end to their trouble. They will have deep dissatisfaction, unrest, pain, frustration, and eternal loss despite the fact that in the short term and on the surface they might appear trouble free.

Again, how proud I am of you and of your dance performance last week. Although your dancing has greatly improved, what makes me most proud was that you danced despite the sprained ankle. This is a sign of high character–to complete what you started despite the pain. Such a character trait will lead to "obedience" to God–the essential aspect required of those who desire to be His servants and children.

Proverbs 12:22-23 gives good, sound, godly advice. Verse 22 tells us that the heart of our Lord hates lying. Why? Because it is not a result of God's character–character that He desires His creation to emanate. It is instead part of Satan's character and as such will lead to death. God delights in people who seek and portray truth, even when it hurts. Truth is godly and therefore of God's character. To seek it and portray it in our lives moves us toward Him.

Verse 23 summarizes a truth axiom: "The person with the least to say, says the most." The wise and perceptive person uses his wisdom and knowledge in a way that is most helpful and constructive. She waits until the hearer is ready to listen and until she is respected by their character. Create a learning environment by establishing your godly character. Then your knowledge given in a selfless, non-arrogant manner will change people. Alternatively, the thoughts and feelings of one who will not be listened to are blurted out without thought to the state of the hearer. This will cause what they say to be rejected and have no power to change or influence.

By the time you receive this letter many of your exams will be over and your second year of college completed. I have prayed for you several times today, knowing that you had one exam this morning. The passages of Proverbs that I will bring to your attention in this letter are really appropriate to your end-of-year situation. Therefore, I will be claiming them for you and asking God to accomplish them in your life.

Proverbs 12:24-25 are observations and truths that you know. In verse 24 the writer points out that ability or innate strengths are not enough to assure success. One must also be diligent and work hard. This is increasingly so as you move further and further up the ladder in any area. Many people will be equally talented but the edge will always fall to that person who is disciplined and diligent. This applies equally to spiritual growth. Walking closely with God cannot be accomplished without diligence. In God's kingdom, however, there is no competition between His children.

Verse 25 states that worry or fear causes anxiety and a weight on our heart. The writer tells us that we should not think this is not to happen to God's people. Instead we should minister to each other a kind word that could ease this burden and convey our support during this difficult time. (See Hebrews 10:25).

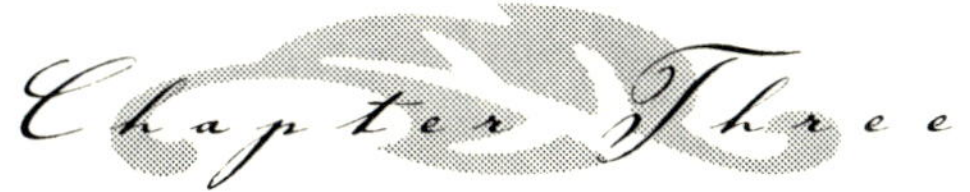

1994—JUNIOR YEAR OF COLLEGE

OXFORD, OHIO

Dear Christine,

Well, now we can resume our study of Proverbs–I missed writing to you of its wisdom. You must be moving quickly to "full speed" in your classes; how are they, how is the research going, how about Crusade–have the small groups begun yet? I have so many questions!

Proverbs 12

We will look today at two unrelated verses. Proverbs 12:26 talks about how we should relate to a friend or neighbor. The godly person will be cautious in his interactions. The Hebrew words are specific–to act in a way that would enhance or positively influence your friend to God. We must be thoughtful, deliberate, and careful in what we say, what we model, how we confront people, and what we do or don't do to and for them. Too often we become lazy or lax in our interactions with our friends and then our humanness leaks out and our weak areas become negative influences. Of course, the best way to approach this is not only to concentrate on external words and actions but also on our inward character. But since we are all "in process," we are exhorted to exercise caution to control our interfacing. Ungodly words and behaviors will lead people away from God.

43

Verse 27 is a bit more obscure. It contrasts the "lazy person" to the "diligent person." The lazy person kills and cooks his game for temporary satiation of his appetite. After eating it, he has none for the future. The diligent man regards these game birds as important for his life now and in the future. He will multiply and improve the breed which will benefit him in an ongoing manner. Likewise, the person who views his life and experiences in the context of God's love and God's Word will grow deep, multiplying and refining himself and his portion of the kingdom.

I hope your three-day holiday has been productive and restful. I looked into the options for Grandpop. I talked with his oncologist in Pittsburgh and was impressed. There is no curative treatment, but I have advised Grandpop to proceed with the suggested treatment. It will have minimal side effects and should be of some help. We all are grieving. I find my mind thinking back over the memories of the years. Mom and I have had some long talks sharing, praying, and shedding tears.

Proverbs 12:28 is a good one to study. The writer reminds us that if we follow God and become more like Him, then we will find life. Life here refers to the abundant life characterized by love, peace, and so on. (Galatians 5:22 and 23.) The world deceives us into believing that true happiness is found through things and accomplishments, but really it is found as we seek God and incorporate Him into all of our plans, actions, and conversations. At the end of the "path" is the ultimate blessing—living with God for eternity. No other path except for the one God designed will lead us there.

Proverbs 13

Verse 13:1 again reminds us that it is profitable to listen to those who are able and called to instruct us. The writer is encouraging the learner to have a teachable heart and also reminds the teacher of his responsibility to mold and shape the lives of those he is called to instruct. God is the ultimate Father, but each of us who walk with Him will at times be the teacher and the person being taught. Remembering this makes one humble and encourages us to use our opportunities to the best advantage. It is the ungodly person who rejects loving interactions of this type. This is sin and will eventually lead to destruction.

I pray for your disciplined study this year, for wisdom and for a healthy share of good fortune. I have thought and prayed several times about the small group Bible study you will be leading. Have you talked with all of the girls yet?

Proverbs 13:2-3 focuses on the use of our words and speech. Proverbs highlights this as one of its main themes—it must be important to godliness. Verse 2 explains that a person's speech will bring back to him good or violence. A faithful person will bear fruit. In other words his positive, constructive effect upon others will bring back to him good things. Words given in love and compassion will cause others to speak and respond likewise to us. In contrast, the person who is self-centered will hatefully and destructively relate to others in such a way as to cause himself destruction and pain.

Verse 3 reinforces the same thought as verse 2. The person who is careful and speaks in a guarded manner will protect his character from the inevitable retaliation and attack of those who are hurt. But if one speaks rashly, he or she will eventually come to ruin.

This past week has been a special one but a tough one as I have had some significant conversations with several people. Once again I can testify to God's marvelous provision when we come in faith to Him (Matt. 6:9-11).

Proverbs 13:4 is a true and wise insight, materially and spiritually. The writer is contrasting the "sluggard" with the "diligent." The sluggard wants, but gets nothing. A person without drive or discipline who is motivated only by sensual self-indulgence will never get his needs met. But the desires of the diligent person are fully satisfied. The concept of satisfying relates to the meeting of deep spiritual needs. Therefore, desires of this type coupled with a hard-working, disciplined manner of effort will lead to fulfillment. We are instructed to first search for the true God-pleasing desires rather than false cravings, and then to apply diligence rather than sluggardly means to accomplish these desires. The result is true contentment.

Thanks for coming home this past weekend. I know it was a long drive for you. Several people from the Sunday school class have already remarked about your spiritual maturity as reflected in your comments. I thank God for the work He is doing in and through your life. Pray for God's strong defense against Satan's attack.

Proverbs 13:5 contrasts one aspect of the righteous versus the wicked. The righteous are following God and they allow God to change them as He indwells them. The wicked, on the other hand, are against God and all He stands for and they seek the world and all false gods. Because the righteous are indwelt by God, they will come to love what is true and detest what is temporary, man-centered, and material. As the wicked pursue false gods, they will eventually show themselves, displaying their true evil character. They will be shamed and disgraced. This is still God's world and He is still our judge. God will not be mocked. He will bring shame and disgrace on the evil ones.

Verse 6 continues by contrasting the character of the righteous and the wicked. A man of integrity is a person whose lifestyle and time utilization reflect his godly perspective. Such a person will bear fruit in his life that is true and right. This fruit will prevent downfall, destruction, and spiritual pain. It will guard the person from inner pain, unhappiness, and anger, and instead he will experience joy, peace and love. On the other hand, he who sins will be brought down, overthrown, and destroyed by his wickedness. Seeking after false gods will destroy. How often can we testify to the terrible downfall of the person who opposes God and His created order? Such a downfall can be public with humiliation and shame but often is an inner rotting of the soul with the existence of quiet desperation and despair.

The weather we have been having is beautiful. There is something about fall that touches my emotional/spiritual being. I find myself more contemplative and in touch with the Lord during these slightly cool, breezy days. Perhaps it is because I was born in October or maybe it is the season that shows off, better than any other, God's creativeness and artistry.

Proverbs 13:7 and 8 seem to be paired. Verse 7 conveys a familiar theme of Scripture–the betrayal of worldly wealth and the redefinition of true riches. The verse contrasts the person who pretends to be rich and the one who pretends to be poor. The word "pretends" is used to convey the divergence of the world's perspective compared to God's perspective: worldly wealth compared to internal joy, peace, and love. Often the two are mutually exclusive. To seek the world's method of approval prevents one from drawing close to God for fear of having to give up what the world has to offer. Wisdom, discernment, and understanding also come not from the world, but from the seeking of heavenly things. Thus, the person marked by worldly wealth is only pretending. In reality, he is quite poor. In contrast, the person that appears poor in worldly standards is really in possession of great wealth. Should we shun worldly wealth? I believe that it takes a person of deep Christian maturity to be able to posses worldly wealth but clearly regard it as far inferior to spiritual wealth. He should be able and willing at any time to walk away from it if God desires.

Verse 8 carries on this concept. The writer states that riches are so important to a person that it "buys" and possesses their life. The world owns them and has bought them with earthly, temporal riches: "ransomed." The poor man will not be possessed by the world. He is safe and able to be in a position to hear God and respond to Him. The rich, young ruler in Matthew 19 was unable to respond to Jesus because he was owned by the world. We must grow in spiritual wealth and become so possessed by Christ that even if we also have worldly riches, we will not be owned by them.

This evening's meal was turkey breast (my birthday choice) and then I had a nice quiet time with your mom on the sofa watching TV (although she didn't let me watch Faulty Towers*). I hope you had a great day. I missed you here but am comforted by knowing that God has you in His hand. I love you and am so proud of the godly woman you have become.*

Proverbs 13:9 calls attention to the fact that what emanates from the righteous person is light and this light will shine brightly. A light that shines bright cannot be suppressed and will conquer darkness. It will show the true nature of things. Implied here also is the notion that such a light will never fade–it is eternal. The "lamp" of the wicked will go out. Notice "lamp" focuses more on the material aspect of that which gives light than on the light itself. This human lamp will be snuffed out.

Proverbs 13:10 is an excellent bit of practical and godly wisdom. Pride will breed quarrels between individuals or within the body of Christ. Pride will seek to get one's own needs met despite the impact and pain that will be inflicted on others. Other people's needs will be shunned, disregarded, or belittled. This will produce, at best, separation and, at worst, outright anger and aggressive behavior. No one gains and everyone loses. This attitude toward God will result in estrangement and eventually judgment and condemnation. It is wise and beneficial to a person to quench strife by being open to taking advice and always seeking to understand and meet the needs of others. Not only does this allow God to bless the union or body, but it also allows each party to grow simultaneously by the action of another. Pride is God's enemy. Learn to conquer pride and be empathetic and respectful of others.

Thanks again for the thoughtful gift certificate and especially for your card—I appreciate your sensitivity and thoughtfulness. My dog, Reilly, has left home—I haven't seen him for three or four days. I fear he will not be coming back. I guess I just can't keep boys around here!

Proverbs 13:11 is worthy of memorizing. The writer is telling us the truth about that which is earned with toil versus that which comes without effort. "Money" can be true dollars and cents or it can represent anything valuable that is sought after—wisdom, courage, intimacy, love, respect, or even truth itself. The author tells us that if we seek to realize or accumulate these things by working hard, by building the right foundation, by taking proper steps at the proper time, and by listening and learning from proper people, then these things will not leave us or escape us. Obtaining God's wisdom through the study and application of His Word is a stepwise, effort-filled process. As it is obtained, it grows and bears fruit and never dwindles away. That which is valuable doesn't come easily or quickly but when it is achieved it will continue to grow and add benefit upon benefit to the one who works hard and waits.

Proverbs 13:12 is a bit more abstract. The "hope" spoken of here is the deep longing inherent in every person that is restored by communion with God our Creator. It is one of Satan's biggest lies that a person doesn't need God, that he can stand alone and be fully satisfied apart from his Creator. By trying to deny this longing of the heart, a person becomes unhealthy–not vigorous and productive. But this longing, when fulfilled through a personal, real relationship with God, will bring life.

Proverbs 13:13 speaks of the basic human sin–pride and self-sufficiency. I think we all are guilty of this sin and perhaps the crux of lordship is in allowing God to displace us as "number one." The person who scorns God's instructions will pay for it. He will not experience the fruits of the Spirit in this life. Often a person will accept God and His Word but reject this same Word being given or represented through another person. This leads to conflict and competitiveness within God's body. Alternatively, the person who listens and responds to God's instruction will be rewarded by a maturing, spirit-filled life along with eternal life in fellowship with God.

Proverbs 13:14 continues this theme. The teachings of a wise person will bring the hearer to a rich, bountiful, eternally-flowing "fountain" that gives life–abundant and eternal. God's wisdom taught and learned is life giving. Not only does it give life, but it also prevents a person from eternal death. Satan kills when he keeps us from accepting Christ's work on the cross.

Thanks for coming home this weekend–it really was a boost for me to spend time with you. Thanks for coming to my Sunday school class. I know you were really rushed Sunday and could have used the time. It means a lot to me to have you attend when you can, but don't feel obligated.

Chapter 13, verse 15 conveys the thought that although most in this world will not acknowledge it, the proper understanding and application of God's Word will win acceptance and admiration from even an ungodly world. Despite man's attempt to remove God's handprint from His creation, he cannot do so and ironically in the end God's ways are the favored ways by all. The person not walking close to God and therefore not acquiring and exemplifying godly qualities will find his walk in this world hard and a place in eternity impossible. Never be fooled, even in an evil world the best way to be found acceptable and win favor is to walk close to God and live a changed life.

Verse 16 continues in a similar vein. Every prudent man learns and applies God's knowledge. A fool will show himself to be unknowing, shortsighted, and shallow when he acts on the basis of "presumed knowledge." Again, be content to be patient. Allow the fool to put the noose around his own neck. It may take time but true character will surface and be in full view.

Thanks for a nice visit Friday/Saturday. I continue to thank God for how He loves and blesses you. Be encouraged to keep your eyes on Him and be obedient. You are, and continue to become, a godly and beautiful young woman. Believe in yourself, rely upon God, and shoot for the stars.

Proverbs 13:17 is an interesting bit of wisdom. A "wicked messenger" is one who acts on his own and carries his own message. Such a message is conceived deviously and is usually counterfeit to what was truly the heart and thoughts of the one sending the message. The result of receiving this counterfeit message will be negative and will bring trouble to the one who receives it–he will be led astray from the truth. Also the messenger will eventually be judged–either by the one misled or by the one misrepresented. The "trustworthy envoy" listens and learns from the source of truth and then carries it well, representing it properly. The result of this communication will be positive and healing to the one receiving it and it will bring reward and fellowship to the faithful messenger. The proverb applies first to the gospel–Christ being the trustworthy envoy and Satan the wicked messenger. We also must be sure we are trustworthy and represent His truth and light properly.

Verse 18 once again reminds us of the value of discipline and correction. God is always concerned with building us into godly men and women. He allows trials and temptations, while giving us His gifts to endure and grow through these difficult times. If we ignore God's training and refining, we will not grow and we will become tempted by Satan to sin. However, "heeding" corrections–that is accepting them as of benefit to our character growth–will be honoring to him who accepts it. To be honored is to grow close to God as we accept His love and directions. We are also honored by serving Him in His kingdom, an opportunity we gain as we are made more mature and trustworthy by His discipline.

I've prayed often since we left you on Saturday concerning your tests on Monday. I was so very proud of you as you participated in the choir concert. I enjoyed the music even though I am far from a critic when it comes to such work. Grandpop finds out more about the state of his cancer tomorrow. I pray it will be good news and for him to know God's joy in this circumstance. We must remember God's promises and trust Him to be a God who answers and keeps His promises.

Proverbs 13:19 is an interesting one with a unique perspective on "desires of the heart." God desires us to have human heart desires or longings but not to be enslaved by them such that Satan can use our longings to tempt us. The proverbs first tell us when a longing is fulfilled it is extremely satisfying–sweet to the soul. It is like the first few bites of some delicious food. Yet, that same food eaten continuously will lose its delicious appeal and go on to make us sick. A longing granted by God is to be sought, never expected, and when received appreciated and savored. A fool is addicted and feels entitled to having his own way and seeking his own pleasures. Satan tempts us to sin by convincing us of our need and entitlement for our own pleasures.

Verse 20 is a real truism. We reflect and are altered/influenced by those people we spend time with and have as role models. A person who walks (relates to strongly and is taught by) with someone reflecting God's ways will become more Christ-like and it will be reflected in his speech, actions, attitudes, and heart. Walking with a fool will lead to ruin–loss of peace, joy, and God's blessings.

I just returned from a funeral. It again demonstrated that the value, meaning, joy, and lasting significance of a life is in the effect it has on other people, especially if that life is acceptable and glorifying to God. Always invest yourself in people, never sell out for inanimate achievements or material goals.

Proverbs 13:21 is true but not always in the short-term analysis. "Misfortune" is to be regarded from a long-term analysis of a life and has to consider the whole person instead of focusing on the world's definition of success. A person may have material wealth and power, yet be utterly miserable in his emotional or spiritual being. While on the other hand, the person living for God will know great prosperity (joy and peace), meaningful relationships, and the assurance of eternity in God's house.

In verse 22 the writer of Proverbs tells us that the good man will leave a great inheritance for the generations to follow. Again, this inheritance is not just worldly wealth but an example of godly character and lifelong instructions on living as one of God's children. The wealth of a sinful man will eventually be lost. It will then be added to the true wealth of the righteous man (see Luke 19:11-26). In the long run, only those who know the Creator and live according to the rules and standards of the Creator will posses and enjoy the creation.

I thought of you several times yesterday, knowing you were dancing and singing. I missed being able to be there with you. It is really hard to believe that next week is finals week at Miami and the end of the first semester of your junior year. I will be praying for you during exam time.

Proverbs 13:23 is a call for a person with godly behavior to use her resources and opportunities wisely, completely, efficiently, and with sober judgment. Even though a godly person may be poor in terms of the worldly, material opportunities or resources, she can produce abundant fruit by wisely and effectively using what she has. It will yield all she needs or more and give opportunity for her to develop prudent and responsible behavior. If she uses her resources in a contrary manner, then she will be lost. Too often a person with very little becomes defeated and irresponsible even with what she has.

Verse 24 is one I know you have heard quoted. The concept is that the person who loves is willing, and feels the responsibility, to do what is required to help the one she loves to mature and develop. "Tough love" is the concept of today. God disciplines us and allows Satan to tempt us in order for us to become more godly. It may hurt, but it is necessary. God can be trusted to know what is right for us despite the way it feels. In raising children, you must do this without exasperating them (Eph. 6:4), even at times to the point of inflicting pain. The challenge is to do this while the recipient is aware that it is being done out of your great love for him.

I know your first final is tomorrow and that you will not get this letter until most of them will be over, but I am and will be praying for you at this important time. I'm confident of God's hand on your life and in your openness to His movement in your life; therefore, I pray in confidence that His will be done this week. I will always love you and be proud of you no matter how your future shapes up.

Proverbs 13:25 describes that which truly satisfies. The wicked will never truly know fulfillment and peace. Only she, who seeks to know God and do His will, will be blessed. To be blessed is outlined well by Christ in Matthew 5. To be blessed is to know comfort and mercy while being part of God's kingdom. Since we are His creation, only when we are reunited with and serving our Creator will we know real contentment.

Proverbs 14

Chapter 14:1 is an excellent one for those women who desire to serve God as a wife and mother. Solomon tells us that the woman who has and applies God's wisdom in her home will strengthen and deepen the home as a fortress and sanctuary for God and His spirit. A woman living apart from God will, through her evil behavior and untrustworthy instruction, weaken and tear down the home.

I'm glad your trip back to Oxford was uneventful. Was it good to see your friends there again? I enjoyed having you home and what a privilege it was for me to have you on "rounds" and at a "teaching session." In the past, I believed you would make a fine doctor, but now I am sure of it. Do not let anything discourage or defeat you in achieving that goal. I know that this semester and the MCATs are "biggies" so I will be praying for your success in them. I shall pray daily.

Let us return to Proverbs. Chapter 14, verse 2 tells us what is logically apparent. When one is disobedient to a standard set of values, then the person who represents these values is rejected and avoided by the disobedient one. It is against human nature to embrace the person but reject what she stands for. We often avoid considering such values and defend our indefensible positions by criticizing or tearing down the people who advocate these values. Verse 2 tells us that the person who walks in a way pleasing to God will be reverent and hold awesome regard for God. But the scoffer, whose ways deviate from God's ways, will protect himself and seek security in his position by hating the originator of these ways (God).

Verse 3 tells us a truth that will be born out in every person's life given enough time. The fool is a godless, self-seeking, worldly person. His talk will eventually backfire on him and he will condemn himself. He is inconsistent, egocentric, untrustworthy, and generally of low character. Eventually this will become evident and he will destroy himself. The speech of the wise will give the soft, selfless answers that turn away others' wrath. They will be trusted and held in high esteem, for they will be known as concerned more for others than themselves.

I hope your trip home was safe and that you and your friends had a good time at Kiawah (despite the rainy weather). I'm looking forward to returning in April.

Proverbs 14:4 is interesting and a good one for a leader or a parent. It uses good, pragmatic symbolism. The "oxen" spoken of here are the problem people or the solid person who is acting at a given time in a rebellious or problematic way. Where these people exist, there will be "messes" or manure to deal with and clean up. Yet we need all these people to work in God's kingdom to maximize His harvest. Therefore, the leader must work to bring an erring brother to repentance and back to the right walk. We must be very reluctant to give up on another–only as a very last resort, if there is continued defiance and mocking rebellion with an unteachable heart, should that person be excluded from fellowship.

I know you are working hard this semester–it will pay off! Continue to pray for both of your summer options (Austria and Mercy Ship)–do not be deterred by the process.

Proverbs 14:6 describes the difference in the truth or wisdom a person obtains as a result of his attitude to the source. A mocker is a person whose heart is skeptical and pre-determined to disbelieve and to justify and legitimize this disbelief. Such an attitude will blind the person to any or all truth that could emanate from the source. But the person who approaches potential truth with sincere desire to know is "discerning" and will know truth easily. The mocker may inquire but will not find out.

Verse 7 follows up this thought by encouraging us to stay away from such people. These people are blinded from the truth and will lead others into condemnation. It does no good to try to reason with such a person. You will not only not find truth from him, but you will make yourself vulnerable to worldly thinking and Satan's devious lies. Pray for discernment as to when such a person is to be avoided, as opposed to making an effort to bring him truth via your witnessing.

I hope you had a great weekend–did you go to a Super Bowl party? We (Mom and I) went to a church gathering and had a good time–too bad the game was not closer. A new group of medical students began today. I always look forward to getting to know each of these students as they rotate through family medicine.

Proverbs 14:8 tells us that the key wisdom of the careful, productive, successful person of God is that she gives time and effort to seeking God's mind on a matter. She carefully listens to God via His Word, via other mature Christians, and directly via the Holy Spirit before committing her ways and actions. The downfall or mistake of the foolish is that she allows herself to be led astray by her self-centeredness and the world's urging. This blindness and foolish deception will be her undoing.

Verse 9 further tells us that the person not seeking God will ridicule and mock any suggestion that she seek repentance and reconciliation. This person has a hard and sarcastic heart. However, if a person accepts God and then His gift of peace and joy, she will recognize God in awesome fear and seek after Him. This person has a contrite heart and will be blessed by God.

Your sister Kara fell on the ice yesterday and hurt her wrist. I X-rayed it today; there were no fractures but I was not going to make the same mistake twice (thinking back to when I didn't think you broke your foot). I continue to be praying for your relationships–let me know further thoughts or insights that would allow me to be more direct in my praying.

At first glance, Proverbs 14:10 is an unusual wisdom. There is a very deep level in each of us where we have joys and sorrows that only we ourselves can understand. No matter how hard we try, we cannot adequately communicate the full meaning and emotional content of feelings at this level to another person. However, as Christians, we know that God has access to this level of our person and that He will hear these issues and feelings. This is a special spiritual level of our relationship to God our Father. During His life on earth, Jesus gave us a good example of how He related to God at this level. Jesus desired to be fully and deeply understood by His Father and He received strength and wisdom at this deeper, "root" level. Jesus, since He knows our human condition, can serve our needs to God as He sits now at God's right hand in heaven.

Verse 11 contrasts a "house," something that seems solid and permanent, with a "tent," which seems transient and flimsy. Those who do not know God via Christ (the "wicked"), live in the house, while those reconciled with God via Christ (the "upright") live in the tent. At first this may seem unjust, but since the house is built on a weak human foundation, it will be destroyed. The upright live in tents here on earth but know that their true home is in heaven, and therefore, in eternity, they will be blessed.

We have lost a great person in your grandfather. He was a man of integrity, fairness, and high moral values; his faith was simple but strong enough to persevere to the end; and he worked hard but valued people and his faith above the things of the world. He ran the race well and finished in a manner pleasing to God. I will miss him but am assured we will be united in heaven as part of Christ's body. He was very proud of you and the woman you have become. He knew of your love for him and he spoke candidly with me of this on the day we last saw him. It is our loss but his gain.

Proverbs 14:12 is a fairly straightforward but resounding truth. Man cannot decide truth, for what seems right to us (without a connectedness to God via Christ) is in reality the way that leads to death (eternal separation from God). Our basic sinful nature is self-focused and judges everything by its impact on ourselves. Decisions and "truth" derived from such a perspective will separate us from God. We will not receive God's solution to our need (Christ) since from a worldly perspective we do not see our need or understand how Christ could meet our needs. Therefore, we move further and further away from the truth–ultimately to spiritual and eternal death.

Proverbs 14:13 tells us of a deep truism that the world denies. Even when people seem to be happy and having a good time ("laughter"), their heart longs to be one with our Creator God. We ache to be at peace and know true joy. The world's "joy" (to be contrasted to deep spiritual joy of knowing God) will end in grief–the pain, terrible loneliness, and suffering of estrangement from the Creator. Worldly "highs" are temporary, counterfeit, and misleading, leading away from true peace/joy. This is hard to explain to a man. We must learn through experience rather than be rationally convinced. Satan offers all sorts of shortcuts and alternative pathways that are seductive, subtle, and tempting. View these with spiritual eyes and "flee from all appearances of evil."

Grammy is doing well. She continued to talk a great deal on the way home, and we were able to help her ventilate and deal with her grief. She was more honest and animated then I have ever seen her. I guess the loss of Grandpop has for now opened a window to her heart.

Proverbs 14:14 contrasts the "faithless" with the "good man." The person without faith and trust in God will be "paid back" for the work that flows out of unfaithfulness. Works or actions flow out of our inner nature. Therefore the works of the unfaithful will be at best hypocritical, and at worst, outright ungodly. God will punish them by not being a presence in this life here on earth and eternal separation in one's future. Contrasted is the "good man" who out of his faith acts in accordance with God's will. His reward is, now and forever, the presence of God.

Verse 15 contrasts the "simple man" and the "prudent man." A simple man here refers to one who can be taken in easily by Satan and the world. This man believes the lies fed to him without taking the time or effort to examine them, and without resistance, heads in that direction. The prudent man is one who really believes there is truth and seeks to know it for himself. Therefore, he examines and puts to the test the seen and unseen facts presented to him. He weighs carefully what man tells him and believes in God's sovereignty and dominion. In this he accepts and puts into practice God's Word.

I think Mom and I are both experiencing the grief of Grandpop's death; we had to be strong for Grammy last week, but now it seems to be creeping into our lives. It is not incapacitating but causes some deep pain and perhaps changes our perspective on life. It is all part of being human and normal. It is really great to have the power and strength of God's Spirit in this time.

Proverbs 14:16 picks up on the "fear" of the Lord theme. To fear the Lord is to recognize His awesome goodness, power, and sovereignty, and to be afraid not to be in a relationship with Him. "Fearing" God changes our person, so that we will naturally desire to shun evil and all that is against Him. Yet a fool (one out of fellowship with God) will allow the world to have dominion in his or her life. Such a person is self-absorbed and heeds nothing beyond himself. She is impulsive and reacts to any given situation without a clear standard or compass to direct her. A compass that consistently and reliably gives a person direction must be fixed by magnetic force on the North Pole. Christ is the North Pole on our compass; therefore, we can reliably have clear direction in life.

Proverbs 14:17. Anger will take over a person's rational senses and nullify right behavior. An angry person is prone to doing things she regrets and which lead her away from God. The "crafty" person is different. She will conspire and conjure up devious means to hurt others and seek self. This person will eventually produce bitterness, repulsion, and hate in those who are the brunt of the craftiness, or who observe the evil impact of it on others. Be aware of the danger of anger and reject all tendencies toward craftiness.

I realize you will not read this until after spring break and your trip to Athens, Georgia, and Kiawah Island, South Carolina. I will be praying for you during your break–for safe travel and a fun, refreshing time with your friends. I'm very happy things are working out with your plans to go to Austria this summer! I never believed they wouldn't; I've asked God to be a part of that time and to bless you in it. Persevere now, Christine, during these last several months of your junior year, and in your preparation for MCATs. I am confident that God desires to use your wonderful character and gifts for Him as a doctor. You have worked hard, do not lose sight of the finish line or become any less than well applied to the tasks at hand.

Proverbs 14:18 contrasts the "simple" with the "prudent" person. A simple person does not have an understanding or commitment to the spiritual truths of God and His kingdom. It is not because he is incapable but because he chooses the things of the world. The simple person believes whatever the world tells him and so he "inherits folly!" He receives from the world only worthless things that do not give joy or peace and pull him farther from God. The prudent person understands that true wisdom comes from "fearing God and shunning evil." The prudent is "crowned " (made part of God's kingdom) as a result of personal acceptance of Christ's work.

Verse 19 tells us the ultimate effect of this choice. The simple or evil man (influenced and controlled by Satan and the world) will eventually acknowledge and bow down to those who wear God's crown. He will remain outside the gates that lead to the place of righteousness where the prudent will be given audience, blessing, and favor with God.

I'm happy your trip to South Carolina was relaxing and fun, and that you have returned to Miami University safely. I hold you in my prayers–especially relative to the MCATs as they approach.

Proverbs 14:20 and 21 are connected. In verse 20, Solomon observes that the people who are "poor" by the world's standards are frequently shunned, looked down upon, criticized, and disregarded by those who encounter them (neighbors). Neighbors are supposed to care for and give aid to those God has placed in their path. But the world's wisdom requires this only if it is good for us and will exalt us. The proverb goes on to say that the rich have many friends. The rich, by the world's standards, attract those to them that are like themselves, egocentric and looking for ways to "get more" for themselves. Are they really friends?

Verse 21 follows and condemns the rich "shunner." She breaks God's royal law that commands us to love our neighbor as ourselves. When the love of God lives within us, it will never allow us to despise the person He places in our path, rich or poor. Instead God empowers us with His Holy Spirit and blesses us when we respond kindly to our neighbor. This blessing of a more personal and intimate relationship with Him leads us to the fruits of His Spirit and heavenly wisdom.

Mom just won the "IGA 25th Anniversary" drawing–she won a $20 gift certificate. Oh well, anything to brighten up a dreary, rainy Monday. I have some leads for your desire for a summer trip overseas–I will pursue them and let you know.

Proverbs 14:22 indicates that that which we give ourselves to in our thoughts, goals, plans, and directions will directly impact what we experience in life. When people allow themselves to think badly of another and "flirt" with how they could cause or allow unkind or destructive things to befall that person, they place themselves in league with the world's standards, which are under the control of Satan. This is dangerous and, given enough time, will be a sure bet that they will be consumed and controlled more and more by the world/Satan and they will go astray. Conversely, those who discipline themselves to think and dwell on what is good for another will experience those fruits of the relationship with God–love, joy, peace, faithfulness, and so on. We must submit to God our attitudes and thoughts toward other people to avoid being controlled by Satan.

Verse 23 is a good, practical bit of wisdom that holds true for God and for societal good. It reminds us that there is no shortcut to achievement in material, relationship, or spiritual areas. Hard work, not mere talk, will be rewarded with insights, deeper relationships, spiritual growth, societal privilege, and opportunities. Mere talk will eventually be seen for what it is and dismissed by others as useless and deceitful.

I really appreciate your coming home this weekend, even though your studies had to take most of your time. It was good to see you, hear of your activities and growth, meet your friends, and pray with you. Although I have a real peace concerning the MCATs and medical school admission, I will pray daily for you in this regard.

Proverbs 14:24 echoes other proverbs we have already looked at, but has a slightly different slant to it. Wealth is that which is worth so much that we conform the rest of our life toward acquiring it. For the "wise" person, the person with God's perspective and heart, wealth for them is a "crown." This signifies becoming royalty in Christ's kingdom now and forever. In contrast, the "fools" are those who measure in human terms and see their wealth as being of this world. This is "folly" or foolishness. The proverb uses this word "folly" twice; the first time to indicate the perspective or attitudes that motivate actions; and the second to indicate that this will go "nowhere." In other words, the attitude behind the actions of the ungodly will yield sad destruction.

Verse 25 tells us that a person who shares her story (a witness), as an example of God's plan of salvation and sanctification, could save another person's life by helping him gain salvation, knowledge of God, and eternal life. An unbelieving person who shares his story in order to detract another from the real truth of God's plan deceives another. Such deceit will rob another person of eternal life and the present blessings of the Holy Spirit. Other scriptures make it plain that we all will be accountable to God for the type of witness we are.

It is hard to believe you are soon to complete your third year of college! It seems like only yesterday we were planning your high school graduation party here. God has blessed you and indwelled you. I am praying now for your summer and that God will use it significantly in your life and for His kingdom's work.

Proverbs 14:26 and 27 are related and interesting. They speak (again) of the "fear of the Lord." This is not fear in a negative, punitive sense but rather "fear" of an awesome God who astounds us daily with His amazing love and whose character is worthy of our full allegiance, obedience, and reverence. We desire to serve

Him and place ourselves totally under His control and guidance. Verse 26 tells us that as we view God in this manner and then, through Christ, place ourselves in His arms, we will have a "secure fortress"–a place of refuge, protection, nurturance, and empowerment that can never be assaulted or penetrated by the world or Satan. It is not a place of slavery or bondage, but a place we seek and delight in. The second line of verse 26 is interesting. It tells us (and this is consistent with other Scripture) that the person who so fears the Lord can claim this same refuge for his/her children. Sure, her children can leave this refuge for the world, but because of the parent's claim, the children have the opportunity to have known the refuge. This is such a blessing and advantage, as opposed to one who had never been brought into God's fortress by others but must enter on his/her own.

Verse 27 tells us that such a fear is a "fountain of life." A fountain never runs dry; so also is the life that flows from such fear–eternal and pure as the water in a fountain. This life-giving fear also leads to instruction and equipping to overcome the sin that leads to spiritual and eternal death and to becoming more like Jesus (righteous).

Well, your third year of college is over! You should feel good that during this year you have really grown and matured in godliness and as an adult seeking to carve out your position, contributions, and role in your life. I am very proud of you and the woman you have become; thank you for allowing me to know you as an adult and to be able to pray specifically for your cares and needs.

Proverbs 14:29 is worthy of special note, and memory. The writer contrasts the "patient man" versus the "quick-tempered man." The patient person is a person with great faith. She is able to not insist on her own way in her time because she believes in a sovereign God who will keep His promises. She is therefore able to learn to wait on God to work in her life and in the life of another person, believing all the time that God will be victorious. Such a person understands that God, Himself patient, will bless (now, in life, and in the future, in eternity) the person who waits in faith. Such a person has great "understanding" of the truth, from God's perspective. But a person who is impatient and self-centered, a person of little knowledge of and faith in God, will "display folly." Folly is wrong speech, actions, and attitude with regard to God's perspective; such a stance leads to a hard existence both for themselves and for others. It moves all away from God.

Verse 30 contrasts "envy" with "a heart at peace," with reference to the state of the body. Pragmatically, I have found it true that the state of the "heart"–whether it is selfless, contrite, and humble or deceptive, conflictual, and self-driven–speaks of the emotional and physical well-being of a person. Spiritually, life can be seen as a vibrant, exciting, "living" existence that is experienced when connected with peace between a person and God. Alternatively is the "rot" that stems from estrangement, spiritually, from God.

1995 — Senior Year
of College
Oxford, Ohio

Dear Christine,
All is going well here. Mom was surprised at my "Mexican an-
niversary celebration." We had a Mexican meal cooked from
scratch. After dinner, she broke her piñata using Erin's baseball
bat; we had stuffed it with fun and serious things. We all had fun.
I wish you could have been able to be here; it would have made
the celebration more fun.

Let us continue our study of Proverbs where we left off at Proverbs 14:31-32. Verse 31 speaks to one character trait of God–that
of His justice and love for all people despite their circumstances.
The writer makes it very clear that those who follow God shall not
show superiority or abuse those who are poor physically, emotionally, or spiritually. Instead, it is our desire (as the Holy Spirit helps
us become more like Him) to be kind and meet their needs in these
various areas. How we do that and the extent to which we do this
will either show contempt or honor to God. The "poor" are not
just the obvious physically or financially devoid person, but we
are all the poor and needy at various times and in various ways.
Do not oppress or make their burden heavier but show empathy
and kindness. This pleases God.

Verse 32 reassures the person who walks with God that when any calamity (even the ultimate calamity of death) occurs, we will be ministered to by God Himself.

The funeral of Jessica Seward was such a testimony. Because the family was assured of where their beloved daughter was, they were able to minister out of strength to others.

God gives those who know Him special privilege, grace, and refuge in our times of need. The people who don't know Him (the "wicked") are destroyed and bitter because their value as people and their "god "(the world) is transient and can be destroyed in an instant. They are brought down.

It was really good to talk with you last night. Thanks for allowing my input to your life. We received all of your recommendations and sent them today. I sense you are having an exciting senior year so far. I really praise God that you have this time to deepen your walk with Him and with fellow members of His body.

Proverbs 14:33 tells us that God's perspective of our world is available and poured out upon the person who seeks it. In fact, God's wisdom is all around us and is seen only by those who are "discerning"–who have their eyes and ears open to it. When such a person comes in contact with God and His wisdom (always together), she will internalize it and place it deep within her heart (neutrality is impossible for one who seriously seeks Him). Such a person is then changed and her behavior reflects this internalized truth. Often such beautiful and right behavior is seen by even an unbeliever and is respected and admired. The foolish (those who follow the world's standards) deeply seek to be re-linked with their Creator and godly behavior touches a chord in their lives.

Verse 34 is from a different perspective. It discusses the impact on a nation of the attitude toward sin held by that nation and its leaders. When the morals of a nation become so ungodly that they are devoid of God consciousness, that nation is a disgrace in the eyes of the Creator. Then it is only a matter of time before God will humble and judge it. On the other hand, the nation who is God-centered and God-conscious is considered righteous and God will bless it. History will bear out this piece of wisdom, even if we confine ourselves to looking at Israel's history.

I'm sorry I was not here when you called yesterday.; I would have liked to have had a moment to say "hi." Mom told me you had been to a Campus Crusade for Christ retreat. Was it beneficial? What things were you confronted with? How is the Bible study you are leading shaping up this semester? Oh well, we can talk about these things soon.

Proverbs 14:35 talks about a "wise servant." There are two aspects here: wisdom (the ability to know and apply truth in practical circumstances) and service (using and applying these truths for the master). The master benefits from the servant's efforts and in turn provides benefits to the servant. You see a reciprocally enjoyable, useful, and rewarding relationship here, even if there must be maintained a stratification of headship. The opposite is that of a servant who is shameful and doesn't possess or use for his master wisdom. He will not be rewarded, but will receive judgment and anger. This principle is easily seen as we use the Holy Spirit's wisdom to be wise servants of God. It is also true as we relate to others in life whom we serve (in one degree or another); remember too that a servant one time is a master the next. Seek wisdom from God and apply it beneficially for the person you serve. You will receive great reward.

Proverbs 15

Chapter 15:1 is one of the most well-known proverbs. It is one I have had to work on since it doesn't come naturally to me. It basically instructs us as to how to react to one who is angry or holds contempt toward us. Be gentle, not harsh. Listen and try to empathetically understand the other's point of view, and pick your words carefully so as not to be accusatory or defensive. Being gentle does not mean you cowardly submit; rather it incorporates strength and a high self-worth (one has to like himself before he will be able to receive another's accusations and displeasure). Harshness indicates a defensive and antagonistic spirit and response. It serves only to stir up the other's anger and further distance the parties involved. Cultivate gentleness in relationships, and especially when another has contempt for you. This trait is critical in marriages that are characterized by low conflict and good communication.

Thanks so much for sharing the story of the man from Texas who became a Christian through the ministry of Miami Crusade. It is so gratifying to me, your earthly father, to see how you seek your heavenly Father. Never let that die and He will bless you richly.

Proverbs 15:2 is another perspective on godly speech, and the use of the tongue. A wise person uses her speech from a basis of knowledge, rather than without forethought. Wise speech knows when to speak and when to be silent. It chooses wording that is helpful, encouraging, challenging, and caring. The mouth of a fool has no rein on her speech, blurting forth anything she feels. Since this perspective always puts self first and others and God a distant second, the words are harmful, destructive, uncaring, insensitive, and a disgrace to God. See Judges 8:1-3 as a positive example.

Verse 3 reminds us again of the sovereignty, omniscience, and omnipresence of God. He is Lord (whether we acknowledge Him or not) over all His creation and is aware of every thought, feeling, and action. He cannot be mocked and He will sit in judgment at the proper time. He is aware of the wicked and the good (this does not refer to right or wrong actions but to a person's heart toward God). He will respond now in comfort with His presence or He will cause pain by His estrangement. He will respond later in more explicit and outward blessings or curses. See Psalm 139 as a good illustration of the proverb.

It was good to talk with you last night and to share some of my thoughts on Colossians. I'm happy you've had a good weekend; I've prayed today for your leading of the Bible study. We will be buying a van soon, since our present one is not safe. I really want to be wise in our choice—reasonable but not extravagant.

Proverbs 15:4 continues Solomon's comments on the tongue. The thoughts we tell ourselves and the words we speak to others can bring healing to individuals and relationships. Have you ever had an inner sense of peace and improved self-worth arise as a result of another person's words to you—reflecting their heart and regard for you? Or have you experienced the unifying and bonding effect on two or more people due to the words spoken and the attitude and heart of the speaker? Alternatively, how destructive to our spirit or relationships are perverse and deceitfully spoken words. See Genesis 13:8 and 2 Samuel 20.

Verse 5 indicates the value of listening to and acting on solid, godly advice. The focus is not that "fathers" are right, but all that is right flows from our true Father in heaven. Those people on earth, who represent these truths, and the Word itself, are to be listened to and heeded. Often we need to ask for humility and discernment to hear the wisdom. To heed this discipline shows a person is aware of where truth and true loving care comes from. The fool will not accept this and thereby cuts herself off from constructive, positive correction.

Thank you for sharing the weekend with us. Did you call Temple? Were you able to set up an interview? Let me know so I can be praying for you; again, try to have your application complete before the interview.

Proverbs 15:6 is a parallel to 14:24. It again makes the point that both living righteously (seeking to know and serve God, not sinless living) and living wickedly (seeking to exclude God and seeking self-centered needs only) have their rewards (treasures and income). The righteous person has in his house (accrued to his or her benefit) an everlasting and greatly valued reward; this reward may not be completely tangible or able to be used or spent in this world. The wicked person has an "income"–tangible and used to gratify his needs; it may be great but only for this world. Both these rewards bring a result–the wonderful, lasting reward; or the worldly "reward" of trouble, not only in this world but after death also.

Verse 7 speaks of what is disseminated by the wise and the fool. What comes from the wise (talk and the accompaning action; remember, the lips reflect the heart) will spread to others not just truth (God's knowledge) but God's love, compassion, and care. The Hebrew word here for knowledge means the complete and wide revelation of God to man. We who have His spirit and are thereby made His body to serve Him, will reveal Him to others and grow and spread His kingdom. Solomon contrasts this curtly by saying "not so the hearts of fools." The heart of the world-centered, self-focused, God-rejecting person will emanate that which destroys, harms, and abuses others, and tears down God's intended creation and His kingdom.

Thanks for calling yesterday and wishing me a "Happy Birthday." I look forward to receiving your card. You and your love are very important to me and your interactions are always appreciated. Hopefully your MCAT scores will come this week; then we can have a better idea of how to proceed on potential interviews.

Proverbs 15:8 and 9 give two things that God "detests." God detests hypocritical sacrifices. Wicked people offer pompous, hollow sacrifices while rejecting God in their hearts. The Jewish leaders at the time of Christ are examples of such people who mocked God with their shows of piety. God loves the deep, heartfelt prayers of His people–those who seek Him and His will for their lives. Such people demonstrate a heart that is believing and trusting of Him and they seek to allow Him to be their God.

God further detests (verse 9) the lifestyles, priorities, motivations, and attitudes of the wicked. The heart manifests such in external behavior. The wicked seek to make themselves god, and thereby mock and affront the true God and Creator. God loves, however, the person who pursues the truth and the origin of the truth, God Himself. To pursue is not just to know but to act in a way that shows we have placed God first in our life.

Thank you so much for the birthday card–you can never know how encouraging and gratifying your words and thoughts are to me. I marvel at your godly character, wisdom, and sensitivity. I am certain God will use you mightily in His kingdom (He already is!). Please be careful in your travel and stay in Philadelphia this weekend; we will miss seeing you but our thoughts and prayers will be with you.

Proverbs 15:10 is frightening for the person who shuns God's lordship in her life. God, the most perfect Father, deeply loves us and, foremost, desires our hearts to conform more and more to that of Jesus. He lovingly corrects, disciplines, molds, exhorts, and influences us toward that goal. If we reject this effort in our lives, we cut ourselves off from the care and protections of the Creator of the universe and place ourselves at the destructive mercy of a fallen world system influenced by Satan. We will spiritually and literally die. God, however, is not ready to give up, and will "sternly" and proactively keep us close to Himself and walking in His path. If we try to leave, He will (in answer to the prayers of those other believers who love us, and the pleading on our behalf of Christ and the Holy Spirit) seek to do whatever is required, in His time, to bring us back. He will not let us walk away.

Verse 11 tells us that our hearts and minds are fully transparent to God's mind. The term "death and destruction" is referring to hell and all that Satan schemes, plans, and carries forth in this world and in hell itself. God has a complete view and knowledge of even this—Satan exists only because God allows him to, and only for the age. Solomon is therefore saying that if God has full privy to the thoughts and actions of the great deceiver, how much more has He full view of the heart and innermost thoughts and motives of us, mere humans. If it wasn't for Christ, these thoughts would convict us and leave a just God no choice but to destroy us, as He will Satan, and all who have not confessed Christ. How thankful we should be that He has sent Christ and is committed to keeping us in His way, on His path.

I thank God daily for the improved MCAT scores and look forward to how He is going to sort all this out—where He wants you next year. I am convinced, since He is a God who hears and answers prayers, that His hand is upon this and His will shall be done. He loves you deeply and will walk with you closely, if you continue to seek Him and go to where He is working. Remember Ruth went to Boaz's field—only then could Boaz bless her and commune with her.

Proverbs 15:12 talks about a "mocker." A mocker is a person who cannot embrace truth but in order to exalt herself, maliciously and hatefully tears down God, His truth, and His revelation. Its quality is opposite to humility, and speaks of insecurity, low self-worth, and a desperate need to build up self by tearing down others. The more authoritative the one that is torn down, the better they feel about themselves. Thus God is a prime target. Such a person spurns and resents (to a visible degree that is exaggerated and fearfully brutal) any interaction with another who (by the very nature of correction) espouses to possess something beneficial and lacking to the mocker. Such a person will actively avoid one who has godly wisdom, fearing her as a challenge to his fragile self-worth. He will not seek truth or wisdom, even if his deep inner being realizes he needs it; he will suffer and die in his self-centeredness and lies rather than open himself up to wise correction from the Creator God.

Verse 13 conveys the thought that what lies in our heart controls and impacts the whole person. The happy heart is a result of one who has found Christ and made Him Lord of his or her life. Such a changed heart will influence one's whole countenance. Thus the term a "cheerful face." A person with a deep, prevailing heartache is a person who rejects and is alienated from God–a person with a hole in the heart that cannot sufficiently be filled with anything of the world. This state of the heart will lead to weariness, discouragement, restlessness, anger, pain, etc.–signs and symptoms of a "crushed spirit." Such a person is broken and lost, useless and defeated. Philippians 4 conveys this idea of how a God-focused and changed heart will change the appearance and actions of a person.

I was interested in your e-mail report on your experience at the Miami University student government meeting. There will always be organized opposition against the cause of Christ. In that setting, we as Christians will feel like the unpopular minority. Yet also in that setting we can rely heavily on Him and give Him opportunity to show His power and sovereignty.

Proverbs 15:14 contrasts a person with a "discerning heart" to the person exhibiting the "mouth of a fool"—the person who "seeks" versus the person who "feeds." The believer, who realizes his or her own human condition and comes to know God's character, will seek (proactively search to obtain what is valuable to break out of her depravity–character growth) knowledge. It is the "heart," not the mind only and certainly not the self-seeking cravings of our appetites ("mouths") that seeks God's Word–the Bible and the spiritual revelations of God through Christ and the Spirit. The Word of God instructs and changes us, but only as we seek His Word with our hearts. The glutinous appetite of our worldly nature (and the worldly women controlled by this nature) consumes ("eats") worldly trash ("folly"). This trash can never satisfy and such a person grows in her emptiness.

Verse 15 tells us the sad truth that the oppressed person's days are terrible–without meaning, peace, or joy. An oppressed person is one controlled by Satan and enslaved to the world's standards. She is (from an eternal standpoint) without hope, and feels the deep emptiness and dissatisfaction of her life now, while on earth. How gloomy and dark are her days. A person with a cheerful heart is one who knows God and is able to rise above her worldly circumstances–who has great peace and deep joy. Such a person has continual bright days, full of adventure and secure in the fact that the Creator of all is in control, and loves her deeply. Her days are like a continual feast, where there is abundance and plenty. Are people controlled by worldly standards and apart from God really happy or tragically sad and hidden from view?

How I enjoyed our weekend with my "college daughters!" I am so proud of you and treasure our friendship. It is good to feel we can share our thoughts, laugh together, seek truth together, debate together, and most of all pray together. I will be praying for you during your interview times.

Verses 16 and 17 of chapter 15 are two verses that compare values–those which come from a walk with God versus those which come from the world. An example of these verses can be found in Daniel, chapter 1. Verse 16 explains that it is better to have comparatively little worldly wealth and the proper relationship with God, than to have great worldly wealth but to be apart from God. The proper relationship with God is predicated on the "fear of God"–the overwhelming awareness of His power, sovereignty, love, and care; and our lacking in comparison. This attitude will allow us to be blessed by Him now and in the future. Our life without God, even if we have much worldly wealth, is a life in turmoil–painful, lacking peace and joy, confusing, and unsatisfying.

Verse 17 expresses the same thought but with food as the analogy. It is more satisfying to our soul (heart, mind, emotion, spirit) to exist with (and be surrounded by) His love (expressed by the Holy Spirit directly and through other believers), even if we must accept less in worldly terms. The world (as opposed to God) offers a "fattened calf" (rich, heavy, fatty food), but we must accept strife, conflict, confusion, turmoil, and hatred. Not only are there these, but the food itself deceives us–it looks appealing but will destroy us as we take it to ourselves. A meal of vegetables is positive and beneficial to our body, even if not appetizing to our senses–likewise God is beneficial to us and our life but not to our five human senses.

I've prayed for you several times today, as I knew you were at your Temple interview. I'm sure you made a great impression. It will be their loss if they don't offer you a position. I really enjoyed the concert at Miami University on Saturday. I must admit that although the music was good, I found myself praying during the concert for you. I was so proud of you and so deeply aware of God's love for you and His desire to use you mightily in His Kingdom.

Proverbs 15:18 is a great truth, one that I have learned and am continuing to learn. A person's anger when expressed (verbally or nonverbally) stirs up conflict and disagreement (dissension). Why do we get angry? Usually because our pride or self has been violated or we are hurt and cope with it by hurting back. The person who is most secure with his value (unconditional) and can care deeply for others has less of a tendency toward anger. Anger sometimes is justified and reflects God's own anger against ungodly actions and words. Anger can in part be genetic or part of an in-born temperament. Such a person must work hard, with God's help, to overcome this tendency. A person who can remain calm, trying to understand the other's position or perspective, will calm a potential conflict and argument. This proverb is very important in marital relationships and between friends.

Verse 19 is interesting and perhaps has several interpretations. I view it this way. A sluggard is a lazy, self-focused, nonproductive individual who can never seem to make any headway in life, and therefore, is of very limited value to God or man. He or she always has multiple reasons (excuses) why he cannot make progress ("thorns") and therefore he is "blocked." The problem is not the path, but he himself is the creature of the thorns which allows him excuses in life. The upright person is a hard-working person of possibility who never gives up and is guided by godly principles. Her road is wide and unobstructed because she will not let her weaknesses or excuses clutter the way. Life will throw obstacles in our way but such a person has resources and trusts in God's strengths such that she will not be overcome.

Proverbs 15:20 is similar to 10:1 which we have already discussed. The fact that it is repeated emphasizes its importance. The actions of an offspring will certainly bring emotion and value to her parents.

Verse 21 also echoes previous ones. Folly is world-centered, sense-oriented actions that are useful only for the moment but cause pain and harm as time unfolds. They are simply transient pleasures. The person who lacks God's perspective and wisdom is prone to seek this, resulting in a "live for the moment," world-standard attitude. The person who understands God, His truths, and His values and conduct, will not be decoyed by sinful pleasures of the world and will remain steady in her course (thoughts and conduct), keeping her eyes upon God.

Verse 22 changes its content. It tells us the value of godly counsel and seeking God's truth/desire by believing He speaks through others. One must be able to recognize who is godly and seek counsel from multiple persons of this level. Without being certain that our plans are consistent with God's plans, and where He is active, we will fail. Failure is not defined in worldly terms but relative to how well God can inhabit the plans and provide us His joy and peace. His body is more than ourselves; it includes others. Be willing to seek counsel from other godly persons and do not be reluctant to share your wisdom and perspectives with others who seek them.

We so enjoyed your dance performance. I was proud of your dance quality—but more than that I was proud of the character of a Christian woman who persevered in her desire and made the dance troop, became its president, chose to be in dance selections that were not degrading or world-focused, and was courageous enough to write in her biography of her involvement in Campus Crusade for Christ. I am confident God has heard and will honor your desire for Him to identify the one medical school He wants you in.

Proverbs 15:23 tells us that a person finds joy and acts in a good manner when he gives an apt reply or a timely word. We are filled with God's joy (that deep gladness and settled feeling of the spirit) when we speak in response to an inquiry of us in the proper season, at the proper time, and in the proper place. Too often a person pushes upon another his opinion or advice–pushing it when the receiver is not listening or is not receptive. This is not only ineffective but also will lead to rejection or controversy/conflict. This is the opposite of joy. In addition to our joy that is received when we reply properly, we also see that proper speech and the proper time and circumstance for that speech lead to goodness for others and God's kingdom.

Verse 24 expresses that the wise person (she who seeks God and His guidance/strength) will have a life that moves in a positive, rewarding direction toward God and His desire for His creation. The opposite is in store for the unwise. It tells us, also, that we cannot ever (in this life) stop seeking God but should commit to shaping our life (with His life) toward knowing and serving Him, or we can be pulled down. We cannot be over-confident or secure in our own efforts and strengths, but must move continuously in this positive, upward, Christ-centered manner.

I trust your return trip went well. Thanks for the visit. I will be praying for your tests and end of semester projects. I know you will do well. Enjoy the rest of your semester and I will be awaiting your return.

Proverbs 15:25 describes vividly how God loves the humble and hates pride, arrogance, and haughtiness. The Scriptures are full of examples of this proverb and I can testify to its truth in our daily modern lives. God "sets His face against" the proud man; He is serious and aggressive against such a person–He will undo the cheap, shallow, meaningless things of life if one seeks himself and his own self-centered desires, as opposed to those of God. Such a person does not seek or depend upon God and moves away from a relationship with Him. God is angry but more than that, grieves the rejection of His loved creation. He often uses the loss of worldly goods to bring a person back to Himself. The widow is an example of a person emptied of worldly goods (in that age) and therefore must seek and depend upon God and His love. God will bless such a person and provide adequately for her in this life.

Verse 26 also contrasts how God sees the wicked and the pure, relative to their thought life. He not only views our actions but knows our thoughts. The worldly, anti-God thoughts of the wicked cause God to "detest" what He sees in their hearts. Detest is very strong dislike and brings forth action. But the thoughts of the pure please Him. Pure thoughts are thoughts that place God and others above ourselves and control our commitments, priorities, actions, and values. They require the pure to stand apart from the world and run the risk of its rejection. Such dependent vulnerability pleases God and causes Him to act on our behalf.

It seems like a long time since you were here at Christmas break–I miss you. I spent the last three days with Nannie. I had many thoughts and feelings–at times joy in her hope and strength as a new Christian, at times fear and sadness as I know of the usual prognosis for this disease, and at times grief that she has come to this time of her life more alone than she should have been. I tried to honor her and respect her while giving strength to her emotionally and spiritually.

Proverbs 15:27 tells us that a greedy person will, in his quest for worldly wealth, bring dishonor, trouble, and pain to the family. Too often I have seen a family torn apart and painfully dealt with by the public because of the ways of one of its members. Such a person has sacrificed her character in order to get her own worldly needs met. She has taken the family down with her in the process. At the very least this confuses or dilutes the godly teaching within the family. Yet, the person who rejects the world's pressure and temptations will not be brought down, but will live a joyful, peaceful, useful life. A life given to God will be meaningful and peaceful, even if not wealthy in worldly terms.

Verse 28 continues the Proverbs teaching on the effect of the tongue and speech. The righteous person considers her words, expressions, and answers in her heart before they are spoken. On the other hand, the wicked will speak before considering the effect of her words on others and upon herself. The mouth "gushes" cruelty, abuse, pride, and revenge before the consequences are reviewed in the heart. There are no restraints or forethought.

Thank you for sharing your struggle, and its outcome, relative to the "research" issue. I am proud of your decision but I am more proud of the process you took to determine the right choice. I sensed you wanted to go this alone. I understand and view this as right and proper. You are "decleaving" from us as you grow in your self-sufficiency and maturity. This is what we raised you to do. I am excited about the medical school interviews coming up. I am praying specifically for them now.

Proverbs 15:29 is a great one that I encourage you to memorize and remember in times of uncertainty or when you feel alone or confused. The wicked have no title to expect or receive anything from God. He will not hear them when they cry out. But she who knows God and whose name is known by God will never have to fear being alone, not being heard or understood. When she cries out to God He does hear and will respond according to His will and His character. You must listen and watch for His response, sometimes very patiently.

Verse 30 is lighter and different. A "cheerful look" and "good news" cause our soul and body to be positively affected. We know joy and physical vigor when we receive from another a cheerful look and good news. Acts 16:29-34 is an example of how Paul and his companions gave joy and deep inner healing to the jailor and his family as they shared their cheerfulness in the Lord and the good news of His work on the cross.

Are you shivering in your bed at night? Have you gotten your house above sixty degrees yet? It sure has gotten cold here. Pray for Nannie. She will be meeting with the oncologist later in the month of February. I anticipate the need for God's grace and power in the months and years to come.

Proverbs 15:31 expounds the "teachable heart and spirit." The person who listens to constructive correction given by one who truly cares for him and his character will become wise. How fortunate the person who has people who deeply care enough to give selfless, life-giving counsel. To listen to such people is to gain wisdom. People who are selfless are so due to a relationship with God and therefore often provide God's wisdom to those who listen. Selfless people also must listen to God as He speaks to them through others and His Word.

Proverbs 15:32 continues this thought. The person who ignores selflessly-given advice and discipline is overly concerned about guarding her own self-worth and is driven by self-pride. She views herself as inferior and of little value–she despises herself. When you see a person shun loving counsel, you are seeing a person of low self-worth. A person who is secure enough in her value can yield herself to correction and will benefit in knowledge about herself, the world, and God. She will also be admired by others as a person of high character.

I've been praying about your next medical school interview at Rockford. I continue to believe that God has a specific school for you and His wisdom is greater than ours. It is exciting to see His action and will unfold in this process.

Proverbs 16

Verse 16:2 is an insightful proverb. We, in our human nature, can justify and rationalize our self-seeking thoughts and actions. We can make ourselves, by Satan-encouraged human justification, believe that even the most ungodly ways are "innocent." The world gives us great freedom to do all sorts of ungodly things, or say ungodly words, under the guise of individualization and tolerance. We are made to feel strict ethics are immature and ignorant while wholeheartedly embracing any and all actions as "innocent." However, God Himself will see clearly, without human rationalization or Satan's lies, the motives and heart of a person. He will judge ("weigh") them against His godly standard, which is unerring. See Daniel 5:25-30 for an example of how God looks into our hearts and judges motives. We must seek His standard; think and act in a way pleasing to Him even if it doesn't in the short run serve our purposes or receive acclaim by the world.

Verse 3 is one that should be memorized and is universally applicable. Give ("commit") completely without reservation everything you do–He is ready and able to take charge and to accept your commitment and desire for His involvement. His promise is that your plans (if they are motivated by a desire to serve Him) will succeed. The definition of success must also be from God's eternal, unconditional love perspective. It obviously doesn't mean we will get all the desires of our human nature (any more than a loving parent will give her child candy all the time, even if the child thinks she wants it). Our plan will succeed to the greatest accomplishment of what is of value and importance to our growth and service. Often, however, this will also please our heart and usually go well beyond this to the achievement of deep joy and peace.

I hope you are not deeply discouraged by Rush's "waiting list" decision. I admit on a surface, human level, I was; but, within a moment God brought back to me what we have been praying all along–that He would make known to you where He wants you, and that you will know, forever, that it was God who gave you the opportunity to serve Him as a physician. You will rejoice in this in a short time, and for the rest of your life.

Proverbs 16:4 speaks to this issue of trusting God for our lives and future plans. The writer assures us, once again, that God "works out everything" for His own ends. He is sovereign and all of His creation will move toward His chosen end–no one is spared. For those whom He loves, His love will deal with your life and will lead you to His path while He fills you with His blessings. He hears our prayers and His love will go beyond our wildest imagination.

Verse 5 changes the theme. I am convinced that "pride" is the most universal and deepest of man's sin. It is at the root of anger, self-centeredness, lack of compassion, and much more. God detests the "proud of heart." He cannot look upon those who place themselves above all others including Him. He knows the pain and the effect of such an attitude of heart. Esther chapter 1 describes

Xerxes who was filled with pride. See Philippians 2:1-11 as the example of Christ's humility.

Congratulations on being recommended by Rockford for medical school admission. I've thought and prayed about this and I feel at peace with this step. How is your spirit feeling? It is really neat to see how God, in answer to prayer, is "playing out this hand" to secure what is best for you, your future family, and His kingdom.

Proverbs 16:6 is a wealthy proverb. Love and faithfulness are the qualities that erase sin from our life and from our interactions with others. Christ in His love for us and in being faithful to His work and mission on earth has atoned for our sin. Additionally, as we love and are faithful in our interactions with others, we can overcome the sin that may have damaged a past relationship. As we receive God's love via Christ, we can love another selflessly and sacrificially. The awesome awareness of God, His power, His desires, His sovereignty, and His authority and the goodness of His spirit available for us, keeps us from regressing to our natural self-centeredness. The wish to please such a worthy God and to receive His blessing encourages us, sustains us, and empowers us to walk with Him and toward Him.

Verse 7 is one that is encouraging to remember when we are hurt or abused by the world. As we seek to know Him and serve Him, He is pleased. God is sovereign over His creation and will, in His time, cause the rebellious, self-seeking enemies to acknowledge Him and His people and to live in peace. He doesn't promise to eliminate enemies from our lives, and He may choose to delay this peace until after the second coming, but peace will occur.

I really enjoyed your visit home this past weekend. I'm sorry the "hair deal" ended on a sour note. I really wanted to pray with you and say "good bye" that night but as I walked up the stairs to your room, I observed you to be upset and decided not to place you in an uncomfortable situation. I'm sorry, for I guess I was the one uncomfortable and wanting to avoid a time of distress. If I let you down, I'm sorry. Be assured though that I came to the Lord that night, earnestly, for you and with you.

Proverbs 16:8 contrasts motives and worldly gain. The writer observes that the effect upon the soul-heart-spirit complex of gaining great wealth and worldly power by unjust means and with self-centered motives is grievous and ultimately destructive. To gain by sacrificing a sense of right and wrong, and at the expense of another person, is loss in the long run—loss of spiritual joy, deep emotional peace, and God's other blessings in this life. It is better to gain little of this world but to do so with compassion and justice in our relationships with others. God will reward us for this, in our soul and in eternity. How many "dollars" or "titles" must be had to balance deep spiritual joy and peace?

Verse 9 tells us that we, as humans, want to be in control of our lives. We want to plan them based upon our current assessment of our needs and desires. Often this is done without God or His wisdom. In reality it is God who will determine our actual steps in life. He is sovereign and will accomplish His purposes in His creation through us or in spite of us. God is sovereign over those who don't acknowledge Him, over the lukewarm Christians, and over those who give themselves fully to Him. It is better to seek His plans, to the extent He is willing to reveal them, and to accept the steps He leads us through to accomplish such plans.

Thank you again for the honor of being at the Crusade gathering last week. I cannot tell you how wonderful and proud I felt as I walked out on stage after your introduction. You are such a blessing to us and more to your heavenly Father. Please enjoy your spring break and your last months at Miami; your time has gone quickly but God has blessed it in marvelous ways. I am praying He will continue to bless your medical school years.

Proverbs 16:12-13 describes the ideal king or the godly leader. It gives us a glimpse of how a person in authority should behave, and the values he should hold. In verse 12, the leader should "detest wrongdoing." This first supposes that he has a value system in place that distinguishes right from wrong. Then the leader must feel and act according to it in regards to those people and behaviors which are negative or contrary to what is right. The leader must be courageous, moral, sensitive, powerful, and proactive.

In verse 13, the leader regards highly the person who speaks honestly and not the person who speaks what he thinks the leader wants to hear. The leader desires truth and honesty along with sensitivity and compassion. James 3:1-12 discusses the need to control the tongue–not by denying the truth but by being compassionate in how you use the truth in your speech. The ideal leader has mastered this and desires it in others as well.

I'm so happy you have returned to Miami safely and had a great time with your special friends from college. You have done this "college thing" extraordinarily well! You have profited and given; you have grown in all aspects of your person; you have been challenged and accepted those challenges; you have built deep, lasting relationships; you have grown daily into a mature and godly woman. God is so proud of you and has an immense vision for you and your life.

Proverbs 16:14 is solid wisdom. The "king" here might mean anyone who is in authority or in a place of power over you. Such a person can do you great harm if he or she is angry at you. This anger activated is "wrath." A wise person will diffuse this anger/wrath by speaking to the problem and helping the king to see it from a different angle. The unwise person will receive anger with anger thereby further distancing the king and begging for the show of wrath. The key here is to be humble and secure. This is only possible from a growing, maturing walk with Christ and a new perspective on your identity, on what is important in life, and on others.

Verse 15 shows the result of such an ability to appease the king. When a person in authority is appeased of his wrath and changes to understanding and respect, he or she can be a source of new opportunity ("life"). The favor that he or she will now bestow on you is not to be profited for our own human gain, but more importantly as a means to influence others for God. I think of Billy Graham and his influence on world leaders because of his wise approach and response to their negative overtures to him.

We sure will miss you this Easter–but I understand the demands upon you this time of the year. Seek to meditate on Christ's passion as it gives us a glimpse of how deep His love for us is. As I have studied what Christ endured, I am overcome with gratitude for Him and I desire to show this gratitude with my life.

Proverbs 16:16 emphasizes the importance of gaining wisdom. Wisdom is truth applied in a way that will move people toward God and His perspective on life. Wisdom is a gift, via God's Holy Spirit, that is His to give to those who seek it and value it. Wisdom at times requires us to put our human interests aside and stretches us into our uncomfortable zone. I believe one has to pray and ask even to be able to recognize true wisdom. This wisdom is better to seek and more precious to possess than the most sought after worldly commodity–epitomized as gold and silver. The world is blinded by the glitter and does not see the preciousness of God's wisdom.

Verse 17 tells us to avoid evil and guard our ways. The way of the persons of God (the upright) will not tempt evil by being in its company; it is easy for man to be side-tracked by the temptation of Satan. Each person has her own vulnerabilities, although there are certain areas that all Christians should avoid. We must guard ourselves from being pulled into temptation by virtue of our own vulnerabilities or by the allure of evil. James 1:14-15 is one of the best teachings on this subject. If you guard yourself from these, you will guard your soul. Satan desires to waylay us and divert us from God's highway.

I really enjoyed our brief visit to your church and breakfast afterward last weekend. Thank you for sharing your Sunday morning and your church with us. Today was a busy day at the office, but being a part of my patients' lives is a great privilege and an opportunity to serve our Lord. Never forget this and you will always love your work and will walk humbly.

Proverbs 16:18 and 19 are important verses, especially for us in medicine since society adorns us with special honor for being a doctor. Pride is a "basic sin." It will yield to other more secondary sins; sexual lust is the other basic sin. Haman, in the book of Esther, is a perfect illustration of the destructive nature of pride. Verse 18 tells us in words what is so painfully apparent to the observant person–pride (the belief that we are better than and deserve more than others) will lead to destruction and a "fall." It is easy, as Christians, to believe God's justice will see to this at the judgment day and during eternity, but it is also true of life here on earth. The "God image" in each of us and in His creation will move against the proud. Even those who deny a personal God will delight in the destruction of a prideful man. Over time such a person will be seen in his true light and his character will be made known and rejected.

The writer, in verse 19, goes so far as to say that it is better to be among those oppressed by the prideful than to be amongst the proud oppressors. It is better to view yourself as less important and thereby maintain a humble spirit. God truly loves such a person and she is attractive to others as well. This attractiveness will open doors of opportunity to others for Christ that are shut to the proud. A prideful Christian is a negative witness for our Lord.

I was so proud of you on Saturday evening–knowing that you worked hard, persevered, believed in yourself, and attained a goal–a goal you could easily have justified not pursuing. I am proud of the friends you have made and the opportunities you have taken to share Christ and be His testimony. Savor the next weeks for God is blessing you with them.

Proverbs 16:20-21 speaks to the need of God's children to be "teachable." This quality is so important and allows one to be molded, shaped, and fashioned by God so we can know His abundant gifts and join Him in an exciting kingdom ministry. We should never stop being teachable–the more one really knows about God the more she seeks to know and realizes the vast amount there is to know.

Verse 20 tells us that the person who "gives heed to instruction" (she hears, accepts, and is changed by it) prospers and is blessed. This may not mean she is blessed in worldly terms and by worldly standards. It can be part of the prosperity He blesses us with (usually God allows worldly rewards because He knows the need of our humanness–He loves His child and grants us this need), but His real blessing is in the giving of His fellowship and His spiritual fruits during this life, and eternal life with Him after death. The person so blessed is blessed because she trusts in God–His character, His promises, His past faithful activity in the lives of His children. Such trust will change our decision, actions–our very lives!

Verse 21 tells us that the person who is wise is "discerning"–that is, ingesting and digesting His Word into their lives. He wrestles with it and allows it to challenge him to higher levels of thinking and acting. It is an adventure with God–one taken with fear and excitement, resting on the confidence that He will be there with him. His "pleasant words" (the words that reflect his hunger and acceptance of His instructions) promote and facilitate Him to mature, challenge, and mold us.

Thank you for sharing your concerns and feelings about medical school at the University of Illinois and leaving Miami University and Campus Crusade. I understand and I will be praying daily for you in this transition. Although I am sure you have chosen rightly and that God's will is being done, it still doesn't spare you from the grief of loss and the challenges of the future. Be reminded that God knows and will abundantly supply all your needs.

Proverbs 16:22 and 23 continue the teachings on wisdom. Verse 22 compares "understanding" and "folly." Understanding is God's perspective into which we tap and thereby see creation and life to a small extent as He sees it. It is the verb that accompanies the noun of wisdom. It gives us a sense of clarity and makes sense of what is otherwise confusing. Folly is blindness to God's perspective that occurs because of our self-centeredness. It is like looking at a forest and seeing only one particular type of tree–we are misled and confused, and thereby make wrong decisions. The result, according to Solomon, of understanding is "living water" (fountain of life)–it is that which refreshes and satisfies yet is active and eternal. It gives peace, joy, and ability to love with God's compassion. Folly will bring punishment–both by God and by the world–for the world (deep inside itself) is God's creation and accepts His standards.

Verse 23 teaches us that it is the condition of the heart that is most critical in being able to glean or receive wisdom from God.

The heart and its sensitivity and receptivity to God's teaching will then guide the mouth–the spoken and unspoken communication rendered. Such interaction of a wise person with another seeking her counsel will be instructive and helpful to the latter.

1996—First Year of Medical School
Savoy, Illinois

Dear Christine,

Well, today was the first day of medical school–a journey that has been in God's plan for you since your creation, and a journey (although challenging) that will lead you to a position of extraordinary opportunity to serve Him and His creation. You are truly on "sacred ground"–walk worthily and with awesome respect. My prayers, wisdom, and knowledge are with you and are always at your service. You thanked us for financing medical school; I responded but didn't point out one point. We do this because we are able and because of our deep love for you. It is our response to and symbolic of God's demonstrated action in paying our debt, via Christ on the cross. He was able and loved so deeply that He paid our debt with His Son's life.

Proverbs 16:24 tells us a practical yet rarely applied truth. Our words are very important. If we make an effort, whenever possible, to say positive, caring, and uplifting words to another they can have a tremendous effect upon another's worth and ability to accomplish. Such words are indeed sweet to our soul and melt the stress and pain of life, while endearing us to another individual. They go even further; they can be instruments of healing to the body. The proper use of our words given in sincerity will be a positive healing factor to one who is ill.

Verse 25 is the same as verse 14:12 and since I have already written on this, I will proceed to verse 26.

Verse 26 says that we are "fallen people" (as a result of the garden of Eden fall) and as such are under the rule of work and toil. Our survival needs, and those under our responsibility, drive us to participate actively in work, toil, and effort; since this is how God has set it up, following our fall. Therefore, it is right and in keeping with the order He has established, that we must work and toil for what we need or enjoy of the world. Wealth and gain gotten without such labor is dangerous and suspiciously out of keeping with God's order and plan. Nothing of this world comes without effort and hard work; only God's gift of salvation and the Holy Spirit are free and not able to be earned. The application of His Spirit to grow us to righteousness, however, takes effort and strain. We should use carefully that which we gain out of our toil, not wasting it foolishly, respecting it as a fruit of our labor, in God's order.

It seems strange writing to you, since I know you are close enough to visit face to face; but there is something unique and complementary (to verbal discussion) about a letter, to one so loved. It is important to me, to our Lord, and I hope to you, that His wisdom is told and set out as our standard for thinking and action. Thus I desire to continue to write you of His proverbs.

Proverbs 16:27 and 28 will be the verses for my meditation. Verse 27 defines a "scoundrel." This term defines a person who is motivated by evil and self-centeredness, to the extent that she goes to great length to counter good and godliness. A scoundrel is Satan-like, and in fact, has been the term often given to Satan himself: the greatest of scoundrels. People who become overwhelmed by Satan's temptations and "dragged away and enticed" (James 1:14) can become more and more controlled by sin, until they become "dead" to righteousness. Such a person not only succumbs to evil but she herself "plots" evil–digs up and creates a circumstance where evil thrives. They delight in evil and are most uncomfortable with godliness. Even their words and speech are destructive, cruel, damning, and actively evil–"like a scorching fire" (hell).

Verse 28 defines two other people types: "perverse" and a "gossip." The perverse person delights in conflict and strife; she delights in seeing peace disrupted and distorts that which is good, pleasing, wholesome, constructive, and honorable. Such a person delights in stirring up dissention and does not have within her God's spirit. The "gossip" is the person who uses words to pervert and cause dissension between two friends. She delights in inventing or distorting truth, or breaching confidences, to harbor in the mind of a person ill motives towards another who had been a friend (a person who had a commitment to uphold another's value, worth, and needs). Nothing delights Satan more than disrupted friendship, since the latter is counter to self-centeredness. Be careful of the scoundrel, the perverse man, and the gossip.

It was good to see you at church, Sunday school, and for lunch. I realized that the time was a sacrifice, but I so appreciated seeing you in the Romans Sunday school class.

Verse 29 of chapter 16 uses the word "entices"–this triggers the verses in James to my mind (James 1:14-15). People will entice those around them; to entice is to be able to manipulate them to a desired mindset or action by saying or doing just the right thing at the right time (at their point of weakness or vulnerability). A person is called "violent" when she does this to the destruction or disadvantage (in God's perspective) of that other person. Smooth speech or a magnetic personality can lead someone in the wrong direction, away from a closer walk with God. Even Christians (no matter how mature) must beware of this, realizing that Satan knows us better than we know ourselves, and will know how and when to tempt us. The only strength we have to defeat him is God's Spirit. Therefore, seek God's discernment and continually ask prayerfully for His victory in your life over such enticements.

Verse 30 gives a visual, slightly allegorical picture of how to recognize this enticement. The writer is encouraging the godly person to "read" others, with the eyes of the Spirit. There are ways of looking, non-verbal behaviors, gestures, attitudes, and approaches that reveal insincerity and destructive motives. The point here is not that winking an eye or pursing the lips are of themselves bad, but that we must be alert and watchful of those around us. We must know what specifically will entice each of us and ask for God's discernment, wisdom, power, and victory over these areas. Prayerfully seek the Lord's mind before decisions are made or emotional actions taken. Be dependent upon Him moment-by-moment.

I hope your studying is going well. I am praying for your study and the tests. Thank you for your participation in the Romans study on Sunday morning. It is so wonderful for a father to have his daughter in such a class.

Proverbs 16:31 is an interesting verse–especially as I get older. "Gray hair" here means not only age, but also wisdom (true wisdom is only God's wisdom and is received only by those who seek it within a relationship with Him, via Christ). Age and wisdom is, in a sense, an earthly reward (as well as providing joy and a deep peacefulness) for walking with God over the years and seeking to grow daily in godliness. It is the mark of one who studies God's Word and experiences Him in a dynamic prayer life–over years and years (perseverance). This "righteous life" is the life that is evolved and which grows out of the discipline of a Christian life. God honors and exalts such a life lived here on earth with age and wisdom (the reverse is not true). Seek such people and become teachable in their presence.

Verse 32 is one of those verses that show us that God's values and perspective are so different from those of the world. In God's eyes, and from a perspective of eternity (from creation until we are all at rest with God in heaven), a patient person who controls her temper is of greater value, is more useful to God, is more glorifying to Christ's name, and is more able to receive and give love, than a victorious warrior who conquers a great city, a politician who wins an election, a businessman who makes a million dollars, a doctor who has power and prestige in society, or an athlete who wins the gold. It is so hard for a person to understand this perspective and to put it into action in life.

I was glad to hear from you today and share your relief that the first major test of medical school is over! It sounds like you felt okay or good about your performance. The patient in my office at the time of your call commented that I appeared happy on the phone. I explained the call to him and he said, "You must be proud to have such a daughter." I really am, Christine!

Proverbs 16:33 is a reassuring bit of wisdom, but one ignored by many (even Christians). It tells us that there really is no such thing as chance or that we are in control of life. "Casting lots" was an ancient way of decision making–believing that some magical means can direct our paths. It rejects the concept that we have a personal God who loves us and desires to direct our ways to our best interest and toward His kingdom's end. Especially we who are adopted children of God, with all the rights and privileges of His true Son, Jesus, should seek Him with all our concerns and decisions. Instead we regard most things as "chance," or feel we (without Him) can know what is right ourselves and ignore Him. Ultimately, it is and will be His decisions that will yield proper results, stand the test of time, and allow Him to bless us. God really is in control of His creation, and as we seek His input to our lives we will live in harmony with Him and know the joy, peace, and reward of such a walk.

Proverbs 17:1 is quite a different proverb. It tells us of the value to our body, mind, and soul of a place without strife or conflict. Even if there is not "a plenty" in material terms in this place, the nurturing and nutritional value (in holistic terms) of a place of peace is far superior to a place of great material comforts full of strife. Often a place with very little in material terms reflects a godly nature of its inhabitants and the peace of that place reflects this nature. Often materialism breeds conflict, strife, competiveness, worldly intrusions–these characterize the people of "self-seeking" natures. In God's perspective and terms, worldly pleasure and materialism do not imply His blessing, necessarily. Strike a balance of enjoying God's creation with a peaceful godly nature.

I praise God that you are off to a great start at medical school. I know for sure in my heart that you will become a physician. I encourage you to view the test results as a confidence booster, a confirmation by God of your choice of life work, and an encouragement to continue to work hard with humility and thanksgiving. I'm also happy you have taken some leadership in the CMDS (Christian Medical Dental Society) group, and that God has provided some spiritual time at the school.

Proverbs 17:2 contrasts a servant with a son. At first glance we think that surely the father will prefer the son. But there are modifiers to these two persons. The writer tells us that the father (the heavenly Father) regards a wise (dependable, selfless, seeking to do her master's will) servant as better than, and with superior position ("rule over") a disgraceful son. What is a disgraceful son? I suspect this would be an arrogant, self-centered man who abuses and manipulates his birth position and his father's love to the destruction of what is right, good, and just. The heavenly Father will choose this servant and he will share in the inheritance as one of the family. For us, our inheritance will be as that of our older brother: Jesus. We Christians are all servants–adopted by God to share all the riches, glory, and honor as God's own children.

Verse 3 talks about the refining process for Christians. The writer tells us that the Lord Himself conducts and is in control of the refining process of His children. He refines the heart by allowing the world to present us with trials and tribulations, choices, decisions, opportunity, and temptation; He offers us His wisdom and strength to use in this process. He is there for us–appropriated by faith. Each time we, in faith, rely on Him, seek Him, choose Him we become more pure and godly–He is "refining" us. All of this is at the heart level. The writer contrasts this refining process with a crucible and a furnace. Both refine by heat and melt the metal–so we must expect "world heat" and to have God use this to melt and to remold us to His image. This is a gradual, progressive process. In addition, the writer implicitly conveys that our heart and soul are of much greater value than silver or gold, because God has chosen (by grace) to involve Himself in our lives.

Thank you again for your card and written thoughts. I so treasure these communications; they are worth more to me than any gift or material item. I appreciate your sensitivity to know this about me, and to bless me so richly.

Proverbs 17:4 tells us that the "wicked" person (the person who rejects God and His dominion in his or her life, and instead follows Satan's lies and worldly agendas) will be influenced or under the control of those people and spirits that encourage evil ways. Evilness is the thoughts, feelings, and actions that result from our deliberate suppression of God's truth and His revelation, accepting Satan and the world's influence working through our self-centered nature. A person who herself lives and speaks lies will heed talk and influences from other people, the world's system, and Satan who desires to destroy our soul, our body, and life eternal. The upright, God-centered and connected heart learns to know the voice of the deceiver, and will shun him.

Verse 5 tells us that when we mock the worldly and humanly poor, we show contempt to God, who created them and has a purpose and love for them. We "mock" by harsh overtly hurtful words and actions, or by ignoring and living like they don't exist. I wonder sometimes whether part of God's purpose in having the poor among us is to teach and stir up within us kindness and compassion, at least to have us see our need in these areas and seek Him (via Christ) for empowerment. The poor can be poor materially, emotionally, spiritually, or mentally. Contempt conveys impatience, negative judgment, haughtiness, self-centeredness, anger, and disrespect. Further we are warned that if we take prideful pleasure ("gloating") when bad things happen to others (even those who have hurt us), we will be punished by God. Will this be punishment at the final judgment or by Him giving us over to the world's ways with its resulting pain and disorder, or both?

I've been thinking and praying for you today, knowing that you had a lab test. I'm excited to see the proofs of the outdoor family pictures; they should be good. I enjoyed being with all of you for that short time. I pray that in the future, our family can celebrate times together often.

Proverbs 17:6. As one ages, the character of one's children is often seen in how they relate, care for, and parent their own children.

The test of one's success or failure is often seen in the character of his grandchildren, although not always since there are other factors that modify this. The caring, loving, nurturing parent is a crown to her own parents; a crown being symbolic of pride and being blessed. Parents, alternatively, should also be a source of pride to their children. The character of the parent will over time be seen as honorable, wise, deeply caring, altruistic, and God-centered. As they become mature adults, children should present with pride their parents to their friends. How sad it is when parents by their own low character are a source of shame to their children. These wonderful dynamics are only possible if the people involved love God and seek Him for themselves and their children.

Verse 7 tells us that arrogant (really better translated as eloquent or good) words ("lips") are not suitable to the self-centered, God-rejecting, worldly-wise person. Words are unsuitable or not fitting because they do not adequately or properly reflect a person's real heart and life. Words that would be suitable as accurately reflecting his true character would be degrading, harsh, and wicked. As sad and hypocritical as this is, it is much worse for one in a position of authority and influence to use words that are untrue to her real desires and motives. Hypocrisy, manipulations, greed, and deceit are clearly manifest when a person in authority is found to be misrepresenting himself or herself with "lying lips." A godly heart and integrity combine to be a certain blessing to others and to God.

Another set of exams done. I heard they were longer and harder. Thanks for your honest thoughts and questions during and after Sunday school last week. Continue to think and prayerfully study His Word and greater wisdom and discernment will be given to you. I sense this year will be one of rapid maturing and self-exploration for you, leading you further toward godliness with powerful opportunities.

Proverbs 17:8 is, at first glance, confusing because of the negative connotation to the concept of the "bribe" in our modern culture. Here a bribe signifies a gift given out of deep affection and love. It is given out of a heart with these emotions, but also in hopes that it would enlist a positive response from the other person. The proverb tells us that such giving will yield success, work "like a charm," in that it will yield that which is of great value. We cannot expect to bring about care and returned affection from another if we treat him negatively and are unwilling or unable to convey positive, loving sentiments or tangible expressions of our love. This proverb encourages people to be "givers" and willing to express their affection. People usually respond in kind, and community as fellowship is built.

Verse 9 is a very practical one with sage advice. The person who is offended by another has a choice. She can either deal directly with the person who offended her, not telling other people or taking slanderous revenge, or she can, to seek her need for revenge or out of envy, spread lies, exaggerations, half truth, or their unipolar perspective to others not involved. The results of each of these choices differ. In the first case, the sincere, honest, personal interaction that is then put aside and forgotten improves trust and understanding and is healing–it promotes love. In the second case, the malicious way of dealing with interpersonal hurt will separate not only the two people involved, but also cause strife between uninvolved people who are smitten with the slanderous gossip.

I'm proud of your test results. Thank you for calling and sharing them with me.

Proverbs 17:10 is really a neat bit of wisdom. A woman who is intuitive, sensitive, eager to be taught, and with appropriate self-regard will be easily aware of the communication of others. A rebuke (a mild, gentle, constructive, negative communication) will have enormous effect on a discerning woman and harsh, confrontational, and destructive overtones will not be necessary to communicate and teach such a one. This is in opposition to the "thick-headed" nature and unteachable personality of one who is so self-focused ("fool") that he cannot see or hear other people and their needs. Such a fool will require harsh communication to get through to him and convey these needs. Although there is a personality factor involved here, the spirit can soften and make a heart more sensitive and "other-centered."

Verse 11 can be understood in civil terms, but really it speaks to us in spiritual terms. An "evil man" (one sold out to getting what he wants despite the pain and destruction to God and others) is determined to not be a team player and seek a common good, and therefore will resist command, regimentation, and common good in favor of his self-needs. Eventually a strong official will be sent to discipline and correct this man–in whatever harsh terms are needed. Likewise, a person separated from God will seek her own will and rebel against God's standards and counter God's vision. Such a person will someday be subject to harsh judgment and discipline at Christ's second coming.

It was good to be with you and your friends Saturday evening. You are blessed to have good friends like them.

Proverbs 17:12 is an interesting slice of wisdom. A mother bear robbed of her cubs becomes aggressive, hostile, intense, fanatical, and undeterable. Such a bear is strengthened by her passion for her offspring–there is a deep, inseparable union with her offspring–to remove her offspring is to tear her apart. Similarly, a fool (one who is self-focused, not God-focused, and whose behavior reflects pride and her distorted perspective of life) is attached to her folly. The folly of a fool is that desperate, aggressive, impassioned behavior and activity that are designed to enhance her worth or value. It is folly because it will never achieve this; because value apart from God is hollow and will never satisfy. But a fool will be aggressive, hostile, intense, and passionate in this valueless behavior. Be careful not to contend with a fool acting out her folly.

Verse 13 is one of several proverbs that tell us that once we entwine ourselves with evil, it can affect us and our whole household. If a person in greed, out of pride and self-centeredness, dishonors goodness by harming or degrading the other person, or God, then she chooses evil over good. Once we open ourselves and our household to this choice, it is difficult to ever remove its "foothold" from our life and that of our family. The sins of the parent are visited on generations to come. Evil so permeates, distorts, devalues, and colors all we think, feel, and do, that it becomes intertwined in all aspects of our lives. It is like yeast in bread. Be in constant prayer to be wise and prevent evil from entering by your choices and your life.

I'm sorry we didn't get to talk much Sunday morning. I looked for you after Sunday school but I suspect you felt a need to get to the "books." It is so special for me to have you in the Romans study. It is a very powerful book of the Bible. It helps us as Christians to have a firm grasp on what we believe and why.

Proverbs 17:14 is sound advice. A quarrel usually begins with one or both persons hastily and without thought expressing in words hurt and anger (see Proverbs 12:18). The words are multiplied by a whole bank of emotion from past and present experiences, and fueled by Satan lying to us about their meaning and the intent or motive of the other person. Soon we counter by spoken or unspoken words to hurt back or "set them straight;" these then cause a similar response in the first person; or we sink into silence, nurturing our pain, hurt, and anger to the point of building large barriers to ever retrieving the relationship. And so it goes! It is like pounding a hole in a dam–water pours out, at first slow, then the hole widens under pressure from the water and the force and amount of water progressively increase. The water never seems to end–it goes on forever! Proverbs tells us to short-circuit this process by never letting a quarrel escalate.

Verse 15 makes the points that God is a just God, and we as His children must seek justice. We, as He, cannot acquit or justify sin unless there is a contrite heart that seeks atonement. We must, in love and with patience, help a person to see her guilt and to desire to change. Although we may be rejected (at least at first) in this effort, we must try. We must not overlook sin and godlessness. Likewise we must not allow an innocent person to be condemned–to impute evil and the burden of guilt where it is not found or earned. We must protect those who are abused or neglected by others or society, for reasons that are not fair or that they have not earned. God detests abuse and neglect because He is wise, just, and righteous. As we become more like Christ we should view these likewise.

I trust that by the time you receive this letter you will be back to the school routine after a brief Thanksgiving interlude. I know you feel a sense of sadness now as you transition from college to real life.

I know you miss your friendships, but I'm confident God will provide new ones as you wait on Him. Nevertheless, I will continue to pray with you on this subject. Practice thinking on the good things and challenge yourself not to be captured by worry (Phil. 4:8).

Proverbs 17:16 is, I think, interesting. The proverb speaks of "money" as a resource that can get things done, influence others, open doors, create opportunities, and strategically place one in this world. If a fool (one who shuns God in favor of her own human and self-focused desires/needs) has such resources, they will be squandered or, worse, used against God's purposes to seek the world's wisdom. They will not seek God's wisdom (the way He desires His creation to live and apply truth) and therefore are of no "use" to God or His world, as seen from His perspective. Resources in the hand of a fool will only degrade God and bring ruin upon the fool and others she influences. I believe, in general, that godly men and women do receive resources (as defined above) from God and are accountable to Him as to how they use them. Seek to use the resources God has given you to get wisdom for yourself, your loved ones, and those whom you influence.

Verse 17 can be applied to Jesus or to a Christian person with whom we are in relationship. A "friend" and a "brother" are roles of intimacy and commitment that require a higher and more costly level of involvement. Jesus can be (and is) our best friend and will love us at all times, in every situation, and without strings attached ("unconditional"). His love is energizing, healing, and understanding–it encourages us in difficulties and rejoices with our joys! A friend (human) who is in relationship with us because of our common bond of Christ, can approach this level of loving–the ultimate being the love of your spouse and parents. Jesus also is our brother and is committed to us by His blood (there is no option to be otherwise); such a commitment can be counted upon in our hour of need–in all adversities. Likewise there are relationships (because of kinship through Christ) that are as deep as a blood brother, and who can be counted upon to stick with us no matter what the circumstances, and to support us when we hurt or are hurt by the world.

I enjoyed the music Sunday morning. It was good to see you playing the flute again. I am praying for you during your study time, and for the exams coming up. I am confident in you, but I know the hard work and hours of study involved. I pray God will sustain you, bless you, and bring toward fruition His work that He has begun in you. I framed the picture you brought me from Venice last summer. It looks nice and is hanging in our bedroom.

Proverbs 17:18 is interesting and somewhat "anti-humanistic;" at first it appears self-centered and ungiving. A fuller explanation is found in Proverbs 6:1-5, and is referred to again in 11:15. Examples are found in Philippians 18 and 19 and Genesis 42:37 and 44:32. The writer advises against entering into pledges (and putting up your resources for another–even a neighbor), of all types. Such generalized, before the fact, commitments are made often before full knowledge of the circumstances, the various and possible actions and direction, and the implications of all these various possibilities can be known and evaluated. Generally, it is out of the need to be seen as helpful (at best) or prideful, able to meet lesser people's needs (at worst). We move to bring about people's dependency upon us, in order to gain greater self-worth and feel our pride. Often this arrangement, with pledges made with this motivation, will backfire and we will be hurt, rejected, taken advantage of, find we are objects of the other's resentment, and cheat those who are truly dependent upon us (family) of our time and resources. Be cautious in this area.

Thanks for reporting your test scores to me. As always I am very proud of you and see God's continual confirmation on you being a physician and serving Him in medicine.

Proverbs 17:19 is sage advice. The person who loves conflict and quarrels is a person who delights in contention. Such a person has a high estimate of himself and judges others by this standard; he is unable to seek to understand or have empathy for another's circumstance or perspective. Such an attitude is based on pride. Pride is the mother of sin and is at the root of Satan's evilness and our fallen sinful nature. Be careful, then, in your conflicts and judgments. Likewise, the proverb tells us that the person who exalts himself ("builds a high gate") and implicitly judges and rejects others will eventually fall and have his pride broken. It is only a matter of time. Such a position is lonely and when the fall comes it hurts deeply.

Verse 20 is proven true in life, not always in the short-term analysis of a person's life, but definitely over the long-term analysis. Even though there is great evil in the world, God's moral fiber is in His creation and, whether one admits it or not, each person holds another to a godly standard, and rejects the self-seeking person. The person with a perverse heart is one who desires to see hardship befall another and delights in the destruction of what is good, healthy, and beautiful. She desires to pervert such to seek destruction, harm, and evil. A person with a deceitful tongue is one whose speech and communication is untrustworthy and egocentric, it is devoid of faithfulness and is manipulative to get his own way and build himself up at the expense of the other. Such people will, in the long run, not prosper and will get into trouble, even by those who don't personally know God. Ultimately of course, God will judge them and His wrath will be appropriated.

I heard from Mom that the speaker at the CMDS retreat was good. I wish I could have been there. I would love to hear from you what he said. Did you meet any new people from other campuses? How's school going so far this semester? I pray for you daily.

Proverbs 17:21 talks about the effect a foolish child has upon his parent. A fool is a person not recognizing or accepting truth. Since truth always comes from God, or is consistent with God's view or pattern, a fool does not accept God and God's moral order. Such a person buys into the world's order, morality, standards, and view of existence; she makes her choices and decisions with such a perspective. This ultimately, often immediately, brings harm and destruction to herself and grief (as in grieving a great loss) to her parents, who apart from God, love her most in this world and want the best for her. A parent's deep joy is to see his child seek truth and walk in this perspective. A parent often will judge his own value or achievement by that of his child, thus bringing either grief or joy.

Verse 22 is mainly talking about spiritual/emotional health, although often quoted in relation to physical health. The "cheerful heart" here is related to a heart that is full of joy, peace, optimism, hope, and contentment; such an inner perspective is only possible out of a relationship with God. This perspective obviously restores our relationship with our Creator-Father, but also provides an attitude and emotional balance that allows us to rise above, or make the best of difficult worldly circumstances. It is also infectious to others and provides healing medicine for them as well. A "crushed spirit" is one of discouragement, lack of peace, pessimism, and hopelessness; this occurs when one is apart from God and has chosen the world and its viewpoint as his own. His whole system is brittle and will easily break under the pressures and circumstances of life.

As I said on the phone, I am happy to share at a CMDS meeting if you would like me to. Let me know a date so I can schedule it and let's talk a little about what might be relevant to their needs. I will be praying for the group, as I sense there is some confusion and conflict on some level.

Proverbs 17:23 depicts the state of humanity where our self-centeredness and self-focus once again pervert godly morality. Justice is important to God–He is just and He will judge us according to our faith and our faith walk. He despises the person who for selfish purposes will interfere with justice, even here on earth. Satan and the world (apart from God) know that bribes (undeserved gifts given to manipulate us) will interfere with objective and truthful testimony and confuse or distort the outcome of any effort to bring justice. There are many subtle types of bribes that are designed to influence us in a way that is unfair or unjust. We have a tendency to justify them when they provide special favor for us, even if it ultimately will be at the expense of others.

Verse 24 contrasts, again, a discerning man and a fool. A person who (by God's Spirit) is able to know that true wisdom comes from an ongoing and growing relationship with God is "discerning." Such a person will not move from one thing to another, desperately or even frantically seeking truth, but will keep her eye upon God (or Jesus–see Hebrews 12:1-2). God's Word (Bible) will always be in her view and accessible for her direction, vision, needs, nurturing, knowledge, and discipline. Contrast such a one with a fool. Her eyes and mind and heart wander from one thing to another, never settled, always being disappointed or disillusioned, as she seeks after truth and a fulfilling relationship with her Creator. She seeks in vain through her own worldly knowledge, trusting not in God who has given His secure and faithful revelation in His Word, but in human perspective, understanding, and fickle feelings. Ground yourself firmly in His Word and see it as the only true and consistent source of truth and wisdom,

I hope the lab test today went well. I am confident in you and your academic ability but pray for you during test time (although I pray for you daily on many issues).

Proverbs 17:25 is deep in spiritual, as well as human, insight. When a son or daughter turns from God and seeks his or her own self-interests he cuts himself off from truth, true wisdom, spiritual discernment, joy, peace, and ability to love. He hurts himself and moves towards despair, loneliness, confusion, callousness, and relativism (he is foolish–doing what harms himself). However, his choices and life do not only affect him but they affect those who love him. God loves him the most and it brings deep pain to Him as He sees His creation and work walk or run from Him; how deeply He hurts can never be known by man, since we can't fathom how deeply He loves. Next to God, the person's parents are deeply hurt, because they love the child the most (second to God). The father feels grief–the loss of his hopes, desires, and expectations for his daughter; as if she in part dies. The mother, who gave life to the child, feels bitterness to life and a world where what was/is so much a part of her, rejects her and what she stands for. The bitterness leads to depression and hopelessness–it is as if her life has been invalidated.

Verse 26 is an understatement that seems self-evident, but the world has distorted and perverted this truth. To distort or pervert justice is evil, it is wrong and against God's creative order and moral law. To punish an innocent person because of the untruthfulness of the world or the logistics of humanity is wrong in God's eyes. To punish a person for moral or relationship integrity is equally an abomination to God. Yet, we condone and equip our society with the tools, perspective, and attitude that allow such schizophrenic behavior (to punish the right and sanction the wrong). God's justice will someday correct but until then, this is the world's way. We should not be surprised by it.

I'm glad you had a good time in Ohio. It is such a blessing to have friends like you have! I will be praying for you as you seek God's will for you this summer. Mom tells me you have a "date" with Jeremy this weekend–let me know how it works out.

Proverbs 17:27 and 28 are true pearls of wisdom; character traits which almost all people find attractive, and which permit God to use us effectively in the lives of other people.

Verse 27 tells us that a person of knowledge (facts and insights about truth, from God's perspective) is a person who listens intently and with humility (not overtaken with self-superiority) and teach-ability; she weighs her words carefully, realizing that words once said cannot be erased and will have deep and lasting repercussions. Even words must be accounted for, and take their toll. Likewise, a "man of understanding" is a person who understands the heart and emotional/spiritual needs of others. Such understanding can help one not "react" emotionally (not even tempered) because this understanding depersonalizes the other person's emotions (i.e., anger, fear, defensiveness, etc.). Words and actions said or done during an emotional reaction are likely to be destructive and reap pain and regret. The key to stability is security and humility in our walk with God.

Verse 28 furthers these points. Even a person with limited knowledge and insight will be regarded as wise if she listens, learns, reflects, and seeks clarification, rather than putting forth an unlearned, unwise opinion in an effort to be impressive to others. How much more will a wise person (possessing God's perspective and truth) be viewed with respect and high regard, if she listens more and contributes less, and only when the timing and spiritual urgings so dictate. She must be discerning as to when to speak and what to say. This ability is a result of the indwelling of God's Spirit and growing godliness. Such discernment yields greater wisdom and greater sensitivity to others and will ingratiate one to the world so he may be an effective witness. Godly men and women demonstrate these character traits.

It felt a little like spring today. Too bad it wouldn't last until spring really gets here. I continue to appreciate your participation and insights during Sunday school class. I hope the study of Romans has been helpful; it has been very beneficial to me as I study and teach it. I am praying for your "guy" situation and for you to be able to relinquish control of it to God–it is hard. Suffering to develop character?!

Proverbs 18

Proverbs 18:1 describes some features of an "unfriendly man." Such a person is one who exalts himself, is prideful and above others, and persues his own will and way, manipulatively and insensitively despite others. He seeks his own "selfish ends" and will not be teachable by God's wisdom, or submit to God's will or the will of the general body of Christ. He will rationalize away truth and true wisdom, in favor of his will. Such a person causes conflict, separation, and schism within the church or in any organization. He is useless to God and an abomination in His sight. See 1 Timothy 1:20 and 2 Timothy 4:14-15. Not all unfriendliness (socially) is due to this issue, but be discerning to observe pridefully motivated "unfriendliness."

Verse 2 states that the person who seeks to "understand"–either truth or another person–is wise. A fool is one who is so full of himself that he misses or rejects God's truth in his life; as a result he is filled with pride. A prideful person doesn't seek to understand and if forced to do so, takes no pleasure in it. A fool has contempt toward instructions and is not teachable; he wants to be heard, to be able to pompously render his own opinions. He gets his delight in this, not in learning or growing through instructions and corrections. I wonder whether such people even really hear others; whether they can read God's Word and miss His truth and wisdom. The root of this difficulty, as in all other sins, is pride and self-focus. There is nothing more refreshing than a person truly seeking to be taught and therefore a good listener. We can strive to be a listener–to God's wisdom in the Word or as He reveals it via other people.

I continue to pray for you–especially for your medical school studies, your relationships with the men you are getting to know (and for the one God will bring to you), your summer's activities, and the things God desires to teach you this summer, and for your CMDS leadership responsibilities. I so appreciate being a part of your life and the privilege of being able to pray for you and with you.

Proverbs 18:3 identifies first wickedness with contempt. Rejecting the Lord for your own self-centered, sinful desires is the route of all wickedness and evil. A person with such motivation will talk and act in such a way that will resist any spiritual subjection to God. For to subject our will and control to God, believing Him to be all wise and wishing to benefit us with His blessing, is to embrace Him as Lord over our life. This is opposite of the concept of "contempt." Wicked people show contempt (anger, bitterness, resentment, stubborn opposition) to God because He requires us to seek Him and His way, not our own. As a result of wickedness, we will know shame. The evil we speak or act is contrary to our internal moral code (there because we were made in God's image), therefore, shame arises (often against our wishes). Wickedness also brings disgrace to the person and her family. The world, ironically, values godliness and disgraces the self-centered, godless person.

Verse 4 is a word picture and contrasting analogies using water. The "words of a man's mouth" is to be seen as human, man-derived, often evil and commonly destructive counsel and advice. This is like "deep water"–water where we can sink and drown, water that is still and black—not living or moving, it is stagnant and not refreshing. But the "fountain of wisdom" (Christ and the Holy Spirit within us) is like a "bubbling brook"–water that is clean, fresh, refreshing, life-giving, moving, and active, where we are safe, water that takes us somewhere. This is an analogy of the difference between man's and Christ's wisdom and counsel. See John 7:37-38 as an example of the analogy.

I really appreciated your call last Saturday, just to talk for a while. Our relationship is so precious and important to me. I strive to achieve the balance of involvement and progressive "decleaving" as you and your sisters mature. I wish to always be a father and will never stop loving you. I continue to pray for your studies and your relationship(s) to godly men. I am confident that God is at work in both these areas.

Proverbs 18:5 is a call for toughness and willingness to stand forth, even when there could be personal implications. The writer points out that "it is not good" (since only God is good, to not be good is to be against God and God's morality and ethical view of life), to be favorable or give preference to the wicked. That is, it is not in keeping with God's view (and therefore not able to please Him or receive His blessing) that we encourage, promote, or even recognize the person who seeks self above all others. We should, instead, seek to even the score and aid the innocent victims of the world's sin order. Great injustices are being done to the innocent of the world (those who didn't personally earn the pain and penalty they suffer) at the hand of greedy, powerful, self-centered people. God will someday justly deal with this, but for now we as His body should seek justice, actively and without personal fear.

Verse 6 focuses again on the words and speech of a "fool" (a person apart from God, who doesn't have a godly nature; she is outside of a relationship with God via Christ). Such a person will use her mouth, as it reflects her unbridled self-centered emotions and desires, to deal viciously with the world. Her words invite, from other ungodly persons, rebuke, revenge, anger, and painful words and actions. It will cause her strife and be as if she was beaten–humiliated, rejected, insulted, disgraced, and could even result in bodily symptoms. Once again the writer highlights the effect of the tongue on us and upon others in the world.

I've prayed for you several times today, as you were doing your midterms. I hope everything has gone well. I'm also praying for your summer and your relationship with Jeremy. Have you heard anything on the Campus Crusade for Christ project?

Proverbs 18:7 focuses on a fool's mouth and lips–this is not just speech but has to include our inner talk, our conscience perspective on things as well as our actual spoken word and non-verbal expressions. The writer is focusing on the fact that what is heard by us from ourselves (often influenced by the evil world, Satan, and the rebellious flesh) is the source of our outward expression. Words and body expressions do not develop spontaneously but are a result of deeper, mind-oriented thought. To listen to godless (the characteristic of a "fool") messages will "pull down" the person's deeper identity ("soul") and lead to a downward spiral of separation from God ("wrath") and the resultant lack of joy, peace, wisdom, and compassion. The result is a depraved mind.

Verse 8 focuses on "gossip." The "old self" (before salvation joins us to Christ to become a new creation) is attracted to anything that will harm or lead to destruction of another person (the result of sin is death). Gossip seeks to harm by lies, exaggeration, selective reporting (not the whole truth), or focusing on a negative (we all have them). It tries to influence others to view the object of gossip negatively, and it is non-selective (you, the present gossiper will be the object in due time). This desire to harm another is tied to a deep human trait that began at the time of the fall. It touches deeply something in the fiber of the old self and man's sinful nature (inclination to sin). It is one of those things that cannot be controlled and is better left completely alone. Flee from gossip or it will entrench you; it is seductive.

I hope all went well at Jeremy's family Easter celebration. I'm sure you were the center of attention! Did you do well under the spotlight? What do you think about his family; the dynamics and the relationships Jeremy has with his parents and siblings?

Proverbs 18:9 is an interesting one—it can be interpreted several ways. It is comparing the lazy, dishonest (not giving to his employer or to his clients what they are paying him for), unproductive, low expectation person to one who is intent upon or cooperating with that which leads to destruction. Being "the brother to one who destroys" can mean that a lazy, unresourceful person will knowingly or, more likely, unknowingly aid Satan in his effort to "destroy." Satan destroys as he reduces our potential value, actualized, to use our gifts and opportunities to serve God and build His kingdom.

Being lazy is based upon self-centeredness, low self-worth, un-gratefulness, and fleshly desires that covet the "world." Such sin-producing character traits will destroy our ability to be successful in life–not primarily to gain materially for ourselves but to have opportunity to impact the world for God.

Verse 10 is one of my favorites. It is worth memorizing and recalling often as you walk through life. The "name of the Lord" is a Hebrew term indicating the whole, comprehensive character of God as He presents Himself as the most loving "Father." Here God is recognized as a strong, caring, infinitely wise, refreshing, protecting, and available Father. The "righteous" are His children whom He welcomes to Himself as they "run to Him"–actively seek Him and retreat from a frightening and overwhelming world. The righteous are the Christians (made "perfect" by our union with Christ) who by the indwelling of the Holy Spirit seek to progressively be more holy (more like Christ). As we dwell with Him and apart from the world, we are safe from any temptation of Satan. We can access His strength. I view this proverb as a source of great security, peace, joy, and confidence.

I will be praying for you as you give your testimony at Campus Crusade for Christ. By the time you get the letter you will have already done it. I'm, of course, proud that your walk with God has matured such that you are willing and able to take such a step.

Proverbs 18:11 describes the folly of wealth. In this world money buys power, privilege, outward respect, and security. The rich easily understand how money can be regarded as strong as "a fortified city"–it seems impenetrable in the world of humanity. But this security is a false security and lulls people into not seeing their spiritual need or the responsibility they have to care for others. But it is only transient and temporary, valueless when they die–it cannot secure eternal life, or even abundant life while on earth (how many rich people know true joy and peace?). They will be eternally desolate! It is no wonder that Christ was pessimistic about the rich entering the kingdom of heaven–they become "numb" to their desperate need.

Verse 12 is a well-known one and should be memorized by any serious Christian. Pride is the source of all sin, it is what caused Adam and Eve to sin and what motivates each of us to want to be our own God and not worship the true God; we reject dependency upon Him and seek our own self-centeredness. Only by the power of the Holy Spirit, or as a result of Christ's atoning work, can we ever hope to have victory over this tendency toward pride. The verse states that before the acts of sinfulness that lead to death (emotional, relational, physical, or spiritual) the heart of a person is seeking her own way and self-exaltation. However, the Christian who, via the Spirit, is able to have humility (spirit of meekness) will seek not her own way but first the desire of God, her Father, then, in compassion and care, the needs of other people. Such a person will know honor from other people, Christian and non-Christian alike, and most importantly from God, who she seeks first.

Mom mentioned that you communicated to her that you are feeling increasingly positive to Jeremy and your relationship to him. I am so happy you are happy. I will continue to hold you and the relationship you two have up in prayer. I believe God has a plan for each of your lives and that He is a God of passion, romance, and relationship. I encourage you to discipline yourself in your studies and to finish the year in as strong a manner as you began it.

Proverbs 18:13 is a good one to put into daily use. I believe it is a refreshing trait of a humble person to be a good and active listener. It conveys respect and empathy to the speaker and encourages her in her self-worth. To preempt a person before she is done talking, by answering, is presumptuous and implies that you, in pride, can know what another is thinking. You will jump to wrong conclusions and will miss much verbal and non-verbal communication that may be critical to the needs of the person speaking. Also it is to such person's detriment and loss, because she will not receive valuable information, instruction, observations, and urgings. It will be her loss, and a great shame; it will be "stupid" and self-damaging. Practice listening actively and empathetically; you will be blessed many times more than your effort.

Verse 14 tells us of the sustaining strength of a person's "spirit." This is not just a humanistic strength of character, but goes even further and recognizes that strong, human spirit is derived from a spiritual relationship to God our Father and Creator. Such a spirit will give a person strength, optimism, energy, a "can-do" approach, and will not be defeated by setbacks or obstacles—even sickness. However, a spirit that is not based on or derived from the hope (sure but unrealized belief) of a sustaining and empowering God, will buckle under oppression or in the face of obstacles. This is why true believers can rejoice in the throes of oppression and severe atrocities. A spirit that therefore is crushed (by lack of true God relationship) leads to brokenness and defeat.

I really enjoyed being with you last weekend and together sharing the challenges of the conference. I so appreciate the openness of our relationship and the exciting opportunities we might share in the years to come. I really believe God has great things for you. Continue to seek Him and His will for your life. I continue to pray for you and for the relationship between you and Jeremy.

Proverbs 18:15 describes an inner attitude that is so important to a person who truly desires to know and serve God. The writer describes this person's heart as "discerning"—that is listening, pondering, evaluating, prayerfully considering, and sifting out that which is of God and that which is beneficial to him and to the service of God. He is aware of the many contrary, worldly perspectives and counterfeit truths; he wishes to know and know fully the wisdom of God, and to do such with the intent of placing this knowledge into action. The godly person seeks out wise instruction and knowledge; this is an active, seeking process that is willing to persevere and overcome all obstacles to seek and know the truth. The person who will discern and seek after God will find Him.

Verse 16 is speaking to the proper use of a person's spiritual or ministry gifts. The full use of one's gifts will be an opportunity for God to allow the possessor of the gifts to have the great privilege of serving God in His work on earth and in the spiritual realms. In this cooperative godly work, the person finds herself in the presence of greatness (God Himself and other godly co-workers) experiencing miracles of the Holy Spirit and working in and for eternity. The full use of one's gifts requires the giving up of self and the reliance upon God to do great and mighty works in and through us. It is profitable to learn your gifts and to offer them to God. Then stand amazed as to how He will expand and use them.

We enjoyed our dinner together with you and Jeremy. It seemed comfortable and natural to relate to you as an adult and a good friend, as well as our daughter. This is, I think, the way God intended the "decleaving" process to occur. We are so blessed. Your relationship with Jeremy is healthy and proper.

Proverbs 18:17 is an insightful and practical piece of wisdom. It tells us that when a person presents to another her perspective or view of any situation, it will be presented in a way that usually seems reasonable and right. However, the other person, when she also presents the same situation, will also make it believable. No matter how conscientious and honest a person is, she cannot be 100 percent impartial in the presentation of a perspective. The advice that spins out of this wisdom is that when you are to decide, arbitrate, or understand a situation, have all parties present, face-to-face, in order to settle the issue. See Proverbs 18:13. Do not answer or decide until you hear all voices on the subject.

Verse 18 is interesting. Before we had the full written revelation of God to guide us in decisions and judgments, man was instructed to trust God in a supernatural way. By believing that God loves His people and desires to guide and direct their ways, His people were instructed to "cast lots," not believing in magic or other spirits, but that God would use this means to guide them. Now, however, we have God's full and complete revelation–first in the Old Testament, then in the teaching and example of Christ, then in the inspired writing of the New Testament. No longer do we need to believe that God will inhabit "lots" but that He inhabits His Word and His own Spirit will testify and interpret His Word to us, as we seek to serve Him in His kingdom.

I'm sorry that you were hurt by the situation at the "formal." The assessment was fully untrue but must be seen in spiritual terms. I really believe that your godliness and your growing value in God's kingdom is what has aroused Satan and he has used the forces of the world to attack you at a vulnerable area–your desire to be respected by all. Don't let it shake you, discourage you, or overwhelm you. View it as a high spiritual compliment, realizing the glory you have brought to God.

Proverbs 18:19 is a very interesting one. It is in regards to the relationship between two Christians. When one or both are offended by the other, they withdraw and in deep hurt view the other with suspicion and mistrust. The gulf between the two is much wider than that of "non-brothers;" it is virtually never able to be repaired and the trust restored. The lesson here is first that one must be very cautious in relationships with brothers, weighing one's words carefully, bathing their motives, thoughts, and actions in prayer before they raise words or accusations that could offend. It is hard and risky, but at times required to confront a brother in love and not offend. Second, work out any disputes quickly, aggressively, humbly, and with great empathy before Satan can encourage pride, self-sufficiency, and rejection.

Verse 20 is a more positive one. It encourages the use of our mouths, tongues, and words as a satisfying "fruit" that will fill up or satisfy another. Words seldom fall idly to the ground–they either build up or tear down. Realize that your words can and do satisfy others and can cause offense that will break the most intimate fellowship.

Dear Christine and Jeremy,

I feel it appropriate to write to the two of you now that you are engaged. I have obtained Christine's permission to include you, Jeremy; please accept these thoughts and reflections on Proverbs as a way I use to encourage you both to know and live God's standard. You might talk together on these verses and my reflections, then hold each other accountable for putting them into practice. Remember the greatest desire of God's heart (and mine too) is for you to progressively become more like Christ.

Proverbs 18:21 is a restatement of a theme that recurs throughout the whole of Scripture–including multiple times in Proverbs. This fact alone should tell us how important it is to God. The subject is our tongue–our words and the inflection of our words as we relate to one another. The old saying "sticks and stones will break my bones, but words will never hurt me" can't be further from the truth. The tongue is the mightiest part of the body and can build up or tear down within a split second. The choice of a word, the inflection used, the lack of true listening, the emotion that surrounds the speech, and the timing of our communication are only a few of the ways our tongue can convey much. We should love communication with others. But we must respect speech, discipline our words, allow ourselves to be corrected for our misuse, and learn to listen to others. Practice thinking before you speak a single word, then choose your words wisely. Ask yourself, "Would God be pleased if He were present in our discussion?"

Verse 22 is more to the husband. As you look to your wife, you must realize that she is a gift from God, chosen for you by God and is a manifestation of His love for you. God desires man (most) to have a wife–the gifts, joys, and experiences of much of life is open to married people–God has designed His creation this way. Also the pain of life, its struggles and pressures, are best managed as a married couple. Therefore, He gives you the second greatest gift in life–your wife. How you regard her, build her up, enable her, love her, and disciple her is a reflection of your appreciation to God and should always occur in perspective to your love and obedience to Him.

114

1979-Dave, Elisa, Erin, Christine.

Freshman year at Miami-Christine at top right.

Graduation from Miami–1996.

Christine's wedding–sisters Kara, Elisa, Erin.

Jeremy and Christine married June 20, 1998.

College friends and Christine.

Medical school graduation–2000.

Dave hooding Christine

Dave and first grandchild Annie.

Residency graduation–2003.

Dave "GaGa" on his 60th birthday with Sam (2),
Ellie (5 months) and Annie (4).

1997—Second Year of Medical School

Rockford, Illinois

Dear Christine and Jeremy,

It was a beautiful weekend–I even had my MG out yester-day. I really love the fall. I suspect it is because it speaks of change, transition, life and death, deep thinking, contempla-tion, and emotion. I find I can get deeper into myself and into the Lord during this time of year.

Proverbs 18

Proverbs 18:23 contrasts a "poor man" with the "rich man." These terms are to be taken from a worldly perspective. The poor man is seen by the world as weak and unsuccessful while the rich man is seen as strong. However, the rich man is actually self-centered and out for himself despite the effect upon others while the poor man recognizes his limitations relative to God and has a tender heart for the needs of others. The rich man can harden his heart to his true emotional and spiritual needs, to the needs of others, and to God's power and sovereignty in this world. The poor man, as he recognizes his true state and who God is, will plead for God's mercy. It is more desirable to be a poor man on earth and to know a great spiritual blessing.

Verse 24 is interesting and generally contrary to the accepted goals of younger people. It will require compromise of our character, standards, and lifestyle to be too many things to too many people. It will require tremendous time, effort, and compromise to be a "friend" to many people. Those who seek this generally are insecure in their worth. Having a few friends who are wise and who hold similar standards and goals is precious and these relationships can be closer than many blood relatives. Treasure and cultivate these few God-given friends.

The weather has been great here at Kiawah so far. I hope it continues. Mom is going to look for her dress (for your wedding) tomorrow. I continue to pray for you both daily, and that God is preparing you for your marriage. Resist temptation and seek His guidance in everything.

Proverbs 19

Proverbs 19:3 has sweeping meaning. "A man's follies" are the decisions, thoughts, and means of relating that are done apart from the counsel of God. They are done to achieve self gratification only while ignoring the truths of the Scripture or the advice of Christian friends. The result is a "ruined life"–a life that knows no peace and joy and that is unable to show compassion, kindness, and gentleness. These choices cause pain, sorrow, rejection, and regret. The reason a person chooses a life of folly is that she is in the unrepentant state that "hates" God. Romans 3:9-18 describes such a person. She seeks only her own desires and will never seek God. A contrite, humble heart that seeks God will result in a blessed life.

Verse 4 is a comment on the world in which we live–the world that is fallen and allowed by God to be ruled by sin. It is true that according to the standards of this world, money and wealth will attract people who claim to be friends but really desire only their own profit. A poor person has few friends–the self-seekers desert him and the friends who remain are true. However, wealth used to alleviate misery and show compassion will develop people who at least honor and respect us, and some will be true friends. This whole standard will be changed in the new world here on earth and in heaven. Wealth will not be pivotal for relationships or a stumbling block for spiritual growth.

I'm grateful that your trip to Ohio was safe. I hope you enjoyed your stay and renewal of friendships, as well as the time the two of you spent together.

Proverbs 19:8 relates our emotional health and our material standing to spiritual areas of our being. The person who seeks wisdom is the person who seeks God and His insights relative to who we are, the realities of the world, and our function as His children in the world. We begin to like ourselves and feel good about ourselves because we feel accepted and worthy in God's eyes. His unconditional love gives us self-esteem and emotional health ("loves his soul"). Further, the person who seeks to understand God's truths and how to apply them to life ("understanding") will prosper, even in this fallen world. Frequently, this understanding will bring prosperity in material ways, but always it will yield prosperity in relationships and people ways. God's wisdom and understanding unlock all that is valuable, worthy, and worthwhile in this life. Seek it always. See 1 Timothy 3:14-15.

Verse 9 seems rather straightforward, yet the truth of this is not accepted, or at least personalized, by much of the world. A person who slanders another, testifies unjustly against another (even to one other in the quiet of their conversation: gossip!), manipulates for or against another, takes unfair advantage of, or outright lies to gain for themselves; such a person will be punished. The punishment will, in this life, be at the hands of the ungodly of the world, which will eventually turn against a person of such low character. For the unrepentant, punishment will finally be by God at Christ's second coming. In either case, part or all of such a person will perish. A person who persists, or delights in such behavior cannot have a new spiritual nature, and does not know Christ.

I'm sorry that you have not felt well. I encourage you not to look too far ahead, to feel the need to have all decisions worked out, or to give vent to the natural (and Satan encouraged) ambivalent feelings of the place in life you are at present. It is normal to grieve the loss (or perceived loss) of some aspects of life that must be relinquished by the choices you have made, but you must accept and believe (evidenced by the events of your life to date–response to prayer) that this is God's will, His choices for you. Take each day at a time–with anticipation of the fact that God will meet you there and bless you in new and exciting ways.

Proverbs 19:10 is interesting. The writer is defining a "fool" as someone apart from God who seeks his desires alone; a "slave" as one who is controlled by the world's values and the scheme of the world–self-seeking. The writer, I believe, is viewing life and eternity from God's eyes and speaking not from a moment-to-moment perspective, but from the perspective of the final analysis. God will not permit–eternally and in the final analysis–the fool to know the fullness of blessings or the slave to rule over His chosen royal children ("princes"). In this life, day by day, it may seem this is not the case, but it is God's will or design for this to be so, and for it to be revealed in His kingdom–increasingly now and in eternity.

Verse 11 is a good one to ponder and memorize. Patience grows as part of our character as we become more like Christ. We can increasingly see life from God's perspective and release control for its events to God who is faithful and trustworthy. We can relax and enjoy the day, savoring the moments, confident of His sovereign control on all events. Further, we are exhorted in this proverb to forgive–"overlook an offense." We can better do this as we mature because maturing in godliness is characterized by growing in value in God's eyes, and not by extracting it from the world. We are offended less by others because our value is not dependent on their explicit or implicit approval. To have to punish an offense done against us is to show how fragile our self-worth truly is, and how focused we are on our human needs.

It was good to see you at church and to talk together at lunch. Thanks again for the Rockwell print and especially for your birthday card–your words give me deep joy. I still feel a bit bad that we can't be at the "White Coat Ceremony" next weekend. I'm not sure of its intended meaning, but I believe that you two will be great physicians–sensitive and compassionate, as Christ was as our example.

Proverbs 19:12, I believe, is to be regarded as we view God/Christ as our king. The analogy in life is that a person (king) in authority can be "for" or "against" you. If he is for you, he will benefit, give pleasure and joy, and nourishment. If he is against you, he can destroy you and inflict great pain. The spiritual interpretation is not upon God's wrath (although that is part of His righteous character) but upon His supremacy, authority, and power. It also is upon His ability to use such for the benefit or detriment of His creation. Other scripture tells us that the pivotal point of being positively or negatively dealt with is our heart. Does it seek Him (He who seeks will find) or reject Him? Do we accept the Christ He gave us as our Redeemer, and the Holy Spirit Christ sent as our Comforter? There will also come a time when judgment of the type depicted here will occur. I'm glad we will not experience Him as a lion.

Verse 13 is basically a comment upon the effect a "foolish son" and a "quarrelsome wife" have upon a father/mother and a husband. A "foolish son" is a son or daughter who does not turn to God but lives as if He doesn't exist. Cut off then from truth and wisdom, such a person will make mistakes, poor choices, indulge in sin, and bring disgrace on him who loved her and dedicated his life to her. He (the parent) will feel like a failure and be "ruined" as far as his value as a father. God as our Father grieves deeply when we act foolishly. A quarrelsome wife is forever being negative, fault finding, conflict seeking, rude, and insensitive. The day-by-day diet of this will wear a husband down in a relentless and destructive manner–just as the effect of a constantly dripping faucet has upon our sanity.

It is almost November already; the year is slipping by quickly. It will be the end of the first semester before you know it. I pray your studies and Christian growth are progressing well. Continue to work diligently on maximizing the opportunities God has and is giving you each (and as a couple) in all areas of life. Remember, He has not begun anything in your life that He is not also prepared to finish to His glory.

Proverbs 19:14 is interesting and timely for you two. It tells us that some things of this world, which can be enjoyed, have value and are important, such as things of the home and family. What parents and family teaching does in a person's life is significant, but there are others (maybe even most important ones) that are directly from God. A woman who is a wise, practical, and insightful wife ("prudent"), can only be so by the direct touch and ministry of God in her life. The family and parents may provide the building blocks and example but God puts it together and provides the blueprints and mortar to make her such. Once again we are reminded that we are really God's and, if we allow, He will do a great work in us and through us.

Verse 15 exhorts us to be hardworking, diligent, resourceful, creative, and farsighted. These character traits should characterize us in all aspects of our life–work, family, teaching, hobbies, relationships, and godliness (prayer, study of the Word, ministry, etc). The result of such conduct brings productivity (opposite of "going hungry") and alertness (not sleepiness).

It was an honor, Christine, for you to share with me your pain and emotion relative to medical school. As your father, I covet the opportunity to relate with you at even this level, to think out loud together, to express real feelings and to pray with and for you. As one who has walked the road, I understand and remember those same feelings and can (on this side of it) encourage you confidently to persevere, believing you both to be chosen by God for this ministry of compassion and healing. Remember too what Hebrews tells us, that we have a high priest who can sympathize with us.

Proverbs 19:16 emphasizes obedience. The person who listens, understands, and obeys godly instruction (makes definite changes in her choices, actions, and thoughts as a result of godly teaching) will "guard her soul." This means she will protect herself from the world's persuasion, Satan's attacks, or her fleshly vulnerability and thereby keep herself faithful to her calling and recreated spiritual nature. The person who is hostile to instruction and rejects (scoffingly) obedience to God's ways, will die. Here, *die* means eternal death and death to knowing an abundant life here on earth. He will be attacked and seduced by his flesh, the world, and Satan.

Verse 17 changes the emphasis. It instructs us that when we are kind to those who have less (give out of our material or personal abundance to one who has less–emotion, care, compassion, goods, and relationship), we are acting Christ-like and our actions reflect Him, honor Him, and in fact are received by Him. Christ Himself tells us in the Gospels that when we give to the least of man, we give to Him. Kindness itself is a communicable trait of Christ, given to us by His Holy Spirit–it is not natural to man. Christ is aware and is in those who receive; He will surely reward, both here in our spiritual person and in the future, somehow, in eternity, the person who gives and is compassionate.

Thanks, Christine, for your visit. It was good just to be with you and share in your joy, excitement, agony, and God's work in you. You are doing great and I so love you.

Proverbs 19:18 is a "non-modern" truth for parenting. It encourages active, proactive, thoughtful molding and shaping of your child–"discipline." It exhorts parents to be involved with the child's life, not as a buddy or peer, but as a wiser, more experienced parent, who realizes his accountability before God. Parents must believe that in this lies the hope and expectation that the child will be rescued from the world's (and Satan's) designs and have the fullest opportunity to hear God's calling in her life and respond to it. To not actively shape and point your child toward God and godliness is to be a "party to her death." Death here is total depravation (in this world) and separation from God (this world and the next). You have given up without a fight.

Verse 19 is a bit tough to accept. It tells us that an impulsive, angry, out-of-control person will get herself into trouble, again and again. She will have to pay the penalty–both from an ungodly world that feasts on such people, and from God who gives them over to His wrath, now and in the future. If you actively and altruistically try to shield them from these penalties, they will not learn and you will be forever "bailing them out," absorbing some of their pain, or helping them to rationalize away the consequences of their ungodly behavior.

I pray your week has gone well, without too many "med school frustrations." The first semester will soon be over and you'll have a well-deserved, timely break.

Proverbs 19:20 is clear and to the point–it is the most direct proverb on the concept of teachability. To be taught requires "listening" and "accepting." To listen we must be open, seeking, not pompous, able to acknowledge another's wisdom and experience, not consumed with our own way and pre-established perspective, and respectful. We must actively listen, asking questions that tailor the impact to address our learning edge. To accept also requires emptying one of pride, arrogance, self-sufficiency, and pre-established tendencies. We must listen with intent to implement the counsel; acceptance connotes actions. To listen and accept this instruction will lead one to become wiser–that is, to know more fully God's perspective and heart on the matter. God honors teachability and will fill it when it is sought from a godly person. You, the seeker, will benefit and will in turn become the teacher. We are all learners and teachers of God's wisdom.

Verse 21 encourages us to seek to align our plans with God's purpose. If we plan our life leaving God out and therefore seek only our own will and desires, we cannot expect Him to bless us in the plans. It is when we meld our plans with His purpose that He can be an active part of our lives. We also must remember that the Holy Spirit intercedes for us and can and will intercede to make our plans meld with God's purpose (to bring Him glory and make us more Christ-like). God's purposes will prevail, so if our plans do not correspond, we eventually will fail and be denied true joy and peace.

Thank you both for being part of our Thanksgiving. It was great to have everyone around the table, sharing, remembering, and laughing. I kept thanking God for each of you that evening. He is so good to us, even though we all are undeserving.

Proverbs 19:22 is a hard one to interpret. It appears at first glance as disjointed internally. The writer is talking about greed and doing whatever it takes (including lying) to not be poor in the world. We think (and the experience of ungodly man gives testimony to it) that achieving this level in the world (wealth and privilege) will buy us unconditional, deeply-committed love ("unfailing love"). But in reality, those who know deep unfailing love, know it not because of their wealth and power, but because they are like Christ in some small, growing way. Their selflessness and sacrifice are what brings forth what we all deeply desire and seek—to be loved unconditionally.

Verse 23 is one worthy of memorizing. The "fear of the Lord" is the positive view of God that lets us submit to His authority and lordship in our life, trusting Him and loving Him. That attitude will lead us into an intimate, living relationship with Him—"life" characterized by deep regard for Him and His creation. Such living relationships and emotions will yield deep peace ("content") that cannot be taken away by the troubles of the human state. In fact, life becomes more abundant when God ministers to us, befriends us, and perseveres with us in the midst of difficult times. Christ sent His Spirit as our "Comforter" when He left this earth; He knew the challenges of the world can rob us of peace and joy. The Spirit continues to seek God's gifts for us and to empower us with His wisdom and power, in any and all situations. Proverbs begins with this "fear of the Lord" and now again reminds us of it.

Soon another semester will be finished and Christmas break will be here. I've wondered how the "physical exam" test went and if you both felt good about your performances. I look forward to some time together this holiday season. Perhaps we could talk together about how the relationship is going or study some Scripture together. I'd really like to pray with you, seeking God and His wisdom concerning your life now and in the future.

Proverbs 19:24 is a poetic and graphic way of getting across the point that the lazy person will never accomplish anything, even if it is in his best interest. The illustration basically tells us that a lazy, low productive person will not even bring the food from the plate to his mouth. A person who expects life to serve him, who looks for easy, comfortable, effortless paths will never move toward accomplishment. Although success in accomplishment is valuable, even more valuable in life is the character that is built in a person as she strives and works hard to accomplish the goals she has determined to be worthwhile and right. It is important to know God has confirmed these goals at the beginning, because the path is hard and full of deterrents, and you will need His strength and wisdom.

Verse 25 contrasts "prudence" with "knowledge." Prudence is the ability to be crafty and know what to say or do in order to stay out of trouble or free of judgment by those more powerful than you. There is not *true* deep inner growth of character–they only become "street wise" for survival. Knowledge is deep, character changing, and causes growth and evolution–it is real and has the qualities of honesty and integrity. If you "set straight" a man who seeks knowledge and desires to grow and develop ("discerning"), he will take this rebuke as a means of growing in knowledge. The person who is cynical, a mocker of truth, will, when presented with truth, only learn to be crafty.

It was great to have you both in and out of our home this holiday season. I hope you also enjoyed yourselves and were able to relax in preparation for this new semester. It was good for me to have a male around and to be able to buy tools, etc., but I continue to delight as a father of four beautiful young women.

Proverbs 19:26 describes two detrimental attitudes/actions of a child to the parents–these foster and invite shame and disgrace. A child who "robs" his father refers to the taking away from the father what is rightfully his, for the child's own self-centered needs. Assuming (and this is a large assumption) that the father's motives are honorable in God's sight, a child who withholds respect, appreciation, love, and consideration, or who rejects the father's desire and willingness to share his experiences, wisdom, material benefits, and time brings shame and disgrace to himself, to his father, and to God. Likewise, the child who shuts out her mother from her life (hers and her spouse and children), who thwarts her mother's efforts to find her rightful and needed place will bring them all shame and disgrace. A father and a mother will never cease to be a father or a mother, although their roles and the quality of the relationships may grow and mature. This is part of what is meant by the commandment to honor your father and mother.

Verse 27 is sadly true of too many Christians in our world. It is a clear imperative that to continue to grow and mature in godliness and in our relationship with God, we must be willing (and truly seek) to be taught by the Scripture and by more mature people of God. When one rejects this teaching (humbly and palatably given), she will begin to make choices and live progressively more apart from the way of God. Once again the author is exhorting us to be teachable and to grow in our understanding and application of God's Word.

Well, everyone is back at school now; the house seems empty and there is a sort of sadness about putting away the Christmas decorations. I pray that you both are back to your challenges and seeking God as He meets you there and indwells you. Don't look beyond the "process" (the preparation years) to the "end" (medical practice or marriage) and thereby miss His presence now. He is a God that indwells the process as well as the culmination.

Proverbs 19:28 tells us some things about the ungodly heart and inclination. Justice is a major trait of God. He created a world that must reflect just behavior and decisions. The godly person seeks what is just and honorable, that which rewards what is compatible with God's standards and bears witness to the truth. A "corrupt" person will detest and counter justice, seeking loopholes, exceptions, and clever schemes to avoid what is right and proper. He rejects absolute truth and any standard that will not benefit himself. Further, the wicked (one who rejects God and His standards) has an unquenchable appetite/thirst for that which is against God–evil! The godly person, on the other hand, grows quickly sick when fed evil, worldly, anti-God influences. All of us sin, but the person with a regenerated heart and spiritual nature will not seek or find pleasure in wickedness or evil.

Verse 29 is generally taken to mean that there will be eternal justice for the ungodly (for those not chosen by God, who hate Him and reject Him). God, even before creation, has prepared eternal life and blessing for those He has saved (covered by the blood of

Christ), and He has prepared justice and punishment for those who will be judged without Christ's cleansing blood and thereby found guilty. However, this verse, I have found, is frequently true even on earth. Mockers of God, who choose evil, often violate the personal standards of others and are then rejected and receive personal retribution within their relationships with others. Also the laws of the land often punish mockers because their hearts lead to societal lawlessness.

It seems to me to have been a long time since I've spoken with you deeply and intimately. Part of me feels bad that I haven't been more a part of your growing together during your engagement. Yet, perhaps it is best in the long run that it be so. Be assured that I love you and pray daily for your union and oneness.

Proverbs 20

Proverbs 20:1 gives a strong warning against the overuse of alcohol; it gives two tangible reasons for why this is destructive. Alcohol in excess causes one to degrade others, belittles or disrespects truth and goodness, makes light and mocks that which gives true happiness and joy, and turns one away from meaningful communication with God, our true Father. Alcohol unleashes anger, aggression, and hostility and adds fuel to human ego, pride, and self-centeredness. Care must be used in this area or the user will be led to these behaviors and he can be addicted or socially habituated to them. The result being that his life changes and his focus and priorities are altered away from that which pleases God. This is not wise and cannot be blessed or inhabited by God; that is a very scary place to be.

Verse 2 is a fact and a proverb. It is a fact in that a person who insults and angers the person of great power, who has at his command force and authority, is unwise and will bring pain and destruction upon himself. We must respect human power and authority, even if it is evil and worldly, since it can be lethal to us. As a proverb, we apply this to the King of Kings, to the Author and Creator of the world, the omnipotent and omnipresent God. To resist God, reject Him, or insult Him will anger Him. When angered, God will eventually (at judgment and in daily life as He lets us burn from our self-centered mistakes) judge His enemies. The result will be eternal death, often physical death, and death now emotionally, relationally, and spiritually.

I hope your trip home to Jeremy's family went well and by now you have just about finished another week of your second year. The honeymoon plans sound great. I will be anxious to hear of your stay when you return.

Proverbs 20:3 is a simple but important bit of wisdom. It is worthy of honor, respect, and admiration to be one who avoids strife and conflict. This doesn't mean you can't have a difference of opinion or feel strongly about something, but that this should be held and communicated in an inoffensive, loving, respectful manner, having really listened and heard the other person. The key to be able to do this is in your personal relationship to God. If you feel loved and accepted as His child, and humbly understand who you are (unworthy and a sinner), you will not have the need to force your opinion and stance brutally and unlovingly upon another person. Your pride in yourself is not centered in your greatness and human value but in your oneness with God and His strength in you. Somehow the need to prove yourself at the expense of another grows pale.

Verse 4 again puts forth a truth that is proven continuously in life. The lazy, unresourceful, undisciplined, shortsighted pleasure seeker will not do what she must at the time she must in order to accomplish her goal at the end of the process. The person who takes one step at a time along a well laid out path (that leads to a desired goal) will eventually accomplish her goal. Each step must be done diligently and at the appropriate time.

Mom told me of your conversation today concerning the house you found and liked. I remember the time and effort your mom and I spent finding our first "home" together. It turned out to be the third floor of an older, large home. It was exciting and special. It is important that you find such a special place for your first place together.

Proverbs 20:5 and 6 are both interesting. Verse 5 tells us that a human being is deeply complex with many factors going into his/her personality, choices, circumstances, fears, and life's situations. A person's needs, wishes, motives, and goals are intricate, interwoven, and the summation of many factors. But, the author writes, such can be understood only as a person "draws him or her out." To draw out such deep, personal purposes requires time, a caring heart, and the ability to listen actively and with a spiritual discernment. Here is where I derive such great joy, satisfaction, and purpose in my work and in my life. I encourage you to seek God's wisdom, discernment, and counsel as you learn to draw out others.

Verse 6 tells us that many people can claim deep emotion, care, and love. This is easy and is often counterfeit and misleading–even ultimately damaging to another person. Rare, on the other hand, is the person who is faithful. Being faithful means persevering over time, in many diverse circumstances, and in the midst of the world's temptations, never swerving or faltering, believing always in the other, encouraging and supporting—in short loving her more than she loves herself. Such a person is rare and only God can form the faithful heart. Marriage must claim love but shall be between two faithful people.

It was good to be with you this weekend. God continues to go before you and lay open His path, in love, for you. How blessed you are. Your first "home" sounds great. I look forward to seeing it this weekend. I spent Sunday afternoon working on your sister Elisa's hope chest. I'm building it out of the oak from one of the trees we had cut down several years ago. Its style is similar but not exactly like yours. I hope she likes it.

Proverbs 20:7 can be misunderstood. The "righteous man" of course is the person who exists in a reconciled fellowship with God (via Christ) and is in God's eyes fully clean and without blame. He or she is therefore blameless not because she is sinless but because of faith (God given) that brings her to appropriate Christ's work of salvation. God then can bestow upon her all the blessings He will and is giving to Christ–the only truly self-righteous being. The righteous man then leads a blessed life as a blameless child of God. A father (or parent–male or female) who is so blessed will model, instruct, and pray for his children seeking the same blessed, blameless status for them. God, I feel, hears this prayer, although they must personally procure this blessed, blameless status via faith. Teaching and living the Word of God is how a child will see and hear Christ and have opportunity to respond (Rom. 10:14-17).

Verse 8 tells us that a true king will be able, in his place and position of judge, to sort out good from evil. A true king should be of godly character and has appropriated (been given) gifts of discernment, knowledge, and wisdom. There are many imposter kings (kings that serve without God's choosing) who are ungodly themselves and condone or seek evil and wickedness. A true, God-chosen leader can be identified by her ability to sort evil from good in her role as judge. God, our ultimate judge and most perfect judge, is and will be our perfect example. No evil will escape His eye and He will ferret it out and judge it some day.

We enjoyed being with you last Saturday and appreciated being part of your steps of joy as you move toward your wedding and marriage relationship. It gives us joy to see you both enjoy each other and the marvelous way God has chosen to bless you. We enjoy helping you; don't hesitate to call upon us. It was really neat to be with Jim Conway and to hear and see him minister to you and challenge you in the "realness" of marriage. He is truly one who walks close to God and serves a living God.

Proverbs 20:9 asks a question–one that begs the whole issue of salvation and God's plan to redeem His chosen people. With this question the writer confronts the reader with the reality that there is no one worthy of God's acceptance due to his or her good works and pure life–we all sin outwardly and surely inwardly in our hearts. To acknowledge this and then to be open to God's remedy to this situation leads one to the only means of reconciliation–Christ. Christ is the only one who can answer in the affirmative to this question and that is why He's worthy to be our Savior. This question should humble us and point us to God's answer in His chosen Messiah.

Verse 10 gives us an insight into God's character traits of fairness, equality, justice, and honesty. The thing He detests is any differing standards applied in His created universe. He holds all mankind to the same measure and judges each according to it; but His kindness and grace and mercy led Him to a means of changing us so He could fairly judge us but be able to accept us worthy of His blessing. He desires and holds us responsible to be just and honest and equal in all our dealings with other people, whether they are worthy or not. When possible, we should influence a change in them that would benefit them when fairly dealt with by us. Isn't that what we strive to do as parents to our children?

I hope you both are feeling better. I have been busier seeing acute illness this winter than I ever have been. We look forward to seeing your home now that Jeremy has moved in. Have you done any further painting or "fix up"?

Proverbs 20:11 tells us that a person is known by her actions–her choices, priorities, ways of spending time and money, ways of relating to others, etc. This tells us much about a person. I feel much can be learned about someone by looking at his library and seeing how he spends his leisure time. Our conduct will be either "pure and right" (pleasing and glorifying to God) or self-centered and destructive. Especially as physicians, prominent and revered by the community, we have to be sure our actions point to God and His values and standards. We must stand the test of time; our actions are seen as the example for others. In order to conduct ourselves in this way, we must walk close to God and allow His Spirit to change our actions and us.

Verse 12 is interesting. God has given us hearing and sight but do we really listen and see Him in the world (creation and nature), Him in others and our relationship with others, Him in the events of history, Him in the arts, Him in our science, or Him in our sufferings? How sad it is to have eyes and ears but to miss all that God would like us to comprehend and experience. I believe this is a mark of a spiritual person, who has received God's Spirit. She now is able to see and hear God and to be ministered to by God via her senses. Men and women of the world are blind and deaf to God. He opens their eyes and ears to see and hear Him via faith.

I remember you both frequently during the day as I come to God on your behalf. I have been wrestling with God a bit on this issue, Christine, of your career as a physician/medical student. I also know how difficult it is to be a medical student, and especially you, Christine, as you are beginning the lifelong challenge of physically and emotionally balancing profession, marriage, non-medical ministry, and future children. I have tried to be really open with God and give Him the opportunity to impress me with His Spirit to encourage you away from medicine. To date I have not been granted this impression but on the contrary, sense strongly God's directive for you to remain, persevere, grow in godly maturity, and trust Him to put it all together.

Proverbs 20:13 talks about perseverance, hard work, and vigilance. It commands us, the called and chosen children of God, to stay awake; it seems to compel us to not be lazy, to use the time and opportunity we have to maximum benefit, to withstand the attractiveness and seduction of the easy way, to be alert to how Satan and the world would want to steal from us the opportunity and challenge of godly service and walk with Him, and to be fruitful with our time. The result would be that the "sleeper" becomes poor in spirit and internal character, deplete of opportunity and bereft of joy, peace, and the satisfaction of walking in God's strength, not human strength. The awake person has these benefits and more.

Verse 14 changes the tone and teaching. It encourages us in honesty and integrity. The buyer claims something that she doesn't really believe. She does this apparently to get more from the seller than she is entitled to and to dishonestly influence the seller that his product is not satisfactory. This is dishonest and is harmful to the self-worth of the seller who deserves to have accurate feedback on his product (work, relationship, service, etc.) which really reflects himself. In relationships, it is godly to convey accurately and lovingly our true evaluation and feelings, especially the positive ones that convey our appreciation, esteem, and value of the other person and his or her impact on us.

I pray that you both are continuing to run the race God has called you to steadfastly, diligently, and confidently, although, I know, not without pain.

Proverbs 20:15 compares the value of "knowledge" with gold and rubies. This proverb is looking at this relative value for people here now, living in this life. The "world" seeks material things of value as its goal, believing the acquisition of such will be key to their happiness; the spiritual man seeks "truth" and when he/she is in its presence knows it is of greatest value, joy, peace, and fulfillment. We live in a world of relativism where there is not "truth;" we as Christians know there is truth and should seek to know it by the study of His Word interpreted to us by His Spirit (Rom. 12:2). Those people in our lives who exhort us with truth are to be highly valued, respected, and sought. I encourage you to be truth seekers.

Proverbs 20:16 counsels us to give special place, trust, and recognition to those in our world who give of themselves for the less privileged—the poor, abandoned, misdirected, or needy. Further, we are to trust their efforts with our money, resources, prayer, benefit of the doubt, and encouragement. This is a strong teaching for the support of missions and ministries. Often I wonder, as I give my resources, if the persons receiving them really are using such properly for the needy. I believe this proverb teaches us we must support them and let God evaluate their efforts.

It was good to hear the laughter of the "girlfriends" in our home this past weekend. Christine, you have nice friends who really care for you. I am glad the objective of the Saturday trip to have everyone fitted for the bridesmaid dresses was accomplished—another step toward the wedding on June 20th.

Proverbs 20:17 is really about integrity. It tells us that when we extract gain from the world by dishonest and deceitful means, it will meet an immediate need and taste sweet, but as just a short time goes on, it will cause us pain, turmoil, and disgrace. Satan plays upon our desire for instant gratification and the "feel good now" philosophy of the world. We seek this despite a logically discernable awareness that the price for this is often long-term payment, hardship, and distaste. We seek it despite the cost, and can justify to ourselves that it is okay even if we must cheat, steal, lie, or slander to gain it. How unlike God and Christ is this, how unlike the truth given to us in God's Word.

Verse 18 encourages one of the rarest of godly characteristics: teachability. Teachability really grows out of humility, "sober judgment of yourself" (Rom. 12:3), and ability to recognize wise, godly people, and subject yourself to their counsel. People who can do this save themselves from making mistakes and suffering needless pain, time lost, and breached relationships. The verse encourages us to seek advice and counsel as we make our plans. It doesn't imply that we are "non-people" and simply do what another tells us, but that we become thinking, informed, and contemplative people. Such people will be the wise people of the future and will be used by God to share His deepest truths with those who, in turn, will learn and be teachable.

March is nearly over already and you are both that much closer to finishing your second year and being married. I encourage you to be prayerful as you make decisions and choices, but remember that God cares for you and has a "good, pleasing, and perfect" will (Rom. 12:2) for you in every choice. Hopefully we will be getting our kitchen finished this week. We want our home to reflect the deep love we have for you, as we have your wedding reception here on June 20th. We are proud of you and want our home to reflect this.

Proverbs 20:19 highlights the sin of gossip. This is one of the unrighteous uses of the tongue and deeply damages our reputation and our relationships. When one gossips he is betraying confidential information entrusted to him. When we betray this trust we do damage to the one who trusted us and to our own reputation. Confidential information shared is harmful to the sharer and receiver. The receiver has her opinion colored by half-truths, complete lies, or truths that are not seasoned by explanations. You the gossiper show yourself to not be trustworthy and your reputation is forever dulled. The hearer will probably never share confidentially with you, believing you may betray him/her as well.

Verse 20 challenges our thinking; it is one of those that seems somewhat illogical and unfair. It, I believe, is emphasizing the godly trait of respect, honor, and unconditional love. Apparently, God blesses or withholds His blessing in part as to how we regard our parents, unrelated to how they have dealt with us or merit our respect. To positively regard parents who have let us down or hurt us requires the power of God and presupposes a relationship through Christ with Him.

We're all feeling, to different degrees, a sense of grief as we get used to the idea that our dog Schnitzel is gone. Your sister Erin especially is hurting. I spoke with her just before I began this letter and she is linking Schnitzel to Grandpop and in a round about way is partially grieving again the loss of her grandfather. In a way I think that is true of Mom and I as well. Time is moving closer to your wedding day. I pray that in these final days of your engagement you both will remain pure and focus on your emotional/relational oneness. Work out the details of your communication and appreciate the beauty of your diversities as well as your commonality.

Proverbs 20:21 refers to the need for work and reasonable self-sufficiency. It tells us basically that a person who is given everything and doesn't work for his/her way and station misses out on much of God's blessing, which is often a part of the hard work of making something happen. On the other hand, a person diligently taking, patiently and with hard work, each step at a time toward a goal will be blessed in this process. It presupposes that he seeks God's path and His power, wisdom, and discernment along the way. I believe we must be reasonable here, for if this is taken to the furthest degree, it will encourage independence of others and ultimately of God. Part of God's blessing is in the relationship, of those who love each other and corporately seek God. Also keep in mind the joy to others of sharing their means and wealth.

Verse 22 discourages us from seeking revenge upon those who do us wrong–to sit in judgment of another although we may not understand his perspective and motives. We do not possess empathy for his circumstances. To judge right and wrong is not to be confined to outward manifestations but must include inward motives, attitudes, and feelings. Only God who knows the deepest thoughts and feelings can judge them. He then is the only one able to repay what is due; now or in the future. He also can deliver us from our circumstances, if we allow Him to be God in our life and seek Him in our need, when other people have done "wrong" toward us.

I really enjoyed the presentation of "The Savior" last Saturday at your church. I don't feel like I adequately expressed to you how wonderful I felt you did that evening, and how proud I was of you. Thanks for sharing that evening with us.

Proverbs 20:23 makes it very clear how God views dishonesty in any form. Dishonesty comes in all forms, from outright, boldface lying to employing a different standard for one person compared to another. The root of all dishonesty is centered in the question "what's in it for me; or what will benefit me the most?" Pride! Dishonesty is one of the most utilized means of self-protection and self-exaltation in the world. God clearly states that He detests dishonesty and can never find pleasure in it. Therefore God cannot be with us or work through us when we employ self-centered means of making ourselves better than another.

Verse 24 makes an observation and then asks a question. For Christians, because of the truth found in the Scripture, we believe that God cares about and directs our ways–in all areas of our lives, big and small. He understands the human walk and wishes His children to know joy and peace in the midst of a fallen world. The whole world is under His control and command. If we believe this truth, then it makes sense that we, as shortsighted men and women, cannot know why and how God will intervene in our lives. We cannot hope to direct our lives anywhere near as well as God. Therefore, we must choose to trust Him, believing He is in control and will move our lives toward that which is "good, pleasing, and perfect."

Once again Jeremy, Judy and I wish you a very happy birthday. I sure hope your day was special in some way. By now at least one or two tests have come and gone; I am confident that you both will be great physicians and will be used by God in this profession.

Proverbs 20:25 warns us not to lightly and "rashly" give something toward a chosen purpose, then later determine that its purpose was wrong, harmful, and ill-advised. When we give of our self (our effort, time, resources, and family) toward a goal, we must be certain this goal is right and able to be blessed by God and inhabited by Him. Really, it should flow the other way; we should seek to know how God is working in and around our lives, and then purpose to be a part of that, dedicating all that we are toward that effort. The road is usually a long and rugged one; it is a shame and a waste to realize we have gone the wrong way halfway down the road.

Verse 26 takes a strongly proactive flavor. The wise person in charge of her life (a king of her life) will actively seek to determine who would lead her astray of God's plan for her life and remove her from influence, even if the extrication is a painful one. The notion here is that we need to be wary and critical of those who would influence us, realizing Satan and the world will attempt to derail us. When we discern these people, we must sever all ties that would jeopardize our work in God's kingdom. It is important whom you work with, for, and whose influence you allow upon your life. Pray and choose critically.

Well, your second year is winding down. Soon the boards (part I) will be over and the wedding will be at hand. I'm sure it is difficult to take these first steps and not to look directly to the events of June 20. However, I know you are aware of the need to make all of these steps maturely, strongly, and with necessary effort.

Proverbs 20:27 is a deep truth that many people don't fully confront as truth. God is our Creator and He knows us better than we know ourselves. His scrutiny is like an exam with a bright light–it reveals everything, even that which we wish to hide or cover up. He knows our real heart and our spirit–whether we seek Him and desire to live godly, pleasing lives, or whether we seek to be deceptive and really seek our own self-centered interests. It is our human nature to flee from His scrutiny for fear that He will deprive us of something we feel is fun or desirable. It is hard for us to believe that His way is far more exciting and pleasing, and that He is kind and good. The way of God begins when we allow Him to see us truly as we are, and proceed to allow Him to lovingly show us a better way.

Verse 28 is an important one for anyone in authority–even a parent with a child. It simply says that a leader (or one with authority) who really loves and is faithful to his or her promises and the role he must fulfill will secure his position. It is this authentic care for those entrusted to him that is regarded, by those under his authority, as constructive, encouraging, selfless (and therefore able to know their needs), and noble; it endears them and establishes their respect and obedience. Authentic love, even when it must be tough, is always refreshing and desired.

I pray all is going well with your relationship together as you enter your final month before the wedding. I feel very positive and certain as I view your relationship. I daily ask God to anoint your union and grow you individually and as a couple. Place God at the center of your life and relationship, and each other second. Do this and you will be blessed.

Proverbs 20:29 speaks of the virtues of youth versus age. For young adults, their value and manifest notable trait are in their strength; they are determined, fearless, full of vitality and optimism. They need, however, direction, balance, finesse, and wisdom. The older adult loses energy, strength, and prowess but his great contribution lies in his experience, discretion, wisdom, realism, perspective, and balanced self-assessment. Often the combination of age and youth give tremendous effectiveness in dealing with life.

Verse 30 is a strange one, often misinterpreted. It does not advocate violence or abuse. Blows, wounds, and beatings are meant to convey the unsympathetic, hostile, at times unpredictable, and unjust pain the world gives to us. Society and human nature respond to our self-centered motives and selfish behavior ("sin and evil") by inflicting pain, maybe not immediately but ultimately. In a way this keeps a balance in the world so that a person (or a social system) cannot dominate and enslave another. Remember this is God's world and even in its unregenerate state, there is a balance and that balance will not tolerate self-centered evil. None of us can be allowed to use our selfish motives to counter God's balance.

Chapter Seven

1998-1999—Third and Fourth Years of Medical School

Rockford, Illinois

Dear Christine and Jeremy,

I'm glad you both are back from your trips–Jeremy to Florida and Christine to Mahomet. My study and teaching of Romans continues this year. What are you two studying? Do not allow life to squeeze out your study of the Word.

Proverbs 21

Proverbs 21:3 is simple and straightforward. Often we feel better about ourselves if we feel we are sacrificing or giving up something for God–feeling we will impress Him such that He will not know what is truly in our heart, or motivates our choices and actions. Frequently sacrifice is a cover-up for godly ambivalence–one foot in the world and one in His kingdom. To choose to act rightly (relative to God's standard, Christ's example) and justly (giving what is due to everyone) is a result of a sincere, unambivalent, God-seeking heart and has an air of humility and responsibility–it is not pompous or hypocritical. God for sure knows the difference because He knows our hearts; spirit-controlled Christians can discern the difference and I believe every person values and is drawn to such refreshing, honest people.

Verse 4 continues this theme. The "wicked" person is self-centered and not God-centered; she cannot hear Him or have room in her heart for His standards and priorities. What "shines forth" ("land of the wicked") from such people, what is seen by the rest of the world, is conceit, superiority, self-centeredness, pridefulness, unkindness, insensitivity, and self-exaltation at the expense of others. This is sin and God will judge it so and such people will be "rewarded" for this work. The world in the short term is fooled by such people and may reward them with power, position, and wealth, but even the world will reject them eventually because of their pride and unkindness. They cannot be trusted and they represent no truth greater than what is good for them now.

We had a good trip to Southern California this past weekend. I learned some useful material and had a great presentation on "Medical Public Speaking." The pace of life there seemed more laid back and materialistic–I think it would be harder to seek and follow God as Lord in that environment.

Proverbs 21:5 endorses diligence, hard work, perseverance, discipline, and time spent in effort. People with this work ethic will see their plans accomplished and blessed. People of this "diligence" are people who see God and subjugate their "plans" to His plans, as they know Him better and are changed "by the renewing of their mind." True blessedness and reasonable worldly success can only be accomplished and realized as our plans coincide with God's plan. The person who rushes, who is not concerned with deep, inner growth and change, who takes to the "world" without questioning; such a person's efforts will not be rewarded by the world or blessed by God. She will be "poor" by any standard and will not seek God or His plan, so will be also "poor in spirit."

Verse 6 reminds us of the truth behind what we witness daily in our world. Deceit, lying, misuse of power and privilege will in the end lead to destruction and pain ("deadly snare"). What little gain realized is superficial, fleeting, and never satisfying. Lying is so attractive because it purports to prevent consequence of ungodly behavior, but it only delays it, complicates it, and magnifies it. A lie can rarely stand alone–it almost always leads to more and more deceit and deeper internal pain, shame, and guilt. The world will then turn on the person who accepts this way of life and reject her, leaving her with nothing.

It was good to see both of you on Sunday, and to be able to spend time with you, Christine, earlier in the weekend. I trust your return to Rockford was uneventful and safe. You are probably nearing the end of another week of "clerkships."

Proverbs 21:7 warns us that there will be times when we will know pain because of our stance for Christ and for godliness. We live in a sin-controlled world and often, at least in the short run, the wicked will prevail against the godly and will control, conquer, and oppress those who choose to do what is right and honoring to God. Evil encourages violence, fear, oppression, and the need to control by domination. Goodness and godliness are threats to the wicked and will provoke this response. We know, however, that this will not prevail forever and justice will be executed both in this life (if God so chooses and orchestrates) and, for sure, at the time of judgment.

Verse 8 contrasts "devious" and "upright." Devious is concealed, manipulative, self-seeking, shameful, deceitful, crafty, and aimed at tearing down another for self gain. Upright is honest, fully visible, scrutinizable, unselfish, not designed to cause pain, and honoring to others and to God. It is only out of a relationship through Christ with God that we can receive a new nature that can hope to act in a progressively more upright manner. We, in such a relationship, are declared innocent of our sin and fully vested with God's spirit. The people who deny Christ and are encrusted in sin remain guilty and cannot move toward upright behavior or conduct.

I continue to pray that God is blessing your marriage in these exciting foundation years. I remember with great fondness those same years long ago. Savor them daily for they will never come again. Plan for the next phase of your life but do not neglect the godly leadings and lessons of these wonderful years.

Proverbs 21:9 is written to the wife, but I feel the teaching is applicable to either member of a marriage. To be "quarrelsome" is to be unhappy–usually and foremost within oneself. In addition, it usually reflects the inability to understand the inner unhappiness (quarrelsome people usually deny this) and therefore they are unable to communicate on this subject. The unhappiness becomes displaced to others and small "triggering" issues evoke disproportionate emotion and conflict. The result is a relationship or a family in turmoil and conflict; no one, not even visitors, are comfortable and secure. The proverb tells us that any amount of material blessing is not worth this and it would be better to trade wealth for a content, positive relationship.

Verse 10 talks about "craving." A wicked person is, according to Romans, one who doesn't choose Christ and is unable to choose Christ (the Spirit has not enabled her to do so) and therefore moves along a progressively painful and pain giving life that leads to depravity. A person who is godless seeks and proactively satisfies a desire to act and relate in a way that is self-destructive and relationally destructive. She appears to be morally dead and insensitive to others and their needs. Even those closest to her will be abused and their needs will fall on deaf ears. We should rejoice and be eternally grateful that God chose us and gave us His ability to hear His Word.

I'm sorry I wasn't at home, Christine, when you called last night. Mom told me of your frustration about medical education and your colleagues. I understand this frustration and have long since given up on finding fulfillment within the sociology of the profession. My deep satisfaction comes when I can care and minister to my patients, the people God has privileged me to have a part in His healing process. In many regards being a physician is a lonely profession. Thank God you two have each other even at that level.

Proverbs 21:11 is an unusual and insightful proverb. First, the "wise man" is one who knows God (via Christ or Holy Spirit) and seeks Him. The "simple" is the person who is blind to God and knows only the world and his own needs/desires. A "mocker" is one who openly disregards and dishonors God; such a person will be punished here on earth–in time. Such punishment comes by God allowing him to suffer the destructive effect of his choices on his life, and that of his family. When a simple person sees this happen to a mocker he can begin to become wiser to God. God lovingly and constructively instructs the wise man, directly or via the world, and he himself gains further understanding of Gods' ways.

Verse 12 is generally taken to refer to the triune God ("Righteous One")–the only truly righteous, good, and kind one to ever exist. He was manifest in the person of Christ here on earth. The proverb tells us that such a God knows His own ("sheep") and knows those who hate and reject Him; further He knows the whole family. As previously taught, God is just and will allow the wicked to be hurt by the natural effect of their choices and actions while here on earth, and He has promised destruction and eternal ruin on them after physical death. God is not mocked and knows His creation.

I pray for you two daily and for the decisions you are making for your lives, individually and as a couple. Jeremy, as you choose your specialty, remember that while family practice holds extraordinary opportunity to impact people for God personally, I believe a godly surgeon can also have great value as an instrument for healing and impacting lives in a different manner. The issue is what is God doing in your heart and where are you suited to serve Him.

Proverbs 21:13 talks about God's justice and His love of all created man. God knows the poor (by the world's standards; there because of their own choice or unchosen factors) and He expects His body to love and care for them. A person who is made new because of her relationship with Christ will become more like Christ and will not be able, as the ungodly do, to close herself to the needs of the poor. Do not let the poor's personal responsibility for their circumstances confuse the requirement of each of us to love them as God loves them. This is hard work because we are ready to judge and condemn irresponsible and non-hardworking people. God enforces this command by telling us in the proverb that He will not hear the prayers of those who shun the poor, because such people are not of Him.

Verse 14 tells us that acknowledging a person who is angry is right, while "buying" with a bribe only delays execution of deep hate. The unconditional giving of a gift is a way of saying you hear and respond to another person's hurt and distress toward you—it soothes with kindness and understanding. It is not done publicly for wrong motives but one-on-one between two parties. It is constructive and brings solution. Bribes (to advance one's own greed and position of power) done behind the scenes (because it is immoral, unjust, unfair, and unkind) will only delay the eventual display of destruction. It doesn't address real issues or seek understanding—it buys power, wealth, and time, but only temporarily.

I trust you both are soon to finish your current clerkship and begin another. I encourage you to choose to view these clerkships positively and as opportunities not only to learn medicine, but also to know yourselves better and to see how God is working in your life. He is molding you to serve Him and to be privileged to know people at the most intimate levels. Pray every day before you leave home that you would be able to see Him and His work that very day.

Proverbs 21:15 is a reassuring one that we would do well to hold on to when we encounter injustice in our lives or in the lives of our godly or innocent brethren. It should also encourage us to seek to be just in all circumstances. It tells us first that justice will be done—the only issue is when. The implication is that we may have to be patient and trust God for His timing and His plan. However, when it does come the justice will have polarizing effects. Justice is the judicial aspect of acknowledging what is of God and consistent with how He created the world and its inhabitants. Only as we know Him through Christ can we seek Him and His world. The seeking of this will be rewarded and blessed with "joy," while the rejection of this will bring "terror."

Proverbs 21:16 exhorts us to stay on the "path of understanding" or we will find ourselves devoid of life. What is this "path of understanding?" It is the seeking of truth indwelled within His Word. After we receive Christ, we are able to seek this truth and gain His understanding, and then choose this in our lives. We walk this path! If we either cannot seek Him (not a Christian) or if we do not discipline ourselves to seek the path of understanding, we will move toward "death." Such death is not physical (since we all will give up this body for another) but emotional, relational, and spiritual. Only God gives life; all else leads to destruction, darkness, sadness, disgrace, guilt, and shame.

I understand you have a new addition to your home: a cat. Christine, you must have done some smooth talking to the landlord to get his "okay." Or maybe it is a statement of his confidence in you and your respectful character.

Proverbs 21:17 teaches us that the seeking of "pleasure" and hedonistic wishes (about other more important and valuable areas) will result in poverty. Certainly this refers to financial poverty but it also depletes the riches of discipline, perseverance, and sacrifices and devalues the pleasure of thought, personal interaction, and contemplation. It further impoverishes one's spirit which doesn't flourish in the midst of over-sensual indulgences. This proverb doesn't advocate a sterile, serious life or worldly denial, but it, along with other teachings of proverbs, teaches balance and prioritization.

Verse 18 is an unusual and thought-provoking statement. It seems to be saying that the wicked and unfaithful (self-centered, ungodly, and God rejecters) are to be expended and regarded as less valuable than the righteous and upright. By whom is this perspective held? Perhaps by the world in general because despite what is betrayed at the surface of society, there is still a high value and priority placed on godly behavior and Christian morality. Also by God; the Scripture teaches that He will take from the wicked and give to the righteous; He will bless His people and destroy those who reject Him. Often He uses the ungodly to be able to demonstrate to His chosen His power, presence, and plan.

Not a day goes by that I don't think of you two, and with those thoughts I pray God is close to you and you are constantly seeking Him and His ways. I am finding myself praying with my patients more and more. It occurs so naturally and I am astounded as to the effect it has on them and me. It gives me the greatest pleasure, sense of value, and joy of anything I do in my day. I am so grateful to God that I have this opportunity.

Proverbs 21:19 is a strong admonishment against marital or family bickering, nagging, quarreling, faultfinding, and ill temperament. Even though it is written about a wife, I feel it is true of either member of a marriage or members of a family. The marriage and family should be the most peaceful and affirming of all places; a place where we can be understood and our weaknesses accepted but lovingly remediated. Fun and humor, creativity, and expressed love should be the tenure, not conflict and pessimism. We all are human and therefore these negative traits will sneak through at times but should not be the rule.

Verse 20 tells us that we should be responsible, planning people who provide for our loved ones. The "foolish" man is basically self-centered (rejects God's rule in His life and therefore has no true love for his family) and will use and consume for his own self-interest and pleasure the things God has allowed him to earn or possess. The "wise" person knows God and therefore sees himself as less important than those in his life and charge (family). He will then use his possessions wisely and frugally for the mutual benefit of all. This proverb is one of the many that illustrates Christ's teaching of the "greatest commandments" (Matt. 22:34-40). We must first love God deeply, then as we change as a result of fellowship with Him, we will be able to love others.

We sure enjoyed our evening with you in Rockford. We made good time getting home, but I found myself down with the flu on Saturday. I was happy to not be able to go to the football game or work on various projects so I could catch up on my letter writing. I wrote to all members of my family personal letters, praying throughout that God would give me the right words and heart to share with each of them.

Proverbs 21:21 tells us a fundamental truth–that "pursuing" righteousness and love is the top priority in life for the godly person. Note the word "pursue" in this verse. It conveys the idea of a proactive, effortful, concerted seeking after, despite difficulty and odds. We are to pursue the state of becoming more and more like Christ as a result of being made "perfect" in our relationship, and we are to pursue love. Love is also fundamental to the Christian walk; it is out of love we were created and brought back to our Creator, and it is out of love that we are to serve Him and then to serve each other. The writer is saying that when we pursue these, we will find life (all of existence apart from God leads to death), prosperity (not necessarily measured in worldly terms), and honor before God and in time before all creation.

Verse 22 must be regarded allegorically. The "wise man" here is the person who knows God and is being led by Him according to His plan. The "mighty" are those who in pride have secured human power and station, but reject God and His claim on their lives. The "city" is their "house of cards"–their philosophy and lies that form the superficial, weak, tenuous structure of their existence. They "trust" in something, usually their own human wisdom, money, power, etc. This is their "stronghold" and is the thing that lies at the center of their city. To defeat or to bring down such a person (as part of God's judgment here on earth, or in order to bring them to Himself), the wise must undo and dispel that basic, central, false belief that directs her whole life.

Proverbs 21:23 is a fairly well known one and again comments on the need to control our words and what we take into our bodies. The tongue speaks words and these words can honor or dishonor God, build up or tear down others, and lead to pain or peace within a life. The mouth takes in that which goes into the deep fabric of our person. We must be careful what we take into our person. The trash the world puts out can, in my experience, slowly and relentlessly divert us away from God and toward depravity and godlessness. Be always vigilant in the use of the tongue and the mouth.

Verse 24 takes aim at the proud and arrogant person. God hates pride because it drives one away from God and to self-centered choices. One who believes she is the center of all will mock God. She will reject any possibility of His ownership in her life and will be unteachable by Him. The proud will not only be spiritually depraved, but because of their selfishness will drive others away and thereby be unable to love or be loved. They will be unhappy, restless, lonely people that increasingly look to themselves to find joy and peace, only to become further from that goal.

It was great having you two here for a portion of the Thanksgiving holiday. It is deeply pleasing for me to have my children around my table. I find myself praising and thanking God for each of you and find myself in awe concerning His plan and sovereignty over His children.

Proverbs 21:25 and 26 talk about the "sluggard." Such a descriptive term is applied to the person who is slow, lazy, nonproductive, leeching upon others, and obsessed with gaining only his own needs. It is an ugly term because such people are ugly to God. This person refuses to work–he contrives and deceives in order not to discipline, sacrifice, or work hard. In his heart he is set against diligence in work and consciously plays out his subconscious refusal to work. Because of this, he instead craftily and slyly extorts from the resourceful and diligent his needs. They really are not "needs" but only wants or "cravings" (wants driven by self-centered emotions). This process will bring him toward depraved behavior and speech that will lead to death (emotional and relational; physical may be accelerated; spiritual having already occurred).

Verse 26 tells us that these cravings will never cease or be satiated. However, because the person of God is spiritually at peace deep within her soul, she is not driven to crave after the worldly "stuff" but is content to accept with appreciation God's good gifts or to give up to others, unselfishly and not according to merit. The Christian has deep joy and peace due to the restored relationship with God and therefore is not desperately seeking (craving), in vain hope, to extract it from the world. What a contrast presented here between the righteous and the ungodly.

Well, how was Hawaii, Jeremy–did you get to enjoy any of the island? Christine, I bet you are feeling a bit anxious at this point relative to the Christmas production. I'm looking forward to seeing you both and enjoying the production (especially the dancing).

Verse 27 of Proverbs 21 tells us what God thinks of the offerings of the wicked person. The very use of the word "wicked" implies His knowledge of his heart toward Him–he rejects His lordship in his life and seeks only what satisfies his human needs or passions. Any offering, even if it appears to be sacrificial, will be rejected by God because of his wicked heart. More so will it infuriate and arouse God's angry rejection, if that wicked person brings any offering with the intent to impress other people (to get his needs met) or to con what he considers a gullible and backwards God. God looks at the heart and motives of the person offering or giving up things for Him. He will not be deceived or mocked.

Verse 28 tells us that the person who slanders, lies, bends the truth, gives only half-truths, or misrepresents truth in any way will perish. This doesn't mean that if we sin, fall short of being Christ-like, we will perish. It means that a person whose heart delights in this and who repetitively pursues this approach cannot have a relationship with God (not a recreated spiritual person), and therefore will not live after this life. Those whom this person influences to follow his direction and pattern will also be destroyed someday. Moreover, even in this life, often such a person is rejected by society, somehow in recognition of the destructive effect of a false witness.

It seems like ages ago that we were at our Kiawah Island house enjoying our Christmas together. I gave a public talk last night on anxiety, depression, and stress. It was well attended and went quite well. I wish I was able to share with them where real peace comes from! It is much easier and more effective to talk individually with my patients on these issues.

Proverbs 21:29 compares (once again) a wicked person and an upright person. The concept of wicked in Proverbs is one who rejects God and His lordship in his life and who therefore acts according to his/her own prideful agenda. Such an agenda leads to pain for himself and others. Such a person must (to insure his prideful, fragile self-worth) present a "front" that implies cover-up and deception (both to himself and to others). The upright person is one who fears God and therefore seeks and finds His wisdom. He/she is teachable and thoughtfully and prayerfully grows and incorporates God's wisdom into her life choices. This person is inwardly stronger, more secure, and growing daily, but is outwardly listening, learning, and flexible.

Verse 30 tells us a non-arguable fact: that if one acts against the Lord, or derives any wisdom, or develops any plan that is counter to God's, he or she will fail. This is non-arguable to the thinking, spiritual person who can see God in history, in the natural world, and in her own experience. The more mature we become, the more this fact is held strongly by us. However, the non-spiritual person is blinded to this and believes that human wisdom and plans are his or hers to derive and that they can succeed. It gets back to the basic sin of pride. We can only pray for him, witness by our words and actions the true perspective.

I hope you both enjoyed your weekend off and were able to be mentally away from medicine and enjoy each other. I was "on-call" this last weekend and had a very quiet one. I believe that the on-call times have been quiet for me because I have asked that of God. I'm not suggesting that He will do that for you, but simply that He wants us to submit our need to Him in prayer, and He, in His wisdom, will answer. He knows us better than we know ourselves, and He will give us what we need, and what will benefit His kingdom. He wants us to ask and believe.

Proverbs 21:31 is a very profound, but simple, truth. It says that we, as God's children on this earth (part of His heavenly kingdom) should prepare, work hard, make right choices, and be willing to proactively engage life. As we grow in maturity, becoming more Christ-like, our choices will be more pleasing to Him. However, we are to be active because there is no place in this kingdom for laziness and irresponsibility–God will not act or achieve victory without our preparedness and action. However, the result and the effect of our action is His. He will bring victory by His definition and according to His timetable. To establish this balance in life is crucial to being a part of His work here on earth.

Proverbs 22

Proverbs 22:1 talks about character and regard or reputation within the world. To be regarded as caring, sensitive, able, wise, effective, and selfless is the greatest of all goals in this life, greater than material riches. Often the media promotes the latter, but in reality humanity places a greater, more lasting regard for qualities of character.

I pray for you two daily as I know the demands and challenges that are a part of your life each day. It is reassuring to me to know confidently that God is the author of your life as it is now, and as it will be in the years to come. He has had His hand upon you both thus far, and He will never stop being your all-knowing, powerful, and loving Father. Rest in that thought each hour of each day.

Proverbs 22:2 is a very simple piece of wisdom that embodies a very healthy and practical viewpoint. It basically says that the biggest worldly differential criterion (wealth) is devoid of value in the presence of God. God looks way beyond worldly wealth as He looks at His creation. He has made us all and our worldly worth is at best an obstacle in our ability to serve and please Him. All of us must bow before Him and acknowledge Him as Creator and Lord of our lives; it is His choice ultimately as to our fate and future. The Word is clear that only in a relationship with Him, through Christ, can we be acceptable and justified—not by wealth, possessions, or power.

Verse 3 describes an attribute of a prudent person. A prudent person is wise, making beneficial, mature decisions that are realistic but not cowardly. These decisions may lead him to push forward relentlessly or to pull back cautiously; he takes into account a higher and loftier perspective (a more godly one) that would benefit himself, but more importantly, his charge. As parents you must be prudent people. At times it is prudent to avoid worldly traps, snares, and dangers—taking refuge and "waiting it out." The non-prudent person ("simple") pushes ahead, to the ultimate detriment to himself and his charge (not to mention, God's desired kingdom's work). He is motivated by unwise, closely focused, self-centered goals and needs. Be cautious of such people and do not allow them to influence you or your children. Press your envelope of vision but always be prudent.

I trust you both are near completing another week of clerkships. Each week brings you closer to completion. I pray that you both will not only persevere and finish but that you will enjoy your training and work, and that God will expand and add color to your vision and His will. Always be asking the question, "How can I be His instrument in this specific medical setting, today?"

Proverbs 22:4 and 5 are to be understood, I believe, from a non-worldly perspective. To believe that by acting more and more as Christ acted will bring worldly wealth and human honor while avoiding thorns and snares is to miss other significant parts of Scripture and to not see the obvious in Christ's life. Humility is the mental perspective that sees themselves (as human beings) as the creation, not as the Creator and acknowledges God as sovereign Lord over our lives, the sole origin of all wisdom and love. He becomes the goal and object of our lives (not worldly wealth and honor). As we see Him as the awesome, powerful, Creator we come to "fear" Him with deep love and place ourself before Him vulnerable but confident in His care. The wealth this brings is spiritual wealth and wealth by definition of the standards of the kingdom of God. The honor is to stand in His presence and for Him to call us by name. Wealth and honor in this life may occur if it is His will in the perspective of His eternity. The one who actively "guards his soul" (see Proverbs 16:17) from evil will avoid thorns and snares. The things that will be avoided are those barriers and obstacles, traps and lies that will serve to reduce our ability to hear and respond to God. It doesn't guarantee that we will avoid suffering in life, although acting in a godly fashion can reduce some suffering.

Not a day goes by without one of my patients, looking at the picture of you, asking me about each of you. I find that no matter how busy I am, I fondly take time and tell all they care to know, with great pride. Any further thoughts on specific practice profiles for your future? I think this will increasingly become clearer as you continue on in your clinical rotations.

Proverbs 22:6 is probably the best known proverb. "Train up a child" is bigger than lecturing her but involves day-by-day molding, listening, understanding, wise counsel, loving discipline, modeling, and physical warmth. Training a child involves (and requires) both parents and will span the range of emotions, for all involved. The parents must ultimately find strength and wisdom in God and His Word, and must have a strong, growing relationship between them. Train "up" implies a continually evolving, growing set of issues and challenges that must be met—each age having its own blessings, opportunities for godly development, and potential pitfalls. "The way he should go" suggests there is one way and that the parents know it, live by it and hold it visible as what underlies all decisions and actions. It also is the goal of the training and gives all a clear idea of what is desired. The "way" for us is God's way–the only way for joy and peace and total fulfillment. "When he is old" is intentionally variable because "old" here means mature enough to know and choose to live by one's own choices. This varies relative to one's age–some being old at eighteen, others at seventy-five. Perhaps the training in some form or another continues until one is "old." "He will not turn from it" means he has ownership of it for himself and has become a witness that this way is the best way. No matter what the world offers, he will continue in this "way." Often we are in the "training up" of others while we are at the point that we can be certain we will not depart or turn from it. Thus the cycle continues from generation to generation.

It's Nanny's birthday today. I called her at 7:30 to be the first to wish her well on this special day. As per my study of Job, I've learned that birthdays should celebrate God's creative powers in our creation and His love and grace in allowing us to live and continue to be part of His created universe.

Proverbs 22:7 can be regarded at several levels. On the surface is the fact that in this world the "haves" rule over the "have-nots." Is this unjust and not according to God's creative perfect will for His creation? It is the way of the world after the fall and sin. Yet, those who have opportunity to impact the world, through impact-ing lives and policy, are the rich and privileged. To have this posi-tion in the world and to not use it for God's purposes is an offense to him, and one that will be judged. At another level, this proverb may relate to being "rich" in spiritual or emotional ways. This re-quires a relationship with God through Christ and a progressively growing wisdom via His Holy Spirit. We must "lend" this wisdom and spiritual insight to those in spiritual need.

Verse 8 reassures us that God still is in charge of His creation and that justice will prevail someday. There are, and will be, wicked people–they are wicked because they get away (for awhile) with hurting others for their own needs. But, we are told, they are building up trouble for themselves. The Word doesn't tell us when the trouble will befall them or how; that is not our business. It tells us that God has a ledger for the unsaved and that the longer it gets, the more it will be appeased. The means of the wicked's control and abuse of others in this world will be destroyed at God's whim and in His time. It is sometimes necessary for us to remember this proverb.

I was blessed that you sought my input on your decision on whether to go to Ohio. I believe it is a godly trait to seek counsel when making decisions. This will increase the likelihood of making the right and godly decision.

Proverbs 22:9 and 10 are relatively straightforward but often hard to accomplish. Verse 9 tells us that a generous person will be blessed; it gives us an example of how such a one should share his food with the poor. The liberal perspective would highlight the need for social action and the care of the poor. Although this has some merit, I believe the real emphasis is upon the qualities of a person that will result in generosity and sharing with others. Such a person is selfless and humble, believing himself fortunate and blessed by God with possessions or truth. In turn he seeks to share what he doesn't deserve with others. He is blessed by deep relationships, mutual caring and edification, and God's further bestowing of His generosity–material and non-material.

Verse 10 encourages us to not associate with or allow a "mocker" (against God's truth) to be a part of our gathering. Such a person is motivated by self-love and is prideful, arrogant, and will use all means to further himself and his ungodly causes. He causes strife, quarrels, and divisions and is being used by Satan to spread disharmony. Keep your eyes open for such a person and keep your distance from him.

It was good to talk with you, Christine, yesterday. I'm sorry you are ill. I know you both are tired and weary (the gloom of winter doesn't help), but be encouraged. Spring is around the corner! This is true of the weather and also of your professional careers/training. I love you both.

Proverbs 22:11 can be viewed at a human level or at a spiritual one, depending on how you interpret the word "king." Humanly, the people in life who possess and seek to develop a heart that is honest, selfless, and that delights in goodness, such a person is rare and of great and noble character. This person's speech is loving, caring, up-building, and other-focused; this purity in speech is likewise rare. Worldly authorities value such a person because there are no scheming, self-centered plans, and destructive wishes. Spiritually, our relationship with God through Christ is able to give us a new heart that is pure and speech that is considerate. It reflects our friendship with the King of Kings.

Verse 12 offers some interesting considerations for us. The Lord is the origin of all truth, wisdom, and knowledge. He is Lord over all His creation and nothing happens or is said that He has not permitted and intended. All human "knowledge" is known only as He (God) permits and intends. Wrong knowledge (a contradiction in terms) is parlayed by Satan (the deceiver) and God will allow this only for a season and only as it will test and refine His children (bring them into an even deeper relationship with Him). The words and "facts" believed and conveyed to the world by the ungodly ("unfaithful") will not have their intended effect, but in His time will be rejected, unmasked, and devalued. They will be frustrated. It is God's world and He is the Lord.

It is really good, Christine, to hear a more upbeat attitude as you talk about your medical education. I'm glad you were able to be with your patient even through surgery. It was neat that she knew and felt good about your being in the operating room. This is really what it is all about. Once you wade through this man-made system of medicine, it really reduces to two people working together in a trusting, compassionate bond to move toward health.

Proverbs 22:13 is a bit strange in that it doesn't really tell us the point of the proverb. As I have thought about it and understood the term "sluggard," I believe it is saying that one characteristic of a sluggard is that he is pessimistic and full of excuses why he cannot accomplish a goal (even when he acknowledges the goal). There is always some reason why he "can't." Remember this applies not just to the world's societal system, but also to spiritual maturity as well. Too often, a person convinces himself or herself that there are too many obstacles to growing in godliness and seeking to understand God through His Word.

Verse 14 tells us to beware of the enticement of the seductive. There are many "adulteresses" in the world, and each of us has our unique vulnerabilities to the enticements around us. When we turn away from God, and do not seek Him as the Lord of our lives, we will be allowed to feel the natural consequences of this choice. The adulteress of our lives will entice us and suck us into the sin and evil she perpetuates. It is very hard to excavate ourselves from this "pit," so we are advised to stay close to God to avoid painful snares.

Have you had any further thoughts on residency programs? It is an exciting and important time in your lives and one that needs a great deal of prayer. I am confident that God will direct you in this decision, in answer to faithful prayer. I will continue to serve you in this prayer journey. Please convey specifics to me as they become available.

Proverbs 22:15 is an interesting one and counters the notions that "man is basically and naturally good" and that discipline is not necessary to establish "habits of godliness." The proverb clearly tells us that even in the child there is "folly"–that is the desire to rebel against God and His ways. This human/sin nature is deeply rooted in the "heart" of the child; it is not just learned (although learned ways further reinforce our natural anti-God perspective) or a result of poor parenting or "dysfunctional families." In fact, godly parenting must cooperate with God, being led by the discernment and wisdom of His Spirit. Discipline is broader than punishment and its motivation is different. It is continual, requires vigilance, wisdom, discernment, prayer, humility, strength, and compassion.

Verse 16 is a warning that God can (if this is His choice) bring to destruction and worldly poverty any He chooses. God hates those who are proud and who oppress the unfortunate and socially rejected; He hates those who seek their own ways and fortunes by courting the worldly rich, despite the cost to their integrity. He can bring them down, while they are here on earth, and destroy and impoverish them. Certainly, His justice will be served at judgment, if not here on earth. These people even if worldly rich are spiritually poor and know deep pain all through their lives.

I will be praying for you as you take your subject exams for this clerkship. I am glad you have finished one of the two long ones, and will soon be well under way to completion of your third year. Your residency choosing process should be an enjoyable one; exciting when we once again realize that God has the right program for you both, in the right part of the country. I urge you to daily, in prayer, seek His direction. Remember God has called you into medicine, and miraculously given you opportunities in order that you can serve Him and be His hands as you touch the lives of your patients.

Proverbs 22:17-21 is an introduction to the "sayings of the wise;" these are to be placed deeply in your hearts and minds, retrievable and used to teach and give reliable truths to others.

Verses 22 and 23 tell us not to take advantage or use our social power to suppress and discourage the poor and needy. The society here in America gives power, position, and reward to those who have wealth and material possession. It is expected that these people are to be regarded as "better" than those who have not. Sure they have greater opportunity and education, but are not loved more by God, than the poor. In fact, the poor and needy will be protected by God and He will seek punishment on the powerful if they harm the underprivileged.

Verses 24 and 25 tell us not to be in very close relationship with the one who is "hot-tempered" and "easily angered." We are easily influenced and the ways of others impact how we act and speak. If the godly person spends time with angry, cynical, aggressive, defensive people, she will begin to see the world as they do and adopt their ways. When she becomes more like them she will bring misery and judgment upon herself–she will hurt people and incite anger or revenge in the ungodly community. With the Spirit's gift of discernment, identify and avoid angry people, or you can weaken your walk and witness as a godly Christ-centered person.

I appreciate your sharing with me your developing thoughts on residency programs. The one in Charlotte sounds like it has potential.

As I mentioned tonight on the phone, I believe you will definitely see the hand of God in the process and decision. He has brought the two of you this far and will not abandon you now or in the future.

Proverbs 22:26-27 advises against getting into debt beyond your ability to repay it. It is easy these days to get into such a level of debt and even to find (put up) enough down payment or collateral to obtain a loan. But it must be paid off and you must have the ability, opportunity, and secure position to pay off the loan. If there is any question to any of these three categories, you should never begin the process. The world deals harshly with those who default and will take your very home, if you default. This has implications not only for you but also for your family, those who depend upon you and trust your wisdom. This area of finance is one the Bible is not silent on and here we have firm spiritual direction.

Verse 28 is an interesting and intriguing one. It tells us to trust the wisdom of those who have gone before us and the decisions they have made, the guidelines they have given us, the ethics they have lived and died by, and their teaching from their collective years of experience. It is presumptuous and unwise to think we in this (or any) single generation can be right and counter to the wisdom of the past. Be very careful if you find yourself countering or modifying the teaching of those before you. Yes, at times it is right to do so but be sure God is speaking loudly to you and you know it is His voice.

It was good to have you with us last weekend. As a father it is an exciting challenge to be a part of the lives of my daughters (and their husbands) as God directs and moves you along in this life. To see His hand and to understand His will requires each of us in trusting faith to pray, seek godly counsel, study His Word, and ask the Spirit to open our eyes to His movement.

Proverbs 22:29 talks about the quality of one's work. It encourages us to do our work to the best possible extent, as skillfully as possible. God has given every person ability, talent, and a passion for a work. Some of us need to work harder than others to accomplish a high level of performance. The recognition of these skills, talents, and passions is required, then the discipline and hard work to develop and find application for them are demanded. God wishes his people to (in a balanced way) maximize our skills, for this will give us opportunity and influence, while being a vessel for God to use to have compassion for others. God will use the most skilled in the area He deems most crucial and necessary. In this proverb, He will have the greatly skilled worker in the presence of kings, not ordinary people. However, I don't think this means that only at visible social levels does He use His skilled people, but where He deems they are most crucially needed.

Proverbs 23

Proverbs 23:1-2 tells us to be aware of what situations God puts us in, and who we are in the presence of, and that our actions and words are important in that setting. Be a thinking Christian who is aware that God will often place you in circumstances where you can be either a positive or negative influence on key people. "Note well"–look around and consider each circumstance and the people or matter present. Then act in a godly manner that will serve to influence people or the issue in a way that is pleasing and honoring to Him. "Gluttony" here is an example of a negative influence and a negative witness for God.

It is always a pleasure to be asked for my opinion on decisions you two are considering. Christine, I view your seeking of counsel as a sign of security in yourself, respect for others who have experience and wisdom, and just plain "smart." You will make fewer mistakes with less future regrets, and maintain better interpersonal relationships by listening to others' input.

Proverbs 23:3 refers back to "dining with rulers." It warns us not to crave, or seek relentlessly after, his delicacies. Delicacies are regarded as those things in life that are indulgences that when sought after can divert a person from true values and diligent efforts in the right areas of life. The writer cautions us not to be led astray by others, especially those who live by a different (and less God-centered) standard. To seek what they seek will lead us away from God and deceive us as to the real needs and goals of our lives. We must always keep our priorities straight, as they are formed and ordered as a result of our walk with God. Even then, if we are with others with different priorities, we can maintain godly choices.

Verses 4 and 5 warn against seeking riches and wealth for their own sake–they will vanish and leave us quickly, either here on earth if we make poor economic choices and surely after death, in the life to come in heaven. Balance seeking wealth with "restraint" in order to pursue equal or greater goals and life requirements. This restraint and ability to balance is a result of God's wisdom, procured through our walk with Him and His Word. Certainly it is good, responsible, and necessary to work to have wealth enough to build up God's kingdom and to give your children what is their due to maximize their ability and opportunities. This is different from seeking riches for yourself alone.

Jeremy, I do hope you had a great birthday. It was good to talk with you both this weekend. I hope you both had a good chance to rest–the emotional and (at some moments) physical drains of being a medical student are not easy and can be discouraging or disheartening. I understand this and encourage you that these emotions are acceptable and understandable–express them but then put them aside as you move forward. Either to deny they exist or dwell on them excessively is detrimental to you and adds burden to your tasks at hand.

Proverbs 23:6-8 is an interesting bit of wisdom. There are people in this world who at their very core are self-focused, self-seeking, greedy, protective of "their things," and plain stingy. They may try to overcome this and press themselves to verbally be more giving and selfless, but their non-verbal communication or their real true feelings which come to light down the line, will betray their true perspective. At times, they are self-centered to the extent that they are money focused, seeing your consumption of their things as "stealing from them." When their true feelings come to light, you will feel literally ill and regret any complimentary way you had thought of them. I believe this is a spiritual problem. As we seek God for God Himself and not for what He gives us, and as we become changed and less self-focused, I believe we become more generous, other-centered, and seek relationships and not things.

I am deeply grieved and stunned at the latest killing at the school in Colorado. I have found myself rethinking my perspectives on this world, this country, the values of our society, and the impact on the generations. It should be frightening, disheartening, frustrating, and unpleasant for the godly person to encounter the world in its raw, depraved state. But it then challenges us to determine how to live and function in this world to serve God, enjoy life, and raise our children to be godly.

Proverbs 23:9 in effect says not to waste your words, effort, or time on the ungodly who live apart from God and reject even the aroma of His presence. They may react against the godly person vehemently and cruelly. It is important to discern (a gift of the Spirit—to be prayed for) who these people are; and then to not invest yourself in them, not be affected by their cruelty, and at times to "run" from them. Your godly wisdom and efforts to love them will not only be rejected but also will be misinterpreted and used to hurt you. This must be balanced with Christ's example to love others. Seek God's wisdom in each person's case but do not be disappointed when rejected.

Verses 10 and 11 are best understood from a spiritual perspective. The key words here are "defender" and "fatherless." These refer to Satan (the proprietor and defender of the world and the worldly) and to those who are cut off from God the Father, and who obey the values and directives of the Satan-ruled world. Be careful as you interact with these people and especially if you, with your godliness, threaten their worldly, anti-Christ equilibrium. Satan himself will counter and seek to discourage and disarm you.

I'm looking forward to this weekend, at your sister Elisa's graduation, when we can all be together again for a brief time. I'm sorry that your weekend will end up being a crowded one. I appreciate your willingness to drive to Ohio.

Proverbs 23:12 is a general encouragement to the godly person to be open to instruction and the teaching of truth. To be "teachable" is in my opinion one of the most godly of all characteristics. The proverb asks for openness of our heart–our attitude must be positive and seeking of godly wisdom and guidance, while our mind (the ears are one main avenue to the brain) has to take in truth and personally let it make a difference in our lives. Teachability is directly proportional to our relationship to God and inversely proportionate to our human pride and need for ego preservation.

Verses 13 and 14 tell of the benefit to the growing child in a family of strong discipline. Punishment can never be used destructively (to the spirit and self-worth of another) or to elevate ourselves at the cost to another. Punishment here means strong and painful discipline with the goal always in mind to benefit the child–to prevent his destruction (morally, emotionally, relationally, or even physically). Ultimately such discipline can penetrate a young person when nothing else can or will, and it may well turn him or her away from a path that embraces the world and rejects God. In this sense it will save her soul. Strong, painful discipline must not occur in anger (a difficult thing to accomplish) and must be respected and handled very responsibly and discerningly. It can be dangerous or damaging but is at times necessary and courageous.

Well, now you are "four"–the two of you, a cat and a puppy! Thank you for your anniversary card and your words. As you know, that means more to me than anything one could ever do for me. We love you both. Mom and I went out to dinner. I marvel at how comfortable we feel with each other; yet the passion we have for one another has not diminished over the thirty years. We both pray that we have thirty more years together. We need to be doing some serious planning for the Europe trip. I really want you two to take the lead since it is our gift to you (for your graduation) and because it will make us happy if you are happy.

Proverbs 23:15 and 16 express well the deep concern and desire Christian parents have for their children. The desire is that their hearts would be wise and their lips speak what is right. This would mean to seek God both as Savior and Lord. Only then can a heart be wise–to see life from God's perspective and understand truth and true life. Wisdom comes only out of a dynamic relationship with God, through Christ. Lips that speak the truth show the other side of the godly coin–the side of action and effort. For the ancient people the words of the mouth were equivalent to all effort, actions, work, behavior, and use of time. To use all of this for right is to let God be Lord of our lives and permit Him to live in and through us in our daily lives. For the parent, when her children do this, she knows a glad heart and an innermost joy. We feel and know a small fraction of God's delight when we, His children, walk in righteousness.

I just got off the phone with you, Christine. It was good to talk with you and to once again marvel at how God is preparing you to move on to the next stage of your life. I sensed you have in your mind begun the transition out of medical school, looking ahead for new opportunities and challenges. The last several years have left you with various emotions, thoughts, and self-revelations. I encourage you to regard all of this with thanksgiving to God, because each of these has been orchestrated or allowed by Him, out of His great love for you.

Proverbs 23:17 speaks directly to a "rub" many of us Christians experience–our human nature will at times envy the worldly success and outward "happiness" of many who reject God and His Son. We lose sight of what really matters in the eternity of things and get confused about true peace and joy, versus worldly happiness and human passion. This proverb reminds us that we are to be "zealous" for the awesome power of our Lord. This is a continual battle and I believe requires constant reminders, accountability from other Christians, ongoing immersion in His Word, and ongoing prayer.

Verse 18 reminds us of the certain hope we have as a part of God's plan. Hope is an assured truth that has yet to be made tangible in life. It is certain and can never be diverted or challenged and all of the earth's kingdoms and even Satan cannot prevail against it. It is a personal hope, one that God has for each of us, His chosen children, and is consistent and supplementary to that of His other children (especially those He has placed us together with). It is this hope that comforts and sustains us in times of difficulty or confusion.

It's hard to believe that you will soon take the second part of national boards and will enter the final lap of medical school. You have both excelled; not only in the eyes of the world but also in the eyes of God and His children here on earth.

Proverbs 23:19-21 seem at first to focus on the evils of too much wine and food. Certainly excess in these specific areas will reduce the ability to serve Him, but the teaching can be generalized to "worldly/human excesses" of any sort. The writer exhorts the reader to "keep his heart on the right path." The heart is the driving part of our person; where our heart is will be where we go and how we conduct ourselves. To keep the heart on the right path requires we seek God and in doing so allow Him to change and mold our heart and become more like Christ. As this takes place, we will want to walk His path, which is the "right" path. This path leads to our blessing, blessing of others, and most importantly the glory of God. Many excesses hinder us from seeking God and then to navigate the road He leads us on–individually and specifically drunkeness and obesity are physical and character drains on us as we view ourselves and work with perseverance and discipline in God's calling. Aside from these two obvious ones, there can be similar, but more subtle, excesses that tempt us and then hinder us from being effective in His kingdom.

I find my heart is easily squeezed and that my thoughts both savor and ruminate over the human qualities and relationships I have known. Mom and you two (as well as the other sisters) are at the center of my heart. Last night I had a good and cleansing time of prayer on my knees beside each of your beds. I continue to look forward to years ahead and the times our lives will touch and intertwine. I love you both.

Proverbs 23:22-25 conveys instruction from the heart's perspective that I have just shared with you. Verses 24 and 25 indicate the deep and essential value and importance the son/daughter has to the well-being of the parents, and their ability to be joyful and to know the deep "delight" that can only come from such a relationship. The parents delight and know joy because of the "wise son/daughter." To be wise is to know God and His truth and to seek to serve Him. To have your child mature to this level is the greatest joy a parent can have. For the son/daughter to be "righteous" is to follow God's precepts, commands, and leading. What great joy it is for the parent of this person. If this is true of human relationships, what does it say of God's heart to us His children, when we seek or reject Him and His ways?

Verses 22 and 23 outline the means that a parent brings about wisdom and righteousness in a child. Parents teach; they invest themselves; they represent the "truth" and try to bring the child to the point of acceptance of these truths. They encourage their child to seek to obtain wisdom and understanding. All of this is not an exercise done out of obligation but out of a deeply committed and loving heart. The giving of "life" is more than breath, but also has to do with the soul and spirit.

Having your sisters Elisa, Erin, and Kara home this weekend was a joy and a source of vitality for me. In a strange way, I find myself having more purpose and meaning when I can think about, pray about, and interact upon the issues in their lives. To live alone with my own interests seems not to hold the meaning for me that being a father does. Yet to interact appropriately and sensitively, and to effectively impact a life is a difficult balance to maintain when your children are becoming independent adults.

Proverbs 23:26-28 can be regarded/understood in the practical, real-life term it appears, or be seen more allegorically. Certainly, as we have all witnessed by the public exposure of Bill Clinton (and many other leaders over the history of the world), the temptation of sex and unfaithfulness has damaged those involved, their spouses and families and countless others who see them as role models or pace-setters. However, to succumb to these temptations leads many into a deep pit of sin, lies, deception, pain, and personal destruction, while it offers only a thin, narrow, transient moment of thrill and bodily passion. Satan often uses this means to multiply the destruction of many men, their families, and countless lives. Allegorically, we can substitute sex, prostitute, and wayward wife with any temptation strong enough that one is led to make destructive choices and decisions that will hurt them and their families.

Ultimately they will be wedges between man and the God who loves them and desires fellowship with them. Be alert to the traps and snares of the prostitute in this world that would desire to entice and destroy you in your home, family, and walk with God.

I really enjoyed having you here last week. It felt so natural, warm, and comfortable. I hope you both felt at home and welcome. We will certainly respect your privacy and relational priorities. I personally will look to God for His continued wisdom here, as in the other areas of my life.

Proverbs 23:29-35 is interesting but not too applicable to our personal situation. The passage speaks of alcohol addiction and alludes to DTs after discontinuation. It would be acceptable to generalize on this specific substance addiction to addiction to any substance, or to any area of life. Satan will use temptation, and its resulting addiction, to lure one into destructive choices and priorities. Verses 30-31 make the moments of alcohol use seem attractive and harmless; in a similar manner, any destructive life choice can be made by Satan to look alluring and tempting. It may seem harmless or even satisfying at the time. However, verses 29, 32-35a tell us the real story–the effect of the choice after the momentary sensual pleasure; the pain, both physically and emotionally, comes inevitably upon the heels of the moment's pleasure. Verse 35b describes the irrational urge to choose to do the very thing again that has caused such great pain. Medically, even in those times, addiction was well described and warning given. The only true way out of Satan's use of temptations and addiction to destroy us, is to seek God, His wisdom, and His strength.

I'm in my usual location for early mornings while here at our house on Kiawah Island–the wicker chair on the front porch. We hope all is going well there in Mahomet and with your respective clerkships. Have you heard from any more residencies or made any further arrangements for site visits?

Proverbs 24

Proverbs 24:1-2 addresses the issue of who we keep company with and who are our role models. "Wicked" people are those who reject God and His lordship in their lives; they place themselves on the center throne of their lives and all their decisions, actions, motives, and words are directed by their self-seeking and prideful inner selves. They are impulsive, worldly, sense/experience-oriented, shallow, and ignorant of God and His Word. Discerning people and wise people do not regard them highly and realize they are destructive–both to themselves and to others. For the people of God who desire to become more like Christ, it is imperative that we see these people for who they are, identify them by name, be careful not to spend much time with them or listen to their perspectives, and to pray for them (as God lays them upon our hearts). Even if they seem to be superficially happy or successful, we should not envy them or desire to adopt their ways. Ultimately, such people are seeking destruction, conflict, and turmoil; and will know pain and death (emotionally and relationally). Their words are slanderous, critical, accusatory, and self-exalting. It is not necessarily that they plot or consciously choose this, but because they are estranged from God they follow only their human nature; they are not controlled by a spiritual nature.

Today was for me a bittersweet day. Often the thing that can give the greatest pleasure can also give the greatest distress. Yet I believe as Christians we are always called to exist at this edge or within this tension. For when we are stretched, we lean on Him the most. Today I felt the demand of our sixty-five patients and fifty telephone concerns. I felt at times overwhelmed and depleted. Yet within this time, I felt moments when I truly touched a life, shared Christ's compassion, and witnessed His power through my medical encounters.

Proverbs 24:3 and 4 are great verses–two of my favorites. A "house" here is not a home or necessarily a family place; a house here is one's work, service, godly activity, and use of his gifts and opportunities. Through the "fear of God" (wisdom) one discovers and discerns his house; apart from seeking God we cannot really know our true reason for existence. As we understand more (God illuminates and deepens our understanding and application of our service) our work and its impact on others and the rest of God's creation are entrenched and deeply embedded in the fabric of God's world (established). As we understand and procure our house and establish it in God's work, we gain deeper knowledge or real truth and spiritual self-discovery. These are beautiful, precious, and gained only for those who allow God to stretch them and use them. They give the deep peace, joy, fulfillment, life, and love that nothing else on earth can give–true treasures. They are rare and beautiful.

Someone in the last few days asked me how it was having our "married daughter and her husband" living with us. They expected, I think, to hear me speak of awkwardness and difficulty adapting to a new relational role. I reflected quite the opposite. It seems so natural, comfortable, and appropriate that I hardly consider it difficult.

Proverbs 24:5 tells us what is hidden from the world becomes increasingly obvious to us who seek God. Wisdom and knowledge refer to our knowledge of truth and its application in life, as a result of, and proportionate to, our walk with God. We find that this can give great power, not in worldly standards but in our impact upon others, bringing them more spiritual peace, joy, and love, and taking them into God's deep, broad, and miraculous sovereignty of this (His) creation. We become strong as people of character who represent the really good of human kindness, setting an implicit and soulfully-envied standard.

Verse 6 goes on to state that in our "fight" against evil, wickedness, negative influence in our relationships, and the prevailing worldly standards, we need the help of other godly men and women. We need guidance and advice; we should covet godly opinion, input, and perspective. We believe God works and speaks clearly through others as well as through us as individuals. Yes, we must always filter input through the sifter of prayer and the teaching of the Word, but we must be sponges for godly teaching and input. Only then can we have victory over the world and evil's domain.

I'm glad you had a good and affirming first interview in Arkansas. The decisions you will make (relative to residency programs) will have great importance and significance for you and for God's plan to be allowed to reach fullest fruition. Be continually in prayer as you interview and look for His direct leading in this process. You will see His hand if you pray and seek spiritual eyes in this matter. Perhaps we could, from time to time, pray together to bring clarity to this matter.

Proverbs 24:7 is interesting. The "fool" is one who rejects God's lordship in her life. Therefore, true wisdom (only God's wisdom is true wisdom) is not hers and she cannot connect at the level of godly men and women. In Jewish history, the wisest of the wise (the elders) would gather at the Jerusalem gate to decide matters of importance. Here, the gate might be the gate to heaven; here God's wisest (wise because of their relationship to Him) gather to rule with Him. The fool cannot be there.

Verses 8-9 decry and judge the ungodly who plot to do evil. The heart of such a one is wicked (doesn't desire to please God) and his ways are counter to God's ways. He, when turned from God, actively plots his evil, ungodly ways–they are schemes and he is a schemer. Such plans are made in the heart of him who rejects God and will lead to destruction of himself, others, and the ongoing re-crucifixion of Christ. They are then sin! Ironically, not only does God detest the sin and the schemes of the wicked person, but so also do other people. People who scheme to do evil "mock" and devalue other people; they see them as lesser than themselves. This attitude, when perceived by others, causes people to reject and detest the schemer. The evil person loses on all accounts–destruction and death.

I really enjoyed having you, Christine, work with me tonight. I felt honored and a certain sense of paternal pride to see you functioning so well in the profession God has led you into. I know Mom was really grateful and joyful over her time with three of her daughters last Saturday. She was also touched, Christine, by your attendance at her concert. Thank you, Jeremy, for allowing Christine to spend the time with the "girls."

Proverbs 24:10 presents an admonition and a challenge. The strength exhibited by a person when all is going well is insignificant and unremarkable. However, the real test of the spiritual, emotional, relational, and physical strength of a person is in the time of trial and trouble. Here is where the true godly character of a person is apparent. In reality, only a growing relationship with

God over time will equip and enable us to overcome and grow in the times of trial. We don't (in our humanness) seek such times, but they will come.

Verses 11-12 speak to us directly and candidly about our response to those who are cruelly treated in our world and our society. The Hebrew words here are indicating innocent people being unjustly taken advantage of or abused by powerful self-seekers. We are to act to prevent this in our world. It is, also, not sufficient to act like we are unaware, for God knows our hearts and the deepest parts of our minds; He knows our motives, fears, and rationalizations. He will exteriorize these and judge them at some time in our future. Although not criteria for salvation, He will reward and punish relative to our actions in these areas.

I've been praying for your recent interview trip. I'm convinced God has a place picked out for the two of you that will prepare you both professionally and spiritually to minister to other people, in the select role of "physician." Be very prayerful and ask for spiritual eyes and ears to hear His leading in this important decision.

Proverbs 24:13 and 14 are poetic and touching verses. The writer first focuses on a human pleasure–one that God has given to us in His created world. Honey is sweet and good; it gives pleasure to our bodies and our humanness. God wishes for His creation to experience this pleasure–that was why He created this amazing world. We should never be ashamed at the beauty and experience of pleasure this world gives–we should rejoice and praise God for it. In a similar way, and an even fuller and more satisfying way, God's wisdom is sweet and provides deep pleasure to us ("sweet to your soul"). The writer encourages us to seek after it and when we experience God's wisdom, we find hope and a satisfying security that only a relationship with Him can give. Where do we look and find wisdom? We find it as we make personal the Word of God and learn to trust Him to make it a living Word. As we walk with Him in life, we learn His wisdom, and feel His strength and faithfulness. We take a teachable stance with those who walk close to God and whose story we know and marvel at. Such is sweeter than honey.

I don't deserve anything, but I am so blessed. I so love my family and live to be a father and a husband. Thanks for being such wonderful "children" and for loving me despite my weaknesses. It was a good Thanksgiving.

Proverbs 24:15-16. The righteous person is one who seeks God as Lord of his life and places his/her trust in God. He/she is not righteous by his own strength or worthiness but by virtue of his willingness to lay hold of God and His goodness. Such a person is secure and protected by God, preserved through all calamity ("storm" of Proverbs 10:25) whether of this natural world or by virtue of God's refining fire or judgment. These verses warn those who wish to do a righteous person harm that he/she will not be harmed by them. The righteous may appear to fall by the world's criteria and for a time to be "down." But they will not stay down, but will rise up again, stronger, godlier, and purer in heart than before. They will see God with more abandonment and fearfulness than previously. However, God's storms (often via the allowance of Satan's clever traps, or natural creation phenomenon) will bring down the wicked person–she will be destroyed, demoralized, dishonored, and farther from God.

I sure like the feel, sight, sounds, and even the smells of Christmas. This one has already been special since the two of you have been here to be a part of our preparations. The Christmas program last Sunday was so beautiful musically and powerful in message. I know Mom really appreciated you being a part of it, Christine. God has really been using Mom powerfully this fall as she plans worship and organizes the music. We had lunch with Carrie Sunday and we alluded to the Israel trip. My heart leaps a bit as I think of the honor I feel to be able to teach his Word in the very area He walked.

Proverbs 24:17-18 speaks to the very heart of man's sinfulness–pride and self-centeredness. The fleshly nature of man (even those who follow Christ) always seeks to build ourselves up at the sake of another. There is an "old, natural man" nature that is addressed when we tear down another or delight in her tragedy. Sure, we don't like to admit this and many people deny it and cover it up with humanistic social work. This dishonesty only layers sin upon sin. Yet it is true that as God's Spirit rules over more and more of our lives, we will become more like Christ and shed the tendency to be like this. This is, however, a life-long process of "becoming." The proverbs tell us not to take pleasure and obtain deep satisfaction when another (even our enemy) falls. Actively fight this human temptation by recognizing it and calling upon God's strength and wisdom. The writer tells us that God is aware of this in each of us and can, if He chooses, turn His judgment and His allowance of Satan's harm upon the other, from the other and to us. God will not be mocked and does discipline His children for their benefit.

It was, and is, great to have you here with us for the holiday season. It has made it a very joyous and exciting Christmas and New Year. I am continuing to pray for your residency interview trip, believing God will reveal His desire for you.

Proverbs 24:19-20 the passage speaks to an area where all of us who know Christ, some time or another, will be found. In the midst of living, in our flesh, in the world, we will at times envy or feel confused by success of the evil man. We, like Job and Jeremiah, look around and see the apparent reward, and lack of outward pain of those who shun God and follow their own self-centered way–tempted and spurred on by Satan. We "fret" because it doesn't seem fair or just that this is the situation. We even at times are annoyed at God for not "taking care of His people" or allowing evil to prosper. Yes we should know (and do in our spiritual nature) that God is just by His standards and in His time; and that persecution and pain will be our lot (at times, in big and small ways) in life just as they were for Christ. They refine and draw us closer to God. These verses also reaffirm our knowledge that really, after this life the evil person has no life, no hope, and no resurrection. We will never know spiritual death and will have a new heavenly body free of the "flesh" and its temptations; we will live and reign with God forever. This is our hope and we must hold on to that as we fight our natural inclination to envy the world's rewards.

We will soon be going to the airport to pick you up. I've prayed that our time together will not only be enjoyable but significant relative to

God's action in your life as He molds you both to His desire. You may come back overwhelmed and confused but be confident that He will inhabit your thoughts and deliberations. The place you should be will emerge. You both have grown and matured wonderfully in your professional training, and as a couple you come across in the most attractive manner. We stand ready to offer our input to you as you compare and deliberate. Let us know how we can help.

Proverbs 24:21-22 speaks of fearing the Lord; "fearing" is a common, recurring concept throughout Scripture. To fear God is to have awesome high regard for His character as and when we come to know them–either in the study of the Word or experientially in our lives. It is the desire, increasingly felt, not to want to live another moment apart from Him–scared of what life is apart from God. The writer tells us to fear the Lord and King. The two words underline two principal views (there are, of course, more) of God. As the "Lord," we see Him as sovereign over His creation and in control of our life as a single individual. He is able but we must give Him access to us, His creation. As the "King," we see His majesty, power, and exalted position. He can use His power to subdue His creation; He has access to legions of forces in the universe. The writer tells us to fear God in these two personas and stay away from those who reject Him, do not fear Him, and desire to live apart from Him. As both Lord and King, He is able, and in the future, will for certainty, send calamity and destruction on those who rebel. God is a God of grace and patience now, in this church age, but someday He will show His power and justice.

I so appreciate the freedom we felt tonight to look at Scripture and allow God's Spirit to teach us together. The Word of God is so rich and deep that a lifetime of study can only scratch its surface. I believe your ranking of residency programs is wise, mature, and completed according to the best of human ability. Our prayer now is that God would be glorified and have His way on this issue. Therefore, you must be willing to accept what His will be–and with great excitement. It is secure and peaceful to know you have been faithful to do your part, and now to allow Him to move according to His great wisdom, power, love, and justice.

Proverbs 24:23-25 encourages us not to be dishonest in our judgments, especially if such dishonesty is motivated by our pride, greed, or passion. To be "partial" means that we are unwilling to judge honestly because we stand to gain more by judging unfairly. If we do this, others will know it, sense it, or suspect it, and will convey to us the use of self-seeking motives. We will be rejected, mistrusted, scorned, and denounced, for even sinful man hates deception and injustice. Those who dare to judge rightly and impartially will be held high and receive the blessing of man, and of God. Each situation demands God's wisdom and presses us to seek Him in prayer and the study of His Word. God will bless us with such wisdom if we seek Him and labor to know Him.

Mom and I had fun on our trip. We enjoyed each other and experienced a slice of life we usually don't experience. We talked about deep issues and she allowed my deep thoughts and reflections. I was impressed by the depth of depravity we saw in the streets and establishments in that city. It provoked for me a need to seek shelter for my family in His domain and under His lordship. Be praying already for your children and the world during their lives.

Proverbs 24:26 gives us an idea of the value, rarity, and needfulness of integrity. In poetic language, the author tells us that speech that is forthright, genuine, and consistent (inwardly) with one's heart and thoughts is deeply welcomed. Further, it is personal, intimate, encouraging, and respectful and gives value and worth to another. It is not depersonalized or manipulative; it is not self-seeking but other-focused; it holds care and honesty in balance for the good of its giver and receiver. Integrity and honesty, given in love, compassion, and sensitivity, are scarce and powerful.

Verse 27 is interesting and intriguing. It encapsulates the priorities that God would have us to keep during our lives here on earth. We are to be responsible and use what we have (have been given) to serve and produce (His crop) before we seek our own interests and desires. There is here an emphasis on hard work, self-sacrifice, and delayed gratification. It is not that God doesn't desire us to have the desires of our heart but they must never precede the development and use of that which He has given us to serve and produce fruit in His kingdom. It takes strength and His power to keep these priorities.

The party Saturday evening was a good thing. Both Christians and non-Christians were present and all had a great time together. After a brief welcome and introduction, I found myself praying with the group, thanking God for them. Looking back at the act, I feel strange about it, but at the time it felt natural. I know God was present and honored; I believe it was a good witness. It was amazing how God chose those who came (eleven couples) and the various common links and backgrounds people had with one another. It again pointed to God and His hand upon the event. How wonderful He is, to be interested even in a fifties party in Mahomet, Illinois.

Proverbs 24:28 tells us to not "testify against your neighbor without cause." This begs a number of queries: who is our neighbor, what is testifying, and what does "without cause" mean? To me my neighbor is the people I cross paths with daily, or people God puts into my life–in happy or unhappy occasions. To testify against is to use my voice and influence to harm them or their reputations, or to destructively criticize and condemn them. "Without cause" means that I must look at my motives–often it is our pride and need to bolster our own ego that leads us to tear another person down. Is there "good cause"? I think so, but we must be careful and hold ourselves very accountable for such testimony. It should be constructive, out of a loving, selfless heart. Our words must be honest before God and man and never used manipulatively to deceive others and gain for ourselves.

It was good to have you two with us on this Valentine's Day. Once again, I am reminded of how much I love you both. How overjoyed I am as I see how God loves you and has led you since the day of your conception. As a couple, you beautifully balance each other and make each other better than you were before your union. God is doing a great work in you and your oneness, and He deserves your utmost honor and gratitude. After thirty-plus years, I find that I love your mom more than ever and cannot contemplate life without her. She is a beautiful, selfless, and capable woman who balances and complements me. I too am better with her than I ever could be by myself. This, perhaps, is the true test of a godly marriage.

Proverbs 24:29 seems to run counter to "the golden rule." It really doesn't, for the golden rule encourages us to do toward others the positive and caring things we would want them to do to and for us. This proverb counters the "eye for eye" approach to human relationships. The sinful human nature is one that places our own selves in the center and seeks to protect the ego and pride by any and all means. Often this leads to vindictive and revengeful attitudes and actions. They "feel" good to this human nature (with "I" in the center) but they are in opposition to a true Christian walk. As a result of receiving a new spiritual nature and placing God at the center of our lives, it becomes unnecessary and distasteful to protect ourselves and desperately do whatever is required to do to ensure our "worth." Consequently, the pain and injustice we experience at the hands of other people are not so important and threatening to our true value and worth. It is not necessary to seek their pain as a way to feed our ego needs and protect a fragile worth. Therefore, the writer of Proverbs implores us to not have this attitude and to seek God and His justice, in His time and with His compassion.

Well, it's hard to believe your five months here will be ending this weekend. I have enjoyed having you with us and welcome you back in the future. The years ahead will be exciting and filled with God's opportunity. We will walk closely with you but will always honor your need to be your own family. Thanks for this special winter.

Proverbs 24:30-34 is one of my favorites–it can be understood pragmatically, in the present world, or relative to spiritual growth and journey. Certainly, the degree of prosperity, produce, and control of our lives is proportionate to the time and effort we put forth. In this life there should never be a time when we rest from our ministry, word, and availed opportunities. Even the slightest relaxation will permit our work to deteriorate and be strangled out. I am, as a result, against the modern American way of "retiring" to seek a life of self-pleasure. In this life, in this world, this should never be–it was lost at the Garden of Eden. Yes, we must take time to be refueled and refreshed, but only briefly. The opportunities will change but our effort should never decline. Spiritually, if we become lazy and rest on our previous efforts, we will be overtaken and what "used to be" will be taken from us by the world's evil and its tendency toward death and confusion. Stay active, diligent, and disciplined in the study of His Word. This is the only way to hedge off the fallen world.

Christine, I am honored to be able to participate in your "hooding"! To be very honest, I had hoped for years that this might happen but held myself back from embracing it as reality. I look forward to that moment. We are working on getting a bike trip developed for the graduation trip to Europe. It looks like we will be doing our own trip, but hope to secure the bikes and Bed and Breakfasts beforehand. We will have an "adventure" and make deep, lasting memories together.

Proverbs 25

Proverbs 25:2 is an interesting and insightful bit of wisdom. It is part of God's nature and character, and part of the way He relates to and governs His creation, that He holds much that is not able to be known by man. It is part of His godliness ("glory of God") to have such deep wisdom, ageless perspective, and timelessness that we cannot hope to understand or even taste of its magnitude and goodness. Besides, to know it would then have us relate to God by "sight" and not by faith. He knows it is essential that we trust Him in His knowledge of the secret things. However, the royal priesthood of believers ("kings") must desire to search out God's mind on things and thereby receive His blessings.

Verse 3 tells us how great and vast are the things of kings. The kings here are those chosen and made regal by God and thereby given a portion of His deep, unsearchable wisdom and compassion. God is the King of Kings (Jesus, as well, as a part of the Trinity) and therefore eclipses any and all earthly kings in His depth of heart. We are "royal priests" of God and as we seek Him in His Word, we can know more and more of the "unsearchable."

I'm looking forward to next week: to visit you there in Rockford and to hear the announcement of the "match." This is a special, once-in-a-lifetime moment that must be savored and remembered, no matter what the outcome. Remember, God is sovereign and He is a God who hears and answers prayers. Believing this, the residency you match with will be His choice for you, having heard your heart in prayer.

Proverbs 25:4 and 5 have an important message within them. The writer uses an analogy to make his point. He first observes that in order for the silversmith to make a fine product he must first remove that which contaminates it or pollutes it. Here we have a Creator wishing to create something fine and of value from raw materials that are contaminated. He must first purify the material by removing that which pollutes. Likewise, the writer observes that a king will be able to act righteously if he has those people removed who would negatively and destructively influence him to act in an ungodly, self-seeking manner. Here we have one who is ascribed royalty, who can act as God desires and decreed only when the wicked are removed from their influence. Perhaps this is a call for us, as Christians, who are chosen by God as His royal children and viewed as precious material that He desires to make into precious items for service, to awaken and actively remove the wicked influences from our lives. The process of such removal is not one we execute, but one we seek God to do in our lives. Look for the impurities, the wicked, and ask Him to remove them so we may be righteous and useful.

Thanks so much for sharing the "Match Day" ceremony last Thursday. I thought it was fun, exciting, and befitting the achievements of you, the graduating class. I know you realize how proud I am of both of you and have the utmost confidence that you will be wonderfully used by God as physicians. Spartanburg is the right place for you. I believe you will see God's wisdom in this choice as you begin the next phase of your life–residency. I have come to the place in my life that I am completely convinced that God is a God of promise, wisdom, and power and that He does answer the prayers of His children. Do not let Satan or the world rob you of the joy and peace of this confidence.

Proverbs 25:6 and 7 are some of my favorite verses. It is human and part of our flesh nature to seek self-exaltation, to maneuver ourselves to positions where we are noticed, acknowledged, and applauded. The world teaches this and rewards those who succeed.

As our spiritual nature gains progressive control of our lives, then the need for this becomes lesser. Of course, Christ is our example of one who rejected this aspect of His humanity and sought humility and self-sacrifice. These proverbs instruct, exhort, and warn us of this area of temptation. We are not to seek, manipulate, slander, lie, or in any way prioritize ourselves to positions of human recognition. Often such people really have not earned the positions they seek, or have harmed so many in their quest that they are unworthy. We are to work hard and serve God in the positions He has called us to and gifted us in; we are to prioritize Him and our families above all else. If in so doing, we are recognized and asked to have human honor, then we go worthy and with God at our side. Great people may never be recognized as such by society or the world, but pomposity will be humbled, sooner or later.

It is Sunday afternoon and you are probably meeting with the real estate person and being introduced to the potential homes. I have confidence God will, once again in your lives, guide you into the right decision. I look forward to His answer to your prayer. I'm beginning to look forward to our France trip in May; we looked at bicycle clothing and backpacks yesterday. It is going to be a fun challenge to make our travel possessions as light as necessary.

Proverbs 25:8 continues with godly practical advice on daily living. The proverb is teaching a truth/wisdom via a specific situation—a legal court situation. It cautions a person to not jump to conclusions or over read into something we see or hear. If we do this to the extent that we are willing to testify to it under oath in a courtroom, with another person's welfare at stake, we must be certain. The proverb tells us that in all life's situations, our senses ("sight") might deceive us and we wholeheartedly buy into what is seen and the ramifications of that, all based on the fact that sight is truth. The result can either be our testimony wrongfully hurting another person or we are eventually shown to be in error and shamed. In life we must not trust only our sight, but be certain as we seek to fully understand, collect all data, understand motives and needs, consider the background issues, and remember that all people are in evolution over time. We must, when there is any doubt, give the benefit of the doubt to that person and seek his full heart.

I know it must be very exciting these days to be soon "graduated" as physicians, to be moving to a new house (your own!!), and to be beginning a new adventure and meeting new people. Please allow yourselves this time of reward and satisfaction. I encourage you to use it to reflect on God and what He has done for you and in your lives.

Proverbs 25:9-10 is solid practical advice and experientially true. It puts forward the need for the godly person to be honest yet trustworthy to the confidences of others. It begins with the possibility that there will be a need to resolve conflict with a person close to you (your neighbor)–that even a godly person must confront and explain her position/perspective to another. If some other person had provided you information or insight, you must not betray her confidence and not reveal this information (or its source) even in the midst of conflict. If you do it would be for the purpose of exalting yourself with the domination of the neighbor. Your neighbor will know that you are not trustworthy to keep a person's confidence and will call attention to this, shaming you for your ungodly choice. Your credibility and honor will be undermined in the eyes of the neighbor and within the mind of all who hear the report. In all things be trustworthy–even if it means you will suffer for the moment.

We enjoyed helping you move into your new home and being able to see Spartanburg. It helps as I pray to be able to visualize in my mind what I am praying for. I am confident the "program" is the very best for you. God has had His hand on both of your lives every step of the way so far, and since there had been much prayer about which program you should be a part of, I know this is His choice and therefore will be great. I will be looking forward, without surprise, to the confirmations He will give you along the way. Your home is perfect for you and once again was a wise, God-directed choice.

Proverbs 25:11 is really a solid bit of wisdom. The power for good and evil of the spoken word is tremendous. This proverb focuses on the beneficial effect of a "word aptly spoken." It implies that not only is the particular word/message important but that the timing of that spoken word is also critical. I believe it is a gift of God and a sign of spiritual maturity when a person can say just the right word at the right time. A continuous growing relationship with God is necessary to be able to choose both the right word and the right time. The impact of this combination on another can be life changing and long remembered.

Verse 12 takes the use of words a different direction. Here the words are used to "rebuke"–that is to lovingly set a person in the right direction and point out the problems of the current direction. It is constructive. Yet the person must have a "listening ear"–that is he must be willing to allow you to affect his life and his choices. Often that "listening ear" is the work of God and in His time; therefore, we should be praying that He prepares the "ear" to hear. Correct rebuke must come out of a wise heart (wise because of God's wisdom).

I guess this is the last letter I will be writing before you officially become physicians. What a great day for you and for those of us who love you. It is a great understatement to tell you that we are immensely proud of you and have great respect for your long hours of study and perseverance. It is hard to put into words the feeling a father and mother have to see their children reach such a high level of accomplishment. But it is even a greater satisfaction to see the character you two have as people, and your godliness as children of God. Most awesome of all thoughts is the awareness that God has chosen and equipped you to be physicians. As such, He desires you to serve Him and bring Him honor in your profession.

Proverbs 25:13 points to the importance of having a person you can trust to carry and convey what is important (to you) to other people. The specific example here in Proverbs is that it is a great relief and encouragement for the "master" to be able to trust a messenger to take his message to another who needs to hear the message. Spiritually, this is the case for the "good news" (gospel); God needs us to be trustworthy, willing and able to carry His good news to other people. Those other people are really important to Him (it matters not whether they are to us, the messengers) and so He wants them to know this truth! This is refreshing to Him and pleasing to His deep character.

In light of your graduation as physicians, I view your going forth as taking the message I stand for and have upheld these twenty-five years to other people. The message is that God loves them and cares for their physical, emotional, and relational persons, and He has ordained physicians to look after this part of His creation. As physicians who know and love God, He finds you trustworthy, and you refresh and please Him in this work.

2000 — RESIDENCY

SPARTANBURG, SOUTH CAROLINA

Dear Christine and Jeremy,

This will be the first letter of the "school year" (although you are no longer really in school); the ninth year of writing to you, Christine. I would encourage you to read my letters with your Bible open to the passage, and expect that God will instruct you. I sense the overall experience so far in Spartanburg has been a good one, and that you are finding support and friendship. Our time in my residency was one of the highlights of our life to date. Please be proactive to seek Christian friends, to study God's Word, and to pray. Have you settled in a church and have you found a way to serve God?

Proverbs 25

Proverbs 25:14 stresses the importance of substance and depth rather than form and allusion. Clouds without rain disappoint, mislead, and betray–they do not have to give what they pretentiously suggest. So also is a person who looks on the surface like she has answers, wisdom, love, and compassion but really is a hollow shell. She disappoints and betrays those who confidently seek her and her gifts. This applies for you as spouses to each other, physicians to your patients, friends to your friends, and parents to your children. Take the time and work hard to be people of substance, with a wealth of gifts and wisdom to share with those who seek you.

Verse 15 emphasizes patience and gentle speech. Even the most ardent holder of a given perspective can be brought to reconsider if you speak to him logically, respectfully, caringly, actively listening and explaining with patience and understanding. The opposition melts like an ice cube on a summer's day. Do not underestimate the power within gentle, caring speech. Hard, painful words can harm and perplex but gentle words build up, correct, and illuminate all who will listen.

It sounds as if you are happy in your new setting and are equal to the challenges of residency and the business of married life. I'm happy, of course, and am pleased that you have not neglected your spiritual persons. We leave in one week for Israel and I am full of feelings. I find myself at times a bit anxious and overwhelmed; I know God has prepared and called me to this place in my life, but my human nature feels weak.

Proverbs 25:16 and 17 give good practical and godly wisdom. Verse 16 encourages us to seek and enjoy the sweet parts of life–the pleasures and indulgences that God allows us (and gives us) as a foretaste of heaven and to balance the pain and perseverance of a Christian life. But He cautions us not to overindulge and over-balance ourselves with too much of it, because it will be harmful and eventually become distasteful to us–it will make us sick. This bespeaks of a balanced life and is His great wisdom as He gives us what is needed (and no more) to allow us to "end the race" in a pleasing, productive way.

Verse 17 likewise, encourages a balanced life as we relate with our friends and neighbors. We are to be a part of their lives, including time in their world, their homes. But if we are there too often, too long, and become an intrusion to their private lives, they will grow to resent us. At that point we cannot positively influence them or have constructive fellowship for mature edification and strength building–Christ was very careful in this area and serves as our example.

It seems like years since we last saw you and heard all that is going on in your life. I'm looking forward to Thanksgiving as a time to catch up and enjoy your fellowship. Mom's and my Sunday school class on Handel's Messiah is going well. It is interesting to co-teach. We are understanding the biblical references and the music, in light of the fulfillment in the person of Christ.

Proverbs 25:18 tells us the pain and destruction embodied in lies and slander. False testimony against one known to us ("neighbor") is done for various self-centered, evil needs and is at the expense of another. Often at its root is pride and a delight in the ungodly. Untruth, either offered actively or conveyed by silence (when words need to be said) is destructive and painful. Slander is untruth conveyed for the designed purpose of hurting another, often to make one's self-regard better. Scripture tells us that God hates these and that He will reckon with those who hasten untruth.

Verse 19 tells us to be careful whom we turn to and rely upon when we have need. The "unfaithful" are those whose character is so poor that they cannot be relied upon to consistently help, or whose motives are spoiled by self-seeking priorities. Such people are not people with a faith walk with God and therefore are not spiritual people. To trust and rely upon such people will lead to disappointment, pain, and uselessness. At worst they will cause us additional pain–they are like a toothache or a broken leg. People whom you can rely upon, trust, and who have your needs at heart are rare people.

I'm so happy you both like your situation and location, despite the anxiety element in the residency program. We downloaded the delivery pictures, Christine; they immediately brought to mind the picture I took of you (an hour or so old) with Mom and the resident who helped deliver you. How miraculous for you, these many years later to be in the position of the resident. I am still remembering and savoring the Israel trip. My preparation for Sunday school was so much easier and deeper because His Word was alive to me. The worship on Sunday was so deeply personal and meaningful, and I was so blessed in His presence. He loves and changes us as we go to His place to meet Him.

Proverbs 25:20 encourages us to deal/help/aid people with their basic human needs and hurts before we ask them to hear the unseen and spiritual. To not help to heal a sad heart, loneliness, dejection, disappointment, shame, etc., but try to feed them spiritual food is only to be unheard and our message invalidated by our lack of human compassion and kindness. Christ took people where they were and dealt first with their human condition, and then they could hear His spiritual truths. This proverb is important to those of us who are physicians.

Verses 21 and 22 tell us to extend kindness even to him/her who seeks to do us wrong (see 1 Sam. 24). Minister to the human need despite the misdirection and evilness of her will or actions. This is so hard for we do the opposite, as natural man—minister to our friends and add misery to our enemies. If we act as this proverb directs, we will show him to be the one who is ungodly and the contrast will reveal his evilness and desire for destruction. He will be rejected by godly men and increasingly by God. God will also reward those who sacrifice themselves and their human entitlement, and chance loss and further pain. God sees and knows; He shall reward in the future.

Thank you for your call before my birthday. One of my true "soft spots" is in the desire to have a deep and expressive relationship with my children. You two are both so valuable and special to me; to share your love is a delight of my life.

Proverbs 25:23 tells us that it is a certainty that sarcastic, harsh, manipulative speech will evoke anger in the recipient. This is as certain as the natural observation that when a north wind blows, rain will come (is this a fact in the Middle East?). It again reminds us that our speech, especially our word choices and the emotion behind these words, will affect another, evoking in him reactionary speech and emotion. We must always police our words and be sure they reflect an emotion that is pleasing to God. We can be honest but our words and feeling must reflect it warmly and lovingly.

Verse 24 encourages us to seek peace, cheerfulness, optimism, acceptance, and self-sacrifice in our marital relationships. Although the verse cites specifically a wife, I believe it equally fits a husband.

Such a peaceful atmosphere in the home is worth more than all the material things of marriage. When we speak to one who has lost this, or never had it, we are reminded of its value. Obviously, only through each person having a growing walk with God and the couple subjecting themselves to His authority, will such peace be found.

Congratulations Jeremy, on your triathlon. I find it hard to imagine the amount of training and discipline needed to accomplish even the participation in such an event. We have thought of you often this fall as we remember that it was a year ago that we were all here together in this house. That was a good time for us. We miss you but know that now is what God has planned for you for your life.

Proverbs 25:25 is an interesting bit of wisdom. It explains the very human joy and deep satisfaction one has when he receives good news from a distant land. Our soul is God indwelled (when we become a Christian) and, just as is true of God, we deeply seek to hear news from our loved ones when they are apart from us and our land. "Good news" is generally that news which speaks of our growing oneness with Christ. To hear of this is refreshing and soothing to our souls, even when life has made us weary.

Verse 26 gives us a word picture as to how we look to God and other more mature Christians when we compromise the cleansed spirit with the pollution of the world. Our "waters" are clean and purified by Christ's work on the cross when we are declared righteousness by Him. When we taste, or dip into the world, we will muddy and pollute these waters. The world's ways are not God's ways and do not mix. Happily, Christ's cleansings never cease and until the time we can no longer be tempted, He is available, when we ask, for further cleansing.

It sure sounds like you both individually and as a couple have put down good and profitable roots there in Spartanburg. Look around yourself daily and in all situations, with a strong foundation of prayer, seeking God's perspective and wisdom. This is a very busy week for me. Pray for me, for His wisdom and strength. At times, I long to have time that I do not have preplanned and can give myself permission to smell the fall air and feel the late summer's cool breeze on my face.

Proverbs 25:27 gives us two admonitions. First, a heavy diet of honey (sugar) is not good for the body, and likewise a disproportionate amount of time and effort in life to obtain pleasure and sensual delights will not be good for our character and usefulness. Sugar and pleasure are to be woven into a life of work, perseverance, struggle, and sober thought—they should accent or be dessert for the main course. Also it is not good for our character and usefulness to make choices primarily to seek self and prideful recognition. One does not demand honor but receives it when she doesn't seek it; it is earned.

Verse 28 is a good one—worthy of committing to memory. A person without self control—whose emotions, actions, words, and thoughts are unbridled by thought, morality, godliness, and kindness, will make herself vulnerable to the attacks, inflicted pain, and destruction of the world. Such self-control is really not from "self" but is a result of being able to subject self and pride to the higher goal of knowing and pleasing God. It can occur only out of a growing, healthy relationship to God, made possible only by Christ's work.

Aren't these fall days wonderful? The soft yellow maple trees in the woods around our house are in full color now; the leaves cover the ground, blanketing the surface and nullifying the demarcation of the surfaces. I wish I could just choose to stay home on one or two of these days. We look forward to seeing you again first at your home and then in Kiawah for Thanksgiving. I fondly remember often the France trip (and London) and thank God for you two.

Proverbs 26:1 is one I like particularly. "Character" or "honor" is one of the highest virtues, one that can only be approached by virtue of a life-changing relationship with God. To be honorable is solid, lasting, deep, and powerful; it is rare and carries with it deep respect and wisdom. The "fool" can never have honor, because he/she has rejected God and His impact on his life. In such a person honor doesn't fit nor can it exist. Without God, we cannot rise above our own selfish needs and wants and do not know truth and true wisdom. Show me a man or woman of honor, and I will show you a person who knows God.

Verse 2 tells us that the world will try to curse the person of God, to accuse unjustly and with malignant intent. They may inflict pain and wound us but such curses will not rest upon us to undo or discourage us for long. Such will come and go but will not stay. As people of God, He will protect us as His own and Satan or evil man cannot destroy our character and our honor. I believe this is God's world and He protects and guides His people.

It is hard to believe that by Christmas you both will have finished a sixth of your residency as you will be halfway through your first year. I'm glad the experience has been positive enough to encourage and sustain you. I'm sensing that your professional futures are being molded and groomed as you experience aspects of primary care practice. I hope you are making deep and lasting friendships and are being challenged spiritually.

Proverbs 26:4 and 5 are to be taken together. They speak about how we are to relate to a "fool." A "fool" is one who is impervious to or rejects God's ownership and lordship in his life. Fools seek their own human wisdom and are self-governed, motivated by self-centered agendas. A fool's folly is his view of life, his priorities, goals, and standards. It also includes the means he chooses to accomplish these foolish goals. The writer warns the persons who seek to be like God, and to allow Him lordship in their lives, not to even participate with and entertain similar thoughts of the fool. It is dangerous to place oneself at the fool's level and in his world, to debate or encounter him at all. The enemy can pull godly people down and begin to cause them to slip into foolishness. Likewise, to participate with a fool in his foolishness will be to encourage him and to convey approval and respect for his folly. This perpetuates him in his sin. As we relate to the fools in life, we are to maintain our distance and be careful in our conversation with them and with any time we spend with them, for their sake and ours.

Proverbs 26:6 emphasizes the importance of the person who carries the message, or the person who performs the function, the one who carries out the intent of the one who sends the message. A "fool" is a person not of honor, integrity, or character and will bend to whatever seems expedient or self-gratifying; he will place his needs above those of the one who sends the message or defines the greater view. God needs us to be good messengers, to represent His heart and desires with strength and integrity. We must use the gifts He has given courageously, fully, and with thanksgiving.

Verse 7 tells us that the character of the one who gives wisdom or advice is critical to whether that wisdom is heard and considered. A fool who gives wisdom is not heard, and any truth he conveys will be counteracted and disbelieved because of who he is. To carry a message that must be heard, not only must we not dilute or counterfeit it in any way, but also we must be people who are regarded highly by the listener. God needs us to be godly men and women, and to bring His truth to the world as He wishes it to be heard.

Thanks so much for sharing your vacation holiday with us at Kiawah Island. It was so good to see your home. It is so comfortable and warm!

Proverbs 26:8 is an interesting proverb. To tie a stone in a sling is to render the purpose of the sling (to propel the stone out) useless and folly. The stone is wasted and it is useless. Likewise to bestow honor upon a fool (a prideful, self seeking person who rejects God's lordship) is to waste this honor and render it meaningless because the character of the person dishonors honor. Our trust, encouragement, respect, positive regard, and belief in her goodness will be devalued, mocked, and abused as she seeks her own self-centered, prideful ways. We can love such a person but we must be careful whom we honor.

Verse 9 tells us that a wise, insightful directive ("proverb") when used by a fool will be misused to the pain of others as the fool seeks to distort it to gain her own self-centered desires. Wisdom must be appropriately applied in the circumstances for which it was intended—it is never for self-glorification but always to lead oneself and others closer to God. Such a use is dangerous and will destroy, not build up. A drunkard cannot be trusted holding a thorn bush, as a fool cannot be trusted with wisdom.

Christmas is fast approaching and soon you will be back in Illinois for the holidays. It will be good to have a house full again as we celebrate Christ's birth. Mom's Messiah presentation was awesome! The choir/orchestra received a standing ovation at the conclusion. She has a very effective and high quality ministry at Twin City Bible Church and within the whole community.

Proverbs 26:10, I think, talks about choosing a person to trust, to work with, and to carry out your directives. The choosing of such a person is very important to your work/ministry and to your peace and internal stability. Such a one must be chosen prayerfully, in light of scriptural directives and discerningly as led by the Spirit. We should also use our wisdom (given by God) to make rational and mature decisions–to weigh the facts objectively. Such a choice should never be made impulsively or randomly, for one could be choosing a "fool" (one who rejects God).

Verse 11 is a familiar one. It is so, but confusingly so, that a person often repeats the mistakes she makes in life. This is so for the "fool"–such a one is not teachable and there is not a chang-ing of his/her heart and soul, so a permanent and lasting change is impossible. Fools therefore will return to their folly again and again. Only God can change us and prevent us from repeating our mistakes. Only He can prepare and equip us for His service, and to please Him.

I hope by now you are back into the routine of residency and moving ahead with your training. I also hope that you have a moment, here and there, to savor the memories of our Christmas together and your time here with your families.

Proverbs 26:12 emphasizes again how God holds high the traits of humility and teachableness to us, His beloved and chosen people. The writer tells us that when a person sees herself as wise, full of knowledge, and filled with pride, there is very little "hope" for her—hope that she can open herself up to input and instruction from others. We all are on a growing curve and none of us have arrived. Satan often uses our human tendency to be proud and self-sufficient to close us off to God and His loving instruction.

Proverbs 26:13 could have several interpretations. A sluggard is a lazy person who doesn't act to grow, mature, or develop in all aspects (or any aspects) of his/her character. In the proverb, we see this person making an observation that danger is close by and is an imminent threat. However, he/she doesn't proactively do anything to rid himself or others in his charge of the danger (he just talks). Also he fails, apparently, to recognize the grave threat. The lion can represent the spiritual foe (Satan) that prowls close by and threatens us and those we love. Christians must recognize the threat and danger to our spiritual walk and be proactive to derail it.

I have thought often, since you returned to Spartanburg, about how your month has been going. I know you both had anticipated a busy one with a minimum of "off time overlap" together. I've been praying for your continued strength, perseverance, and patience during this hectic and demanding training time.

Proverbs 26:14 and 15 continue the comments on the "sluggard." Such a person is one who may verbalize the right things and indicate he is going to accomplish something, but never will accomplish it, finding all kinds of excuses and rationalizations for why he cannot so act.

Verse 14 gives a word picture of this sluggard. A door moves a great deal but goes nowhere, it pivots back and forth going from one direction to the opposite direction (as if it cannot make up its mind), moving in wide arcs, but making absolutely no gain. This is the way of the sluggard–there may be meaningless movement, swinging widely between one direction and the other (as if without principle) and accomplishing nothing. Sluggards complain they work hard and are tired and cannot understand why they are stalled.

Verse 15 shows a different view that also can characterize a sluggard. The epitome of slothfulness, laziness, and inertia is the inability, or lack of motivation, to bring food from a dish to one's own mouth. There is no movement, no energy expended but the result is the same–nothing accomplished not even enough to sustain oneself.

I've thought much about you both this past week as I know that your respective schedules are so time demanding. I'm glad to know you were able to go again to the Biltmore Estate and hopefully you were able to relax and spend quality time together. Time moves quickly so endure, discipline yourselves, and be patient.

Proverbs 26:16 focuses again on the "sluggard," a term used often by the writer of Proverbs. In general it refers to a person who doesn't diligently seek after God and His truth. He accepts and seeks worldly answers and "shortcuts" to true joy, peace, and love. Such a person views himself as wise; I think such a belief begins as a superficial thought that serves to gain (pridefully) his own needs, but later he begins to truly believe the lie and to become a part of it. He at some point really believes he is wiser than others who answer with truth derived from God's Word and activity in their lives. Satan encourages the self-centered, prideful perspective that he is wiser than seven others (seven is a number that means eternity; therefore, he believes he is wiser than everyone and God).

Verse 17 tells us of the dangers to ourselves if we "meddle" in other people's business–especially a conflict between them. To seize a dog by the ear (if the animal doesn't know you or trust you) will result in him turning upon you and biting you. So also if we get involved in two other people's conflict or quarrel, they will turn around and attack us and will try to hurt or destroy us. Be very cautious, no matter how good your intent about becoming involved in others' conflict.

I heard you had a weekend "break" and a stay at a bed and break-fast–a retreat! I hope you were able to relax, get some rest, and build relationships with others in the program. I know you both are working hard and long hours and probably really needed the weekend.

Proverbs 26:18-19 emphasizes the importance of sensitive, consistent interactions with other people with whom we live and work. If, in our self-centered need to build ourselves up, we deceive one placed close to us, or take advantage of him or insensitively harm him in some fashion; then we are actively demeaning him and destroying our relationship with him. Especially so if we, when caught or confronted, belittle the issue by glibly saying "I was only joking." This conveys to another that he is not valuable enough to speak with honesty and sincerity to and that we do not wish a respectful relationship with him.

Verse 20 tells us that we, and people around us, keep a quarrel going by presenting false information, inflammatory words, ascribing wrong motives and hearsay to the already negative and defensive person with whom we are in conflict. Even benign little words dropped at precisely the "right" time with the "right" inflection will stir the pot and make resolution and forgetting harder and harder. To cease adding fuel to the fire, the quarrel may be forgotten or at least it will become less painful or less of a wedge in a relationship.

It is late at night and I am feeling very tired. I look forward to this time all week so I do not want to subtract from its potential. If I sound scattered you will know why.

Proverbs 26:21 talks about "quarrelsome nature;" this is part of our human flesh nature and seems to be more characteristic of some than others. Such a person or any person allowing this part of her humanity to control her, causes hostility, restlessness, and anxiety and arouses emotion and hostility. At the root of this part of our sin nature is (as in all aspects of sin) the issue of pride and self-centeredness. It seems there are some people who delight in causing fires and burning embers within relationships. We all can learn from a clearer understanding of this proverb.

Verse 22 is distressing to me because of its deep insight to the nature of the flesh. The slander of another person that occurs as we participate and embellish gossip somehow brings gratification to a very deep and primitive part of our self-centered nature. It takes concerted effort and God's power to resist participation because it satisfies us so deeply. I believe we all must pray specifically that God would take away this depraved level of need. The person who can so have victory here is one truly wise and understanding of this truth.

Grammy was so pleased and blessed by the birthday card you sent her. I have come to realize that the most meaningful things in life often take the least effort and time on our part. Mom is in Princeton, New Jersey, this week for a church music conference. We are so rarely apart that I feel a loneliness when it occurs. Pretty soon it will be spring and then the end of your first year will be in sight.

Proverbs 26:23 makes a true observation. In ancient times, a glaze over clay was often opaque and made of silver alloy. The result was a relatively worthless piece of pottery made to look expensive and valuable. Likewise, a person whose inner person and heart are self-centered, prideful, haughty, or arrogant can appear to be of high character and compassionately "other focused" because of the words she says or expressions she conveys. It is hard at times to know when such deception is at hand, and often we need to ask for God's discernment. Satan himself can appear attractive from the outer presentation but is evil in his heart.

Verse 24 takes this thought a bit further. A person can be malicious in his real person (desiring to do destruction to others, or delighting in their pain and suffering), but can disguise this with lying words and deceiving emotions. His heart, motivation, and true delight is to deceive another and see him go toward depravity and destruction. God hates such a person, and such is the tool and servant of Satan. He may know worldly success but will ultimately be judged and condemned.

I hope you had a nice stay in Atlanta, and hopefully were able to relax and regroup. Although it may not seem like it on occasion, these years will be among the best years of your life. It is good you can experience different places while you are pre-children.

Proverbs 26:25 warns us to not be misled by a person's smooth and persuasive speech, or words he uses. Satan can use the tongue/lips to charm people to follow his ways and believe his lies. But we must, by God's Spirit, discern man's true heart. We must look beyond the speech to his character as evidenced by his actions, choices, priorities, loves and passions, time usage, and quality of relationships. The proverb then refers back to 6:16-19 that lists seven things that are detestable to the Lord. These seven things (or some portion of them) when present identify the true person and testify against even his charming words.

Verse 26 continues this theme. The writer tells us that this man's evil motives and driving passions are malicious–destructive and prideful. However, he will try to conceal his true malice with deception–he will coat these deeper forces with humanistic and societally-supported verbiage and acts. He is not godly but awakens popular support, and causes the godly who oppose to be shamed and ridiculed by the world. However, as time goes on and greater experience is gained by more and more people, his deception and true evil motives will come to light. Certainly in the heavenly assemblies he will be exposed.

We leave two weeks from today for Israel. The group will be small but we are going to several new places. I have thirteen teachings to do. I continue to love studying God's Word. He always meets me there and blesses me with His wisdom and insights. I must honor His investment in me of the gift of teaching. I will not say no to Him.

Proverbs 26:27 tells us about the consequences of ungodly effort and activity. The examples of the proverb are to "dig a pit" and "roll a stone"–both having to do with attempted means of harming another (traps and ambushes). The proverbs tell us that ultimately these will backfire and will harm us, being destructive to our well-being and future. Spiritually, God is telling us that apart from a new life in Him, we are driven by self-pride and delight in the destruction of others. This will destroy us, if not in this life, certainly in the next. Only as we relate to Him can we truly love and seek the best for another; this will then bring us blessing and life.

Verse 28 again speaks about the tongue as it reflects our heart and true motives. A person who is estranged from God and has only a "flesh nature" seeks to hurt and ruin another, as a way of building her own pride and power. These destructive motives are made manifest by a person who lies and slanders, and who falsely flatters another setting him up for rejection and pain. It is folly to try to tame the tongue for you can never anticipate the situations in life that will trigger its misuse. Our effort has to be on growing in godliness in our hearts and becoming more like Christ.

I am thinking tonight of perseverance as a trait of godliness, and how Satan uses the lack thereof to defeat, discourage, and destroy. To persevere over time in this life is very difficult, since there always is the disillusionment and agony of the "grind."

Proverbs 27

Proverbs 27:1 is a well-used one, usually used to reflect on the uncertainties of life here on earth. Indeed this is part of it, since there are so many unforeseen curves in the road and human vexations in life. But it also can be seen in context of the spiritual world. God is active in life–in giving opportunity and blessing, as well as judging and disciplining. He has a perfect will and we will be a part of His will; this may or may not always line up with what we think we need or want. To boast today that our will is also God's is satisfying, but tomorrow such may not be the case. He loves us continually. We can always be certain of that.

Verse 2 encourages another distinctly human trait, that of self-exaltation and acclaim. The proverbs encourage us to let someone else give us praise, rather than ourselves. To be able to consistently do this, however, requires us to subject our pride and need for approval to a lower level of need. Only when we feel secure in our value and worth in God's sight can we so subject this need. And only in the context of a living relationship, where we get to know God and see how He pours Himself into our life and uses us in His work, can we feel such worth and value.

Soon you will have a vacation–well deserved and earned. I wish you a great time of relaxation and a time of growing in oneness in your relationship. I smile with joy often as I remember our bicycle trip in France. Our Israel trip was very good. My teaching went well and I think stirred many hearts toward God. I sensed they were of value to God because I felt a spiritual opposition both in the preceding months of preparation and also during the trip.

Proverbs 27:3 is an interesting and insightful piece of wisdom. Certain physical weights when lifted will weigh us down, but not like the effect of certain life situations or people upon our spirits. A "fool" is one who rejects God and God's wisdom for his life. If out of concern, care, or love for that person you share God but he rejects you and your message, the burden on your heart is great. Often the rejection is not neutral but emotionally aggressive and oppositional and provokes within us pain and dampening of our spirits. We must do what is right in our positions but at the risk of such pain. Jealousy is an emotion that leads to the most cruel and destructive action; it is a result of a perceived assault upon one's pride and self-focused source of personal value. When one derives her value as a person from the world rather than from a relationship with God, it is fragile, conditional, and insecure. The person must guard it from being weakened and will react aggressively to anyone who threatens it. When our value is based upon the secure unconditional love of God (via Christ) then the world can never threaten it; and jealousy is less and less our emotion.

I do hope your time off has been good and relaxing. Did you play golf in Florida? I am preparing my sermon for the Mahomet Community Sunrise Easter Service. I am going to retell, with practical application, the story when Christ meets the two men on the road to Emmaus (Luke 24). I wish you two were going to be there, but perhaps you will pray for me at that hour.

Proverbs 27:5 is an interesting one; and one often taught against in our modern society. It teaches us, in God's Word, to be honest, involved, and intimate with a chosen few. It encourages us to be expressive of our love and affection for the appropriate people in our lives, and not to keep our feelings closeted and unexpressed. So important is this teaching that the author goes as far as to tell us that it would be better to go as far as "open rebuke" rather than keep our feelings to ourselves. I don't think he is advocating conflict but making the point that we are to express our love for others.

In balance we read verse 6. Here non-genuine expression of affection is a ploy to confuse us and entice us to the destructive schemes of our enemy. Outward, even extreme, show of affection is meant to manipulate and cause us to be vulnerable to destruction. However, true friends will allow themselves to be harmed or hurt as they faithfully uphold and defend us. They would rather personally know pain than for us to be harmed. This is true significant love.

This week begins the last three months of your first year in residency. I know you both have performed well professionally, and I hope are growing as individuals and as a couple under God's leadership. I know from experience that it is often hard to maintain balance and wholeness during residency. However, that is typical of how life is and will be. My prayer for you this whole year has been that you will be able to find the balance.

Proverbs 27:7 gives a very simple truth. When we are so full of the sweet, good, material things of life (and we as a people seek to be filled and overfilled), than we do not appreciate and savor these blessings as we receive them—we are immune to their purpose. God would have us spend the bulk of our time and effort in discipline, perseverance, helping other people, and ministering in His kingdom. He will "spice" up our lives and "treat" us at times (critical, right times as He determines) when we need it and can appreciate it. His Word, though, can be a steady diet and will only grow in goodness and sweetness.

Verse 8 indicates that the proper place for a person is close to where his/her family resides. Certainly this primarily focuses upon the immediate family because of the great responsibility that comes from marriage and children. An absentee parent or spouse (although at times unavoidable) is a tension and compromise to the other members. I think this proverb also addresses the need to have a strong presence and loyalty to the extended family.

Well, spring has really "sprung" here in central Illinois. It is good to see green and flowers again. This is a busy week with "Holy Week" activities. Remember me in your prayers as I give two addresses—Maundy Thursday and Easter Sunrise. It is always a stretch for me but I prefer it that way because then I can truly give God the glory. Mom is busy with church services, Messiah preparation, and taxes. I really appreciate her energy and ability.

Proverbs 27:9 and 10 are about friends. In ancient Israel, perfumed oil soothed the parched, dry body and refreshed the senses, while incense stimulated the mind and spirit to come alive. In this same way a friend's relationship can soothe, refresh, and stimulate our existence and the outcome of our lives. It is in the selfless, concerned, dedicated, unconditional counsel that we find pleasantness and vitality. To know that the heart of a friend is turned toward helping us to become all that God intended, gives joy and hope. Not all counsel is warm and soft but our friend's intentions and motives are all supportive.

Verse 10 accentuates the principle that often a friend can be of more value, loyalty, and in closer proximity than a family member (particularly a sibling). This is not to necessarily be seen as negative to family, for a family member can and should be a friend (maybe even a best friend) as well. When there is trial and pain, a friend, especially one who is close enough to the situation, can really relate to you well and address your needs best. The proverb also tells us that such people can also be friends of your parents–for they have loyalty that extends to the children.

Happy Birthday, Jeremy! I hope you will have a very special day and that the two of you can have some time to celebrate. I'm glad you had a nice Easter and that you were able to take a friend to Easter church with you. God will honor that effort. I pray that seeds were planted that will grow in the months ahead.

Proverbs 27:11 is a unique and honest piece of wisdom. It gives a high value to the importance, to a parent, of a child's choice (or choices) in life. If the child you have loved and nurtured is wise (chooses God and godliness), he will bring deep and lasting joy to the believing parent's heart. There is no greater joy than to see children choosing God for themselves. Armed with such joy, the pain and rejection ("contempt") shown to the parent by other aspects (or people) in life will not overwhelm them or defeat them. The joy of a believing and wise daughter or son will challenge and nullify any ill treatment given by the world.

Verse 12 warns us to be wary, cautious, and decisive when it comes to danger. The danger here is the spiritual challenge and attack of Satan and evil men toward the believer. Respect it, recognize it, avoid it, and run from it. Seek refuge into the safety of God and His Word, and the fellowship of believers. The unwise and unlearned (in things of the Spirit) will try to persevere but will be defeated and know great pain.

You are soon to be finished with surgery. I know at least you, Christine, will be looking forward to that. I bet the area is beautiful this season; have you had a chance to enjoy the outdoors much this spring?

Proverbs 27:13 encourages us to cooperate with and functionally respect the efforts of a person who makes an effort to help a stranger. The giving of a garment is a pledge that you desire and intend to do a certain thing–it is considered binding and accepted from a respected, honest man. When such a man gives his word and pledge that he intends to help one who cannot help herself, we are to accept it without hesitation. The security is in the character of the one pledging. Christ gave His garment (at the cross) signifying His binding intent to provide for us who are lost (strangers). It is His character that binds the action.

Verse 14 warns us against those who overtly and publicly rain praises upon us; they pick times and places where they will be seen by others and are intended to self-acclaim rather than sincerely convey love and respect. They are insensitive to when we are able to hear and be open to their words. One knows when words of praise are insincere and self-magnifying, and we likewise must be sensitive and appropriate in how we compliment and express gratitude, or it will be seen more as a curse.

It is an exciting weekend for our family as your sister Erin is graduating from college! We will be going to Bloomington on Friday evening and graduation Saturday morning. It is a witness to God's hand upon her thus far. I want to congratulate the two of you for nearly completing the first (and hardest) year of your residency. Although I have missed you both this year, I am very proud of you and believe that the situation is good and right. I pray for you both by name every morning at 6 A.M.

Proverbs 27:15-16 speaks about a wife. It is talking about a wife who has a spirit or attitude of bickering, nagging, faultfinding, pessimism, and anxiety. This attitude, and the words and actions it produces, progressively and relentlessly wears away at a relationship to her family (husband especially). It will eventually break the bond. Also it is impossible to externally quell this or restrain it; only from a changed heart can this be altered. That of course must be a result of a relationship with God that renews and brings a new perspective.

Verse 17 speaks about the fact that godly men need other godly men to sharpen them. To make a person sharper is to clean away debris and help him focus on what is important and crucial for life and service. It helps to eliminate that which hinders our ability to be the proper spiritual head and wise leader in our homes and in the world. It helps us to progressively know truth as we know His Word better, and have the confidence and courage to employ it in our lives. We need each other and other godly men.

At times like this, as you wait on the outcome of the pregnancy, it is tough to be a parent who cares so deeply for you. I want to somehow take away your pain and emotional uncertainty but am unable. Because of distance and the need for separate lives, we cannot even be with you in your struggle. Oh I know, it has to be this way in life. I am confident in both of you to care and minister to each other. I also know that God is your real Father and is there with you, able to heal and counsel you. But my heart joins yours as we wait.

Proverbs 27:18 is rather interesting. It, I think, talks about honor, respect, and teachability. It likens a relationship between one who is learning and growing with his/her mentor, to that of how one cares for a "fig tree." To get the best, most refreshing fruit that is of greatest quality, one has to tend to the tree. That requires time, effort, and getting to know fig trees in general, and this one in particular. There requires a certain respect and humility and patience in the tending process. In life, we are learners and as we identify what we desire and is of greatest value to us, we need to put forth the time and effort and have the heart of humility and respect, as we place ourselves under the direction of our "masters."

Verse 19, I think, is a clear and beautifully-stated fact. We are who our heart is. The things that form our person, our character; that which gives us joy and value; that which recruits our time and effort and which draws others to us in love, are the things of our heart. The heart drives our minds and our intellectual pursuits. As we all journey to know who we really are, we must look at these heart issues. I think heart issues are much greater than our passions and emotions and really focus on our true identity. I believe part of our true identity has to do with a need to connect with a Creator God.

Oh how I rejoice over the news that your baby (and pregnancy) are well. I know you don't feel well physically, but your hearts must be aflame as you hear that new heart beating deep within you, Christine. What a fortunate child to have you two as parents, and to be born into a home that knows and loves God.

Proverbs 27:20. Destruction of a person, his or her spiritual emotional, and relational person, his moral and acting person, and his physical person, never ends until all is destroyed and lies dead. This is the way of the world, a world governed by evil and Satan; people who have not placed their confidence and hope in God will be on a destructive decline all their lives. But God does not intend that this will be what a man experiences ("the eyes of man") and offers in a personal relationship with Him the only means to avert this demise and know life in all our persons; except that our physical person will be transformed to a new body at death.

Verse 21 is indeed a wise one and worthy of thought and prayer. A person is refined and tested by how well he or she can remain humble and other-focused (especially God focused) in the midst of praise and acclaim by other men, upon her. One whose identity and value are not strongly linked to God, and whose understanding of himself and the world is not screened through the eyes of God, will be corrupted and compromised by man's praise. I have come to believe that one of God's greatest acts of love to us is when He protects our ears and eyes from hollow praises from worldly men.

By the time you get this letter, Christine, you will be here for Lori's wedding. I really miss you both, remembering two years ago you were living here for several months during your last year in medical school. I came across the "swing" we put up for you, Christine, (over by the barn) when we first moved here in 1986. You wanted a swing in the walnut tree so we put a simple board on a rope, and there it has stayed all these years. I don't have the heart to take it down although I'm sure it is unsafe to use now. My study of Isaiah is really relevant to the circumstances of the world today. I really believe God is taking the events perpetuated by evil men to try and move His creation back to a relationship with Him as the only real solution to its problems.

Proverbs 27:22 is a true statement from my experience. A "fool" is one who is driven and blinded to truth by self-centered pride; his words and actions are destructive but he has not the slightest clue of his ungodly perspectives and choices. Even if he is brought to shame and pain by his choices, he will not connect this consequence with his perspective. Therefore he will cling and persist with the path that has led, and will lead, to further pain and destruction. No matter how much his choices cause him problems, he will persist. Such is the hold Satan has on a heart alienated from God, our true Creator and Lord of our lives.

Verse 23 encourages us, especially who are responsible for the welfare and molding of other people (parents, leaders, teachers, and thinkers), to know for sure at any given moment what the condition and needs are of those entrusted to us. We have to give "careful attention" to everyone in the flock and for the flock as a whole. We need to know their individual states, the relationships between each in the flock and the direction the flock as a whole is going. This is the awesome responsibility of the parents, especially Jeremy, the father.

I hope and trust that your trip home, Christine, was a good one and you are surviving your week and "on call" schedule. Jeremy, I was really pleased to hear your voice on the telephone during our brief interaction. You are my only son at this point and I so appreciate you.

Proverbs 27:24 is a truth that modern man (in fact many of all generations) knows but does not acknowledge or adapt as his operational motive. Quite the opposite really; man has embraced a life that leads hopefully to "riches." He knows with his head that it cannot endure forever and is not secure, but he places it above God in his priority, and above even the people He places in his life. Obviously it is a plan of Satan, in his supreme wickedness and knowledge of the human heart, to tempt us all in our human, flesh nature. He knows that if we worship riches, we will die. Yet we are to provide for the balanced needs of our human existence, realizing God will provide through our labor and choices. Verses 24-27 encourage us to work hard and receive the reward of our labor–to live well and to provide for those entrusted to us. But this should never replace our worship and walk with God—our Creator, maintainer, and supplier of all that is good. There is, from God's perspective, a sometimes fine line between receiving from Him via our labors, and seeking riches in place of Him. Man must prayerfully maintain this distinction and never lose clear sight of who God is and who we are.

I hope all is well with the two of you, as you push further into your second year. I also hope, Christine, that you are beginning to feel better, although it may be a little early in the pregnancy yet for that. I had some good time of conversation and prayer with Nannie last weekend. I sensed as we were leaving that she said to me some "good bye" things. She sort of "rallied" and found strength and wellness for that short visit. It was comfortable and natural and, as I reflect back, I can see the hand of God on the visit.

Proverbs 28

Proverbs 28:1 once again compares the wicked man to the righteous. The wicked is he/she who acts out pride and self-seeking priorities, shunning God's call and ownership of his life. The wicked act progressively more disgracefully, arbitrarily, and hurtfully; they become more depraved, lose courage and self-worth. They run, not from one who actually pursues them, but from their own self-judgment. That "God likeness" that is a part of us (His creation) condemns the flesh nature and the fear, guilt, and shame make us run and hide. But the person who seeks God and allows Him to be Lord of her life, stands firm with courage, without immobilizing fear and free of guilt and shame. Her actions reflect her heart.

Verse 2 tells us that anarchy and confusion dominate a person who lacks understanding. A person cut off from God lacks a secure, consistent standard in life; he has no fundamental truth and there is no unifying and directing basic principle of his life (apart from self-seeking and self-serving). But the person of God has such and therefore all thoughts, desires, decisions, and actions will be in concert with these basic principles. There will be order and clear, consistent priorities in his life. This is how to recognize a godly man or woman.

Nannie continues a rapid deterioration and has become very weak. She is talking about not taking chemo. She and I spoke today of her death. I grieved as we talked.

Proverbs 28:3 is a good piece of advice for all people in a position of leadership–even within the family. To lead and encourage those entrusted to us, to work hard, produce, and become greater is a result of strong, yet personalized and understood sensitivity to the needs and concerns of those led. The leader cannot "strong arm" them to give deeply of themselves without considering their needs; the result will be discouragement, counter-production, rebellion, and hate. Ultimately, they will not produce and the owner-leader will lose out. We, to be good leaders, must submit to God and understand His leadership in our lives. This should be our prototype.

Verse 4 tells us that those who turn from the law will embrace the wicked. The law is God's standard given to help us to fully realize our position as His children and to know how to live in this life to know true joy and peace, and powerful action. If we embrace His directives and wisdom, we will move ahead as He wishes and will avoid seeking that which is against God and destructive to mankind. To reject His law takes away the only true standard; we then are open to the push and tug of various world perspectives–all of which lead to death and destruction.

Time seems to march on at a rapid pace. The fall colors are waning and signs of winter are daily being observed. I do love the season change and marvel at the order and predictability of God's creation.

In Proverbs 28:5 the writer tells us that God's justice can be known and understood only by those who seek Him. God is perfect and sinless and His holy character insists on justice and judgment of sin. All who are not clean and made pure by Christ's blood will be judged. The people who reject God and seek not to know Him ("evil men") cannot understand this justice and in their false humanistic social compassion will place themselves above God and condemn His justice. Only the person who knows God (progressive and life long process) can have His perspective and heart; will bow before His holiness and agree with Him in His righteous acts of judgment.

Verse 6 again makes a point by contrasts. The godly perspective is contrasted with the human, worldly, fleshly perspective. The world proclaims riches as the goal of its inhabitants and allows perverse ways in order to achieve this goal. We are led to believe this is normative and universal, that this is in conjunction with created order and priorities. This is, of course, a lie. From God's created order's divine perspective, the goal is to walk "blameless" (seeking His standard) even if this places you in poverty by the world's standards. Once again, the world has turned righteous order upside down.

It was good to see you and get "updated," laugh, and share at dinner last week. I'm sorry, Jeremy, that it was occasioned by the loss of your grandmother. As we sat together, I felt like time had hardly passed, while at the same time desiring that we could, someday, be close enough to be important to each other day by day. The ultrasound of your baby brought the reality of that wonderful blessing close and it is beginning to be real for me. Maybe I have been protecting myself from disappointment if (as we first were anticipating) for some reason the pregnancy wasn't viable.

Proverbs 28:7 emphasizes the need to be careful with whom we associate. The person who understands God's desire and directives for our friendships will be discerning, if in addition he behaves and chooses according to these understood directives. Discernment is not only understanding but also includes behavior modified by such understanding. Such a person will be regarded highly by those people in life who love him and have taught him (parents). But if we choose as companions those who violate God's ethics and morals, we are a source of disgrace to those who have prayed for and taught us right from wrong.

Verse 8 reveals the folly of spending a life (or having as an overriding priority) seeking to amass wealth by putting all one's effort to that purpose. The wealth will not benefit you (the person who sought it) but will someday fall to the discretion of others to dispose of it as they see fit. Because they do not have the same priority, interest, and investment in it that you do, it will be given away to those who need it. In the final analysis, a life spent in such an endeavor will be valueless and forgotten within a generation or two.

I continue to be amazed at the depth of truth and wisdom in the Word of God. I never dreamed that the prophet Isaiah had so much to say about the character of God and about the plan He has for His creation.

Proverbs 28:9 underscores that God is a God of order and justice. He has created a world where (after Adam has sinned and rejected the internal spiritual order) there must be law and consequences in order to prevent anarchy and oppression. God will indwell this order and will meet His creation as we submit to His law. He also expects His children (via Christ's sacrifice) to submit to order and consequences–even if they seem unjustified. Even Jesus submitted to law, order, and consequences though He didn't earn them Himself. If we refuse to submit, it is a symptom of pride and God cannot relate to a pride-driven creation. When our walks are characterized by pride, our prayers cannot be answered as they are given. Further, this lawlessness and pride-driven walk can lead others astray–away from submission and obedience into evil self-indulgence and injustice. Such a person will eventually find himself being judged and acted upon by another who is driven by pride and lawlessness. The one who submits to God, His law and order, will find Him and be offered great blessing.

I'm sorry that I was not at home when you called last weekend. I, of course, would love to talk with you on any subject, and provide any thoughts I have. I hesitate to call you for fear that I may awaken you. I guess I remember my years as a resident when I was sleeping most times I was at home. I'm finding it confusing and strange going through my mother's dying process with her. I'm trying to understand God and His grace for those He loves, while at the same time trying to support Nannie and express my heart to her. Please pray for us both.

Proverbs 28:11 is certainly proven true in my experience. A person who seeks wealth and power in the world's terms can easily be deluded to believe he is wise, bright, successful, etc., because he excels as measured by the world's yardsticks. He is playing by the world's rules and he is judged a winner by this standard. However, the rules and standards are superficial at best and depraved at worst. But the person who seeks God's standards rejects the world's perspective and "discerning" because he sees through and beyond the flesh and physical world. Such a person knows that true wisdom must be found in God's game and by His rules.

Verse 12 observes that mankind at a certain level desires in its leadership (of those in power) righteousness, not wickedness. People in authority who rule with God's morals, His truth, His justice, and His mercy will bring security and fairness to all they rule. But the wicked ruler brings a threat of insecurity, arbitrariness, injustice, and oppression; he is motivated by self-seeking agendas. It is better to hide from such rulers.

I hope you are both settled back again after the fast trip to Pittsburgh for Nannie's funeral. I very much appreciated your sacrifice for Nannie and for me. She would have enjoyed the gathering and the times we had together as a family.

Proverbs 28:13 is rather straightforward but a basic tenet of our faith. Confession of our sinful nature, acts, thoughts, and words presupposes that we understand and accept God's standard for right and wrong. We must, in order to confess, feel accepted and valuable to God (our judge), and not fear Him rejecting us. Then we act to humble ourselves before Him, and at times before other men, to acknowledge these sins, express our desire to not sin further, and renounce these acts (so they are set apart from us). In this we receive mercy and forgiveness. Further, in this God can prosper us–by His definition and not by the world's.

Similarly, verse 14 tells us that we can experience the blessed state (feel and experience God's goodness toward us) unlocked when we fear Him. Of course, fear here is not a "cowering in fear of destruction" but an awe and respect and acknowledgment of His supreme power and authority over all creation. In contrast, the person whose heart is hardened toward God (when he refuses to let God be the powerful Creator God, challenging His authority) will fall into trouble. His life will move toward chaos and depravity; from light to darkness; from life to death.

Once again today, I realized as I prayed with three patients, how deeply touched they are by the merging of medicine with the spiritual power of God's healing hand. How grateful I am to Him who chose me for this privilege.

Proverbs 28:15 states what history has, many times, borne out. When a wicked man is the ruler, the subjects (especially the lesser privileged) are oppressed and are objects of the ruler's need for satisfying his ego and pride. A "wicked" person delights in all behavior that seeks his own selfish needs without regard for God's way and at the expense of other more helpless people. He will oppress and act unjustly in a violent, hostile, intimidating manner (like a roaring lion or charging bear). God has, in history, and will continue to depose and destroy such a ruler and have compassion on the helpless. Only as a ruler can parallel God's governance will he/she thrive, succeed, and prosper.

Verse 16 tells us two things about such an unjust, tyrannical ruler. Firstly, such a person is blinded to proper perspectives and judgments concerning affairs and those he is given rule over. He will not stand for true wisdom and truth, instead seeking his own ego needs. Secondly, the person who does seek God's standard and appropriates His wisdom will rule long and enjoy a long and satisfying life. The wicked man will be destroyed.

It seems so long ago that you were here for the holidays. Dr. Moberg e-mailed me and expressed very positive feedback concerning his meeting with you both. We will wait and see how God will work all these possibilities out; we will remain flexible and confident that His will will be right, wherever that leads you.

Proverbs 28:17 talks about guilt and righteous social action. Sin (in this verse=murder) brings internal guilt; guilt because we are made in God's image and we (when we sin) create internal dissidence. This leads to anxiety, guilt, shame, and restlessness. This torments us and robs us of the joy and peace available in the alignment of our souls with God's. We will spend the rest of our lives searching and seeking this lost peace and a solution to our guilt/shame. Only by returning to God in repentance and then His cleansing, will we reestablish the created equilibrium. We should not try to give false peace, hope, and substitute joy to those who are guilty. This is to reduce God's efforts to bring reconciliation.

Verse 18 tells us that our choice of ways of living and acting has natural consequences in God's created world. When we align ourselves with His standards, in His world, we are internally void of blame and in many ways kept safe—safe from our own guilt/shame and self-destruction, safe from the persecution and rejection of the rest of God's world, safe from the impact of our perverse ways on our bodies, and safe from that spiritual alienation (now and in the future).

I hope all is well with you both, and with the pregnancy ("Annie"). Time marches on and soon it will be May. Mom still is reluctant to admit she is going to be a Grandma. I think it will hit her hard when she finally holds Annie in her arms.

Proverbs 28:19 generally advocates for hard work toward practical provision for life. I believe this is important for us to understand and adopt personally. Too many people are looking for the "short cut" to avoid hard, persevering, and often grueling effort. They usually never quite make it happen and if they do hit it lucky, it is not satisfying to their "god-patterned" soul. God allows us abundance but we must work for it; and our character grows and matures at the same time. But I also believe that there is a time for "chasing fantasies." It makes us interesting and balances the grueling aspects of life. But this must be seen as the "spice" of life and not the "meat and potatoes."

Verse 20 continues this theme, but places a spiritual twist on it. The "faithful" man is one who walks with God (in faith). He makes the right decisions at the right time out of a growing walk with God. In these choices, in his work and perseverance, he feels and knows the presence of God–he is blessed. But he who seeks his own wealth and worldly success (who has no need for God) will know the discipline of a universe created in concert with God the Creator, and will answer to God throughout and at the end of his life.

Thanks for sharing your heart's concerns, Christine, tonight on the phone, relative to Annie. I remember the same thoughts and fears as Mom carried each of you girls. I never felt I could voice them for fear of causing Mom distress. Keep your eyes and heart on God, be honest and open with Him, thank Him for the blessings He provides, and trust Him in whatever path the future will bring. Enjoy and be blessed by this pregnancy and the process of creating life; don't let Satan rob you.

Proverbs 28:21 is a piece of wisdom that speaks to mercy. Often in the world's eyes it is better to be fair, equal, and objective, showing no differential between people based on their life's circumstances. We pride ourselves (and it is about our pride) on showing no partiality in our individual encounters with others, even if life in general has brought about inequality. This proverb tells us that in God's eyes there is a higher principle to be understood. People are flesh and when their very existence and well-being is challenged, they will choose unrighteous behaviors. We must, in compassion and in mercy, differentially provide for people to prevent them from following a destructive and devaluating path of behavior. Mercy implies recognizing and accommodating different needs.

Verse 22 once again reminds us that self-seeking behavior will in the end bring about destruction and want. This must be understood from a total "whole" person understanding. Stingy behavior is based on pride and self-centeredness; a life of that will rob a person of the ability to seek after God and humble herself to God. Further, she will never know the satisfaction of human relationships, nor the joy and peace of a godly life.

What a good idea to write Scripture on the walls behind the wainscoting in Annie's room. It is like an invisible shield around her as she sleeps vulnerably in her bed, protecting her from Satan and his deceptions and surrounding her with the living Word.

Proverbs 28:23 is true in my experience, although we who do not like conflict try to avoid this piece of wisdom. To "rebuke" is to set straight and to bring clarity to the way one should go (consistent with God's standards, laws, and statutes). It can and should be done with strength and conviction while being concerned, caring, and understanding. To rebuke another may cause some initial conflict but will cause the other to regard you highly and with deep appreciation. This is much more valuable than a flattering tongue. To rebuke in this way is a large part of being wise.

Verse 24 is interesting. The writer uses an example (to rob one's mother and father) that is clearly wrong and sinful. Such a person who does this must deal with his guilt/shame. A common man-devised way to deal with this is via denial or justification. That which is obviously wrong is seen as not wrong. Such denial will lead to self destruction—we lose our self respect, our ability to be honest with ourselves, our trustworthiness to others, and our ability to see right and wrong.

I took three of the pictures of our family to the office today—one for each of my exam rooms. I really like the picture and already many of my patients have called attention to the picture. I am so blessed to have such a family. I pray daily for each of you in the picture. Having the picture there makes me aware throughout the day of how I seek God for each of us.

Proverbs 28:25 contrasts a greedy man with one who trusts the Lord. A greedy man is motivated for self-acquisition. He has flagrant disregard for others and their welfare. He uses gossip, slander, and anger as weapons of control and manipulation. The result is dissension, disorder, and destruction. But the person who trusts in God is placing God higher than herself and has dealt with pride and self-seeking. She is growing in God's likeness and employing His ethic, standards, and laws. The laws are at the root of the creation. To adhere to them will lead to blessings.

Verse 26 furthers this. The person who trusts in God and seeks His wisdom will know safety. To be kept safe is not to avoid the pain of living in this world, but to know nothing will take away our true joy and peace and that death has been conquered. The person who trusts instead in himself will not know true wisdom and will never experience life abundant or eternal.

Of course, you both (and Annie) have been in my thoughts and prayers all week long. I thank God that the labor has stopped for now and that Annie is safe. I thank God that you were well cared for in your time of need. I pray God will visit you in a very special way, Christine, as you rest and know a quiet you haven't known often before. Congratulations, Jeremy, on your selection to be one of the chief residents. It is an honor and certainly speaks of high respect from those around you—respect of your character and your trustworthiness. I believe you will do a great job.

Proverbs 28:27 calls us to care for the poor. Most of us will cringe a little with this one since we often choose to be oblivious to the needs of the poor or, worse yet, justify this behavior by blaming them and holding them responsible for their situations. Although that may in part be true, that is not the point—it is the counterpoint encouraged by Satan. The point is that we are to give to the poor because we have received from the King and giving to others in need is our participation in His kingdom. It is not necessary, usually, to go out of our way, but just to be sensitive and responsive to those God places on our path. If we do this, He can bless us greatly.

Verse 28 tells us that the wicked in places of power will use that power destructively and for self-centered means. Those who have been changed and have a heart seeking to be more like Christ will retreat from this wickedness and the specific threat they represent. When these wicked people are taken away, the righteous ones will blossom and thrive. Ultimately this will be at Christ's second coming.

I pray for you two and Annie throughout my day; I am thanking God for every day you are not in labor. I know it is very hard now and that you are being asked to sacrificially love your daughter by giving up your life's activities to stay in bed. Unilateral and complete trust of your daughter to God is the most important and valuable lesson you will ever learn. How blessed you are for Him to teach this to you even before day one of Annie's life.

Proverbs 29

Proverbs 29:1 tells us a very scary truth. God's patience has limits. He will repeatedly confront a person with her sin and lack of repentance, her stubbornness and self-centeredness; but, there will come a time that she is judged unteachable since she continues to choose her flesh nature over her spiritual nature. She will not or cannot hear, learn, and respond to God. (See Rom. 1.) Then God will give her over to her destructive ways and she will be destroyed. He will not rescue her; she will be refined by fire. Each of us must remain sensitive to this tension in our lives and hear God as He rebukes us, so we will turn and not be destroyed.

Verse 2 tells us a self-evident truth. When God's right way prevails in life, when people act according to His standards, then the people rejoice. To rejoice is to know deep inner peace and joy, aware that the Creator God of the universe is directing the ways of His creation. When we as a people walk in step with His ways, we thrive. When evil and wickedness rule the ways and directive of the people, then the people feel deep pain and groan, mourning the lack of peace and joy.

Well, you are nearly thirty-three weeks along now!! Well done! Keep up the good work. I trust all is going well with baby Annie and that her room is looking good. As it gets closer to the time of her birth, I am becoming more excited to be a "Grandad." I continue to love my study of Isaiah; I wish I would have studied it long ago but maybe I was not ready to know its truths or to teach it properly before this time.

Proverbs 29:3 seems at first disjointed and internally unrelated; but there is sense to it. It compares the great value and ongoing reward that comes from seeking after and savoring "wisdom," versus the absolute folly and wastefulness that come from a life of meaningless sensuality. Wisdom is meant to mean that ability to know God's truths and apply them in everyday life in such a way that others grow and blossom, and God is glorified. Wisdom so sought and applied is the deep desire of a godly father for his son or daughter. Squandering yourself and your resources on the passions of the flesh brings only destitution and personal destruction.

Verse 4 reveals that integrity, justice, compassion, and self-sacrifice in a leader will cause his charge to prosper, remain stable, and enjoy a strong future. Groups, countries, or kingdoms of the world are all "wired" the same by God. The fact is that they (like us individually) work better when they are led according to God's strategies, plans, laws, and ethics. If the wiring is instead self-centeredness, self-seeking, "get rich," and injustice, then that country or people group will ultimately fail. They are on a downward spiral that only God can fix.

Well, almost thirty-four weeks. I'm thanking God for this time for Annie. Probably, Christine, you will be back at work part-time when you receive this letter. The end is in sight but every day still is good for Annie. Easter here was good. I prayed several times for you and the woman you took to church—how did she respond? I'm sorry, Jeremy, that you had to work.

Proverbs 29:5 speaks about integrity and the proper use of words. Flattery carries with it the concept of manipulation through speaking false positive statements about another. These statements may be built on half truths, enough that they can be believed by one who wishes to believe the best about himself. The goal is to "get" for ourselves by manipulating another. When one uses flattery for this purpose he is really intent on causing loss or destruction of some degree to the person he flatters. At first it may seem sweet to the neighbor, but without being aware she is being "set-up," taken advantage of, or controlled. When she realizes it, it is often too late and the damage is done. This is not pleasing to God.

Verse 6 takes this a series of steps further. The one who abuses the neighbor is an "evil man." He may succeed then, or maybe even repeatedly, and maybe for years and years. But eventually the cast of his sin will be apparent. He will be exposed, rejected by others, become internally ill with guilt, shame, and restlessness, and maybe even punished by man's law. God will bring justice to the oppressed. He that walks rightly and who pleases God will know joy and peace. Reward, not judgment, will be his.

Another week closer for you to be parents and another week longer for Annie to be further developed. I really thank God for this time and pray for the both of you as you prepare to be parents of God's greatest gift. Mom tells me, Christine, that you sort of like this "part-time" doctoring. It sure has some advantages and also calls into question the issues of priorities, self-realization, role definition, personal versus family needs, and vying internal pressures. God will help you sort it out as you walk this road over the next year or so.

Proverbs 29:7 and 8 are parallel verses to two others earlier in Proverbs. God's people, who are indwelled with His Spirit and who are trying to become more like Jesus, will care about seeing just treatment of the poor, needy, and oppressed. This can be worked out in many specific ways depending on our environment, jobs, opportunities, and internal security. But we are expected to care about it, to think about it, to plan for it, and to run counter (if needed) to society in order to give it. Those who are not changed by God do not hold such care.

People who are wise have God's perspective, His discernment, and a measure of His knowledge. With this they can speak and act in such a way as to quell discontentment, hostility, anger, and aggression. Their soft, godly manner and expressions abort an angry person's aggression. However, those who mock God, His ways, and His truth will act in a way, or speak in a way to stir up discord, hostility, anger, and aggression.

Thirty-six weeks today! Great! I've been really thanking God and praying for the delivery and for baby Annie. So many people here are asking about you and the pregnancy. I know there has been much prayer over these weeks.

Proverbs 29:9 tells us not to go to court with "a fool," and why. A fool is one who doesn't know God and rejects Him as lord of his life. He is motivated by self-centered ideals and is chronically in internal turmoil, unhappy, and angry. He hates correction, mocks ethical rightness, and rejects God-given truth. Spiritually, he is influenced by Satan and being so, he has great contempt for the children of God (the Jews and those of us who are grafted into the covenant). To go to court to settle a dispute will provide an opportunity and a platform for him to "rage and scoff" and to spread his turmoil; he will move the whole court and the people there away from peace.

Verse 10 is an extension of the above thoughts. "Bloodthirsty" men are people who are so completely cut off from God's truth and ethical standards that they seek to harm others. They are motivated to do so in order to further their own passions and self-centeredness, but mainly because of a deep hatred of God and any people committed to Him. Satan sensitizes such a person to know (recognize) godly people and "the man of integrity" and then gives him his (Satan's) hate that motivates his actions. There is a spiritual warfare raging and we are often the recipients of the battle objectives. We must pray and defend ourselves with God's Word.

With this letter, I shall resume my weekly writing, sharing some personal thoughts and continuing our study of Proverbs. I believe we shall finish the book this year. I am open and desirous of continuing this level of interaction and would appreciate your input.

Proverbs 29:11 is a simply stated and simply understood statement of wisdom, but it is very hard to consistently put into action. It is true and the evidence in each of our lives is abundant, that anger never is profitable or valuable to the nurturing of God's kingdom. Beyond that, vented anger is a mark of pride and self-focus–we become angry when we cannot make things happen for our gain or to our glory. We want to be gods and thereby reject God's genuine right to be the only Lord in our lives and others'. Or maybe we just won't trust Him and take control and insensitively and unlovingly push our agendas to the surface. If we walk wisely, we submit our anger daily to God's control.

Verse 12 brings to our mind the effect the character and action a leader has on those he leads and controls. In this example, if the leader will listen to and be made to believe false things (not able to demand and discern truth), then this encourages those before him to manipulate him and his power for their benefit, by evilly slandering, lying, and deceiving the leader. His character weakness and action have encouraged them to walk in the wickedness, to their future detriment.

I trust you enjoyed your long weekend at Kiawah Island. Congratulations, Jeremy, on completing another triathlon and improving your time. I hope Annie is beginning to fall in love with the beach and the Kiawah pace, as we have. I look forward to when she can build sand castles and chase the sand birds.

Proverbs 29:13 is one of the pieces of wisdom that equalizes people of different socio-economic levels of life. To God there are many levels of His creation that are similar despite the artificial and meaningless distinctions we put on ourselves. Here he looks at the "poor man" (disadvantaged and viewed as lowly by the world's yardstick of importance) and the "oppressor" (the socially advantaged person who may have gotten there by taking advantage of others—even the poor man). To God, both do not of themselves have the ability to know truth and to see spiritual, eternal significance. Only as they turn and seek Him will they gain this ability, knowledge, and insight. It is His gift to give but we must seek Him; it is often easier for the poor to seek than the rich.

Verse 14 underlines how God feels about justice and compassion. If one in authority or in power (at any and all levels of life—family, work, social, church, etc.) takes advantage of his position and judges harshly and oppresses unjustly, his time of authority will be limited and he will lie someday in ruin and disgrace. However, if one uses this position to deal fairly and compassionately with those beneath him, he will be allowed to be in authority for a long time and leave with respect and gratitude. It is impossible to do this in our own strength—we must seek God and His spiritual power.

Here we are again at Kiawah Island. Oh, how I love it here. We have been bicycling and enjoying the beach. I have already logged several hours on the front porch thinking, praying, studying, and talking with Mom. This is the first time we have had an extended time here with just the two of us. I'm convinced God has given our family this place as a refuge over the years. On the dock I have felt closer to Him and heard His heart toward me and our family clearer than any other place in my life.

Proverbs 29:15 and 17 can be taken together. They talk about correction and discipline of your child. There is great benefit to our children in this undertaking. It is true (and I am finding this out in greater ways every day) that God really is our children's father and mother and only to the extent that we tie into His heart and mind will we properly raise these gifts from Him. However, to correct wrong ways, thinking patterns, and decisions will bring to our child "wisdom"–wisdom is knowledge that practically works in life; we need to press our children to do and think what is right so they are able to know wisdom. Verse 17 tells us that a child so corrected and disciplined, who knows and employs wisdom, will bring peace to our hearts and delight to our inner persons. Since we deeply love our child, the demonstration of wisdom in her life brings us great satisfaction. How much greater does God desire (as our real parent) for we as His children to learn His ways and employ His wisdom? How He must delight in our walking in His ways!

Verse 16 simply retells us that she who seeks her own way and exalts self over God ("wicked") will sin against God's standards and ways. Eventually such people will come to ruin–in this life and for eternity.

I'm so happy you both are feeling better. I've been praying that Annie would not get the virus. I love my study of Isaiah. I am learning so much about who God is. I will miss going to Israel this fall. I feel particularly close to God there and can gain a different perspective on our world. I look forward to returning soon. I would love for you to join us someday.

Proverbs 29:18 is a familiar one, and a deep truth. The writer is observing that when people do not have "vision" or revelation of God's plan for His creation and for us personally, they will not be properly grounded or have a sense of security, purpose, and logic that eclipses human reason. It is a great blessing for each of us when we grow to understand that God has a plan and an ethic that when embraced will give us security, joy, and peace. The "how" is God's plan and His eternal wise logic; we cannot understand it except as we grow in our relationship with Him and begin to have His vision for the world and its creation. To tie into God-sightedness gives us security, confidence, optimism, and a sense of assurance that keeps us able to persevere through the vicissitudes of human life. We feel grounded (not perishing or without restraint); we know there is a greater truth that eclipses human fickle truth, one that gives vision that transcends our human sight. This sustains us in the hills and valleys of life and allows a peace that transcends worldly transient happiness.

I found the "Camp Webbegone" sign we made, and put it above the door to my barn pinball room. As I cleaned and repaired things in the barn, my mind recalled memories of our family from years gone by. I was touched.

Proverbs 29:19 is one of my favorites—useful for raising children and leading others. The question it addresses is how one changes the behavior of a person who is in her charge or under her influence. The proverb itself is in the negative, telling us that instructing another with only our words will not change his behavior. He will hear the words and intellectually understand, but will not respond. By implication, we are brought to understand that in addition to words, we must have a heart of love and acceptance, and the exemplary demonstration of our verbal directives in the lives we lead. The warmth of the relationship and the example of our lives will bring another to choose to respond to our words.

Verse 20 reminds us to be very careful in our response to another, especially relative to the words we speak. We must control our responses by a heart of love and a deep understanding of human needs and response. A verbal communication done without thought and consideration, but reflexively and full of self-focused emotions, will cause damage and be counter-productive. Here again, only via God's control of our lives and a transformation to being more Christ-like, will such a preferred response be possible.

It is so great of you to keep us updated with Annie's progress and "new" steps of life. I sense that even at her very young age she is favored by God and will touch the hearts of people she contacts.

Proverbs 29:21 is one that can lend itself to multiple interpretations. One that I favor is that which would bring about disruption of relationships because of confusion of roles and expectations. A servant is one who must serve another; the better equipped he is to do this, the better will he be regarded and rewarded. It is cruel and misleading to "pamper" a servant in his early years and then to expect (and judge) him to perform as a servant in later years. He is confused, unprepared, and angry at being suddenly demoted. You will be unhappy with his performance and discipline him whom you once pampered. It is right to care for and love your servant but prepare Him to do and be what he was intended to be. The parallels here must be seen as we are God's servants, His beloved servants, yes, but we must serve well.

Verse 22 is a familiar one. A person's anger and the words and actions that result from his anger cause conflict, misunderstandings, cruel action, hurtful words, and disrupted relationships. The "hot-tempered one" cannot think or reason well and opens himself up to the influence of Satan through the weaknesses of the flesh, to sin against others and against God. Anger and ill-temper are a result of self-centeredness; it is a "thin-iced" place to be and will result in sin and destruction.

The laugh of a six-month-old on the answering machine made the worries and concerns of the day fade and a huge smile come across my face. That is one of the sweetest sounds in life–treasure it.

Proverbs 29:23 tells us the worldly consequences of pride. Although it may be hard often to tell, this world is God's creation and its infrastructure operates by God's ethical and moral code. Satan has confused and distorted this by encouraging us (according to our spoiled flesh nature) to seek our own glorification and to want to be god! This is called pride. It is a sin and unless crucified with Christ will cause us eternal separation from our Creator. Pride, when it motivates human action in real life, will eventually harm and conflict with others (and their pride); then the person will be disgraced, rejected, and disadvantaged. While a person who sees himself as God sees him will seek repentance and walk humbly among men. The world honors such a person; they, at their deep nature, recognize true moral goodness.

Verse 24 makes a point that those who support, aid, or facilitate wrongful action or sinful behavior are also part of the crime and are to be judged accordingly. When confronted and if they tell the truth ("put under oath and testify") they will act to destroy themselves. The spiritual point is that to do anything short of opposing wrong and sin in this world is to be part of the problem and will be judged guilty and punished. This is godly behavior taken a step further.

I have been praying that South Bend would grant Jeremy an interview but realize that God's wisdom goes beyond ours and that He might have other plans for your family next year.

Proverbs 29:25 is an often-heard statement of truth but, as in many things relative to human hearts, it is under utilized and under claimed. In this world with the human pressures and the temptations to our walk with God, we are more concerned with the fear of men than the fear of God. We act in response to the power, authority, wealth, and position of men trying to elevate ourselves and avoid worldly pain. Ironically, in so doing we are inviting judgment from the God of the universe. Because in reality, if we trust in God (in reverent fear of His character) we will know deep joy and peace, and protection from the world. (See Phil. 4:6 and 7.)

Verse 26 extends this thought. The way of the world is to seek to find favor with the powerful and authorities of this world. This is really backward, since the goal should be to seek a hearing from God; because it is only through God's plan for creation that all things will be set right and justice prevail in this world.

Verse 27 makes a simple but painfully true observation. There is a spiritual war going on and these forces work through us, the creation of the world. Those who are of God and who seek His will and lordship "detest" the people who oppose Him (the "wicked").

I sure miss you both, and my granddaughter. I think often of you all and wish it were possible even now to be only a short distance away.

Proverbs 30

Proverbs 30 begins a chapter a bit different in its wisdom. Verses 2-4 present the heart of the writer, and show us his deep humility and reverence for God. We also see that, even in these ancient times, he reflects the truth that involved God and His Son! I sense the writer has been changed forever due to an encounter with God Himself (similar to Isaiah in chapter 6), where he grasps a deeper sense of who he is and who God is.

Verses 2-3 tell us that he sees himself as innately less than other men, not having their understanding or wisdom learned. I suspect he is comparing himself to others in those ancient days who encountered God personally and had been given deeper wisdom and understanding. He writes as one who has been filled up by God but he knows that this is just a mere fraction of God's fullness.

Verse 4 begins to give words to how he has been impressed with his encounter with God. He poetically alludes to God's sovereignty over all of creation, and His coming and going at His will, in His created world. He challenges anyone to tell him "what is His name" or "the name of His Son." In the name of a person is his identity; can any man tell about God's identity, or the identity of his son, Jesus?

I put up the "yellow crib." We had stored it in the attic after your sister Kara outgrew it twenty-plus years ago. It was strange for me, since I remember dismantling it and feeling a bit of sadness that the "baby time" in our life was finished. Now I put it back up with great joy and anticipation for the new baby generation.

Proverbs 30:5 and 6 talk about God's "Word." Literally this would be the Scriptures, our Bible, but more broadly it is all the ways God manifests Himself to us as we seek to hear and obey Him. It is the total expression of all that flows from Him. It can be as generalized and unusual as the beautiful fall day where He reveals His masterfulness in creation, to a very personal and individualized touch He has on our hearts or minds. Whatever the nature of His Word, it is flawless. It is complete, lacking nothing, and it contains nothing worthless or incorrect. Not only is it flawless, but it is powerful to protect us and shield us from the world, driven by the evil one, if we choose to take refuge in it. Verse 6 exhorts any man to not add to His Word! No person can have any truth that God doesn't and to presume to be able to complete or correct His wisdom is an abomination to His lordship and evidence of destructive self-pride. Too many philosophies and humanists feel they need to correct God or "contemporize" Him–that His wisdom is naïve or outdated to modern life. God states clearly that this is such an affront that He will rebuke them and show them as liars. This of course will be in His proper time.

So Annie is now sitting up! Wow! How wonderful and miraculous each of these steps are. We really look forward to seeing you three during the Thanksgiving holiday. Of course, the dedication of Annie will be the highlight–to give her publicly to God is a great privilege and the right step for the Christian parent. As we get closer to Thanksgiving, I find myself thinking of Nannie, not just because she died a year ago on that day, but because she so loved the holidays.

Proverbs 30:7-9 expresses the writer's strong feelings that God would grant him/her two things during his/her life. The first request made of God was that God would keep "lies and falsehood from me." The writer knows that he is vulnerable; that he would find it dangerously hard to know right from wrong, truth from falsehood. To believe a lie or falsehood would lead him away from God and His perfect plan. He depends upon God and acknowledges His sovereignty in his life; he asks God to allow him to hear and confront only truth. He depends and finds great comfort in God. Secondly, he asks God to grant him neither riches nor poverty. He recognizes that either state would jeopardize the proper dependency on and regard for his Lord. He asks only that God give him what he needs for that day, no more and no less. He explains that if he has too much he would be prone to self-dependency and reject his need to seek and depend upon God. But if he was poor, he would be tempted to steal and in so doing he would disgrace and dishonor God, whom he claims to know and depend upon. The writer has great insight and wisdom, and we would do well to depend more and more on God, even in these areas.

It was a deep joy and a deeply moving experience for me to see and hear the time of dedication of Annie at Twin City Bible Church Sunday morning. I really felt the hand of God upon you and her and felt His Spirit powerfully within my soul.

Proverbs 30:10 shows a deep understanding of human nature and the lines of allegiance in our world. The verse cautions us against making critical, character-destructive, judgmental, and accusatory comments about a servant to his master. A servant, one who is loyal and committed to his master, was often viewed as part of the family, with all its rights and mutual obligations. To speak this way of a servant was equal to speaking such about the master's own child. The master will defend, protect, and fight for his servant–and the accuser will be rejected and treated as an enemy. God often held Israel this way–He would love, refine, and correct them, but would curse and destroy any nation who harmed His people. We also are His people, grafted into the promised people.

Verse 11 simply tells us that in this world there are people who are so self-consumed and evil that they could even stoop so low in their ethical and moral choices to curse their fathers, and not seek God's blessings on their mothers. They can, without a moment's hesitation, turn against and away from those who love them the most in this life. They are heartless and hardened and place nothing and no one before themselves. Such people are far from having spiritual eyes and soft, teachable hearts.

Proverbs 30:12-14 continues to tell us that the world contains people who act in an unrighteous manner, motivated by self-seeking and destructible hearts. I suspect the writing is making it clear what is indeed the reality of human flesh, after the fall, as it exists apart from a relationship with God. (We must rejoice because we can have, because of Christ, a relationship with God that gives us a new heart and progress toward living a holy life). Verse 12 tells us there are people in this world who see themselves as pure and right, good and wholesome; but in reality they are blinded to their true filthy, spoiled, sinful nature. Since they are unable to see this, they will not seek to be cleansed. Verse 13 tells us that there are people who are so filled up with themselves, prideful, and aloof, that even their eyes and their countenances reflect this haughtiness. When they look at others, and especially the things of God, they look with disdain and contempt. Verse 14 tells us that there are those whose words and whole expression is toward the goal of harming and further depriving the poor and needy of the world. These are the oppressors and those of injustice that God hates.

I know you are beginning to feel frustrated by not yet finding land for building next year. I am confident that the right thing will emerge. God has provided everything for you and your family so far and I believe He will continue to bless. I am keeping my eyes open and will continue to make inquires. Continue to pray.

Proverbs 30:15 and 16 are interesting and very poetic. The theme is that man (after the fall) seeks to be satisfied by the world and its wisdom and pleasures but these can never truly satisfy and we can never get to the place, with what the world offers, that we say, "I'm filled up and satisfied." The first poetic, symbolic example is the leech which voraciously eats its life away on vegetable and flesh, always seemingly wanting more. "Give, give" suggests the attitude and selfish single-mindedness of the leech to want more to eat. Man is like this, apart from God. Next, man (fallen and with a flesh heart) is compared to three things that are never satisfied: the grave that takes all comers and never has a quota (for the unredeemed this is the end), the woman's womb that cannot conceive and all ovum and sperm are spent and wasted, and land parched by lack of water (water when it comes dries up immediately). Man, apart from being a new creation in Christ, can never find satisfaction. To these three things, the writer adds a fourth, symbolic now of that which will never say "enough." Fire will seem to be satisfied when it consumes what is at hand, but always craves more to consume. We as new creations in Christ can be satisfied only by His Spirit.

Congratulations, Jeremy! Pittsburgh next year for a Sports Medicine Fellowship. It sounds like a great program and a good choice; and it should be a nice city to enjoy for a year. Just the thought of it brings back memories of my childhood.

Proverbs 30:17 is a graphic way of making a basic (but often neglected or forgotten in our society) point. The "eye" for the ancient mind was the term referring to the real inner person–it was the pathway to one's soul. If such a person's deep inner being was mocking his/her father and scorning his/her mother, then that person deserves the worst of all punishments. This is not to say that parents are always right or deserving of esteem and respect, but a heart that hates, sets out to hurt, ridicules, and disrespects is not acceptable to God. We, as parents, should strive to be worthy of a high positive regard by our own children.

Verse 18-19 tells about three amazing things of the world to the writer. It speaks of God's creativeness and the great wonder of all that He has created. The mightiness and the power of the sea; the unique and awesome scientific wonder of the "flying" eagle and "slithering" snake–so different but beyond the ability of human creation or even imagination. The writer states that not only are these amazing to him but they defy his understanding. He adds to that which he doesn't understand the relationship between a man and a woman. This truly is a work of God and reflects His ultimate complexity, love, and blessing.

I miss seeing and holding Annie. I look forward to when you will be around these parts so I can see you two and Annie more often. I am continuing to keep my eyes open for property for you. God has the right place at the right time for you, but we continue to seek and search.

Proverbs 30:20 tells us the way of an "adulteress." The use of adulteress is specific for one who commits adultery and general for one who is unfaithful to what is true, right, honorable, and God ordained. In both cases, the person who is so will deeply indulge, then quickly erase from view any reminder of their transgressions. They deny (lie or rationalize away their guilt) they have done any wrong. They desire to reject the sanity of God's way, yet refuse to accept their guilt and its consequences.

Verses 21-23 point out four things that shake the foundations of the world and show the fallibility of man's (world's) ways. When a servant or maidservant can displace a king or a mistress, there is an error in the system. Such people (although maybe good) are not called, trained, tested, or prepared for the high calling of leadership and position of influence. This is a recipe for disaster. A fool (one who seeks only his own way and rejects God's way) should not be "full." In God's wisdom, the fool will fail–this will in fact be the case in the future, at God's time of judgment. Finally, a person unloved should never be in a binding relationship–marriage. This is cruel and a product of improper self-seeking motives.

It brought such joy to my heart to hear Annie laugh over the phone. I so enjoyed my daughters' laughter at the age Annie is now. Thanks for sharing that moment with me.

Proverbs 30:24-28 gives us wisdom through the example of animal behavior. The animals described are small in comparison to other animals or other aspects of creation. Yet, the observation made by the writer/observer about them powerfully illustrates insight to deep wisdom. Ants are tiny and singularly have little (or no) strength; they seem to be helpless, useless, and easily crushed. Yet we are all familiar with their single-mindedness, resourcefulness, and ability to work in community for a common purpose. Here the writer tells us that a community of such weak insects will store up food during the summer for the rest of the year. We can learn much as to how little strength it takes to accomplish a big task if we are single-minded, resourceful, and willing to work together. Conies (rock badgers that live in Israel) are soft, teddy bear-like animals that seem shy and defenseless. They live in small families and in amongst piles of rocks–they live in the crevices and spaces formed by the rocks. They seek shelter not in their own strength but in the strength of the rocks–they find here protection, food, warmth, and shade. We might do well to look to something greater than ourselves to find our strength, protection, and nourishment. For the believer, God is our refuge and all that we need to live. Locusts have (as far as we know) no social order or identified ruler or king. Yet they can do awesome damage and exhibit great power against nature as they naturally organize themselves and rally around a common goal. There is no "self" involved but only doing what they instinctively do. Man would do better to allow the plan and goal to be that of his Creator God, and then to come together without self-serving motives to accomplish this goal. The power and strength would be incredible. Instead the strength is lost by infighting and self-seeking. Finally a lizard in ancient times was a prized palace pet, sought often by royalty and people of high position. But lizards are not there because of their strength or cunning (they can be caught by a person's hand); they are honored as palace animals because they are chosen by the kings. We must celebrate that we are chosen by the King of Kings not because of our personal value but because that is His wish and choice. How honored we are.

We leave next week for Italy, and you leave soon for Costa Rica. We all need a time away from the demands of our lives, for reflection, refreshment, and intimacy with our spouses. Let's plan to share together our individual experiences so we can savor and give praise to God for His blessings.

Proverbs 30:29-31 describes "stateliness"–the presentation outwardly of an inward confidence, security, and belief in one inherent power. Three of them are from nature–stately because God created them in this way–they claim not any of it by their own abilities, and/or "god-likeness." They are like the lion who securely and confidently retreats from nothing, the rooster whose strut, demeanor, and assertiveness exudes confidence and worthiness, and the ram who asserts himself as he seeks a mate and protects his territory. God created them as they are–He is reflected in their masterpiece; they do not claim (or even consider) that they are such for any other reason.

However, the king surrounds himself with his army, in his position of power and prestige because (he believes) he is good, worthy, humanly superior to others. He musters an army around himself to insure that this position is secure. God (except in notable exceptions, for example David) has not created him in this position and the facts are such due to man's fragile self-glorification efforts. God will not bless this and the stately king will be disgraced, scorned, and dethroned. Our royalty is because of God and His work on our behalf via Christ. Only as we recognize this and attribute to God what is His are we truly stately.

I am so happy you enjoyed your stay in Costa Rica. I knew and later heard your distress, Christine, at leaving Annie and heading for a long flight. It was a good but difficult "first time step." As deeply as we love the children God gives us (for a season–for they are really His), the relationship to our spouses must be prime, second only to our relationship with God Himself. It is good and necessary for us to be together as spouses to experience life and have shared adventures that make memories.

Proverbs 30:32 is an interesting bit of wisdom. It tells us what our response should be when (or if) we realize our part in sin. A "fool" is one who regrets God's desire to be Lord of her life and will not acknowledge Him as creator and sustainer of all life. Fools instead seek to place themselves as lord—to exalt themselves over God, in fact to be God. This is the nature of original sin. Also, if one realizes he is part of the act of permitting evil to prevail and control, and not to oppose and destroy it, then he should be appropriately upset, shamed, and regretful. The act of putting a hand over our mouths conveys this feeling.

Verse 33 tells us that there are certain things that will assuredly occur when enough of the right (or wrong) action takes place. Butter will be produced by vigorous churning and blood will come if a nose is twisted far enough. Likewise as certain is that strife will be produced when anger abounds. Anger either overtly expressed, or pent up inside so that it comes out in subtle yet hostile and "warmly destructive" ways, will cause people to be at odds with each other, misinterpret others' words and actions, or slander, gossip, or malign another. All of this causes strife and destruction.

I can't wait to hold Annie again and marvel at her interim development. I do hope she remembers us, or at least recognizes something about us. It's hard to believe that you two only have a couple more months in residency.

Proverbs 31

Proverbs 31:1-7 is a repetition of a mother's wisdom, as she shared this with her son (soon to be king) Lemuel. He was the result of her earnest prayers for a son (who would be king), her flesh and blood. She realizes for him the great responsibility is to lead others and to rule and govern people. We will not be kings, but we are in an extraordinary position to influence, mold, direct and care for other people. We too have a deep and grave responsibility. We are exhorted not to spend our strength and vitality on meaningless, false, and distracting (even tempting to entice us to sin) things of the world. These things will reduce our effectiveness in our roles and lead others to destructive ends. We cannot afford to be less than fully focused and on task in our duties (example here is the effect on us of craving alcohol) for fear that we would not fully enforce God's law and path to righteousness, or defend the oppressed from those who do them injustice.

The effect of alcohol is useful to those who cannot effect change in their lives or do not have influence on others. Here it provides an escape, a means to endure their poverty, misery, sickness, and oppression.

We, who have been given much and are leaders with life changing influence upon others, must guard our minds, our motives, and our example.

I know this is a very busy time for both of you with the upcoming move and the beginning of a new professional step. It is tough to say goodbye and then to have to prove yourself once again to yet another group of people. I will be praying for both of you as you make these transitions.

Proverbs 31:8 and 9 are further instructions given by a godly mother to her son who would be king. He, as the future king, would be in the highest place (of man) and have the greatest influence and control of those he rules. As a king (or leader) one must strive to think and act as closely to the "ideal King" (Christ the King of Kings) as possible. (See Prov. 16:12.) We have an awesome and weighty responsibility.

These verses encourage the king to defend the rights of the lower rung of society–judging fairly and in defense of the defenseless in our midst. He is to provide for those who are poor and needy, and protect them from oppression and injustice. He is to be their spokesman, to see to their interests and human dignity.

The underlying assumption is that natural man is motivated by self-interests and will gratify his perceived needs at the expense of those who are voiceless in power in the world order. It is a king (leader) called by God and empowered by God (given wisdom, discernment, strength, conviction, and peace) who must allow himself to be His agent of justice, mercy, fairness, honesty, and provision. We all must take up this responsibility.

I'm glad your trip to Pittsburgh was successful (in both your interview, Christine, and the apartment search). I'm still pondering the fact that you both will be in Pittsburgh next year-it seems so

God-orchestrated and ironic that you will be where our roots are (even Jeremy has relatives there!). It will be fun to visit you next year. I've so missed seeing Annie; not a day passes that I don't think about her and pray for her. I look forward to when your family will be back in Illinois, and we can see Annie often.

We now begin the "epilogue" of Proverbs. The rest of this book describes the "wife of noble character." Jeremy, you and I are so fortunate to have such women for our wives. Proverbs 31:10 begins by telling us that such a woman is very hard to find; there are very few women of such character and many men look a lifetime without knowing such a person. To be of "noble character" is to be a person who holds and lives her life by a high set of disciplines, standards, and traits; these elevate her to a level set apart from the vast majority of the world–as royalty is set apart and above. What is the value of such a person to her husband and family? No price tag can be put on her, no worldly treasure can even approximate her worth.

Verse 11 tells us that her husband has full confidence in her–trusts her completely, relies upon her, never needs to doubt or worry about her. She will supplement and augment his worth. She exemplifies to him a higher standard and calling. She lacks nothing that is valuable–she is complete and full. She is not sinless, but (especially because of God's Spirit upon her) she grows daily and is loved progressively more.

I love Easter when it occurs in late spring; it seems so fitting that our Lord's resurrection from the grave occurs in April when new life breaks forth from the dark winter. We will miss being with you on Easter but so look forward to the weekend after that when we celebrate another great event–Annie's first birthday. It doesn't seem possible that one year has passed already–it seems like only last week you were calling me from the hospital with the good news.

Proverbs 31:12 continues the description of this wife of noble character. The trait emphasized here is one of motive that engenders a generalized approach toward her husband. At her depth is the desire to see him enjoy prosperity, success, health, peace, joy, and satisfaction; she truly desires no harm, pain, or distress to overtake him. This motive will form the driving force behind her individual daily acts and decisions and will be present her entire life.

Verse 13 emphasizes her work in producing and obtaining clothing for her family. Obviously, a woman then would make the clothing after carefully selecting the right wool and flax. Again, it was driven by her desire to only benefit and be a blessing to her family. Today such a wife purchases the right clothing for her family and keeps the garments clean and complementary. The verse says she works with "eager" hands, again emphasizing her desire to give of herself with great relish to this important but unheralded task.

Oh how I enjoyed the weekend with the family, and especially with Annie. As she gets older, more social, and develops her own personality, I love my time with her even more. The two of you are doing a great job as parents–this is reflected in her spirit and personality. I really look forward to next summer when you will be around and we can build a more ongoing relationship with your family.

Proverbs 31:14 speaks to me of the necessity for a wife and mother to be resourceful and creative. Here it speaks pragmatically of obtaining exotic food and provisions from a ship coming from distant parts of the world. This woman is not content to provide that which is easy and immediately available to her family. She knows the value of newness, creativeness, excitement, expanded horizons, and continual learning. She is not reluctant to go out of her way to enrich her family. This is intended to be expanded beyond food and meals and is a challenge to the reader to approach many things of daily living with the same creativeness and resourcefulness.

Verse 15 tells of her industriousness and ceaseless energy on behalf of her family. To get up early in those days was required to obtain the best of the produce and provisions that were for sale in town. She, out of love and commitment, self-sacrifices and seeks to get the best for her family. She is not lazy or self-focused. This can be only a discipline for otherwise it would soon fade. It is motivated by eagerness and love for those she serves. Note also, it includes those in her household–her servants. They too look to her as an example and for care.

Things must be winding down for you at the residency and in Spartanburg. I know you both are filled with multiple thoughts and feelings–some at odds with each other. Transitions and change are so difficult. I understand and am praying for you on this. I bet Annie will be walking some by the time we get there to visit this coming weekend. It is so miraculous to see her move along in her development.

Proverbs 31:16 is an appropriate one for us as we consider this land. Here a godly woman (who in those days was in charge of the planting and harvesting of crops) is making a decision to expand her work area by buying a field. She "considers" the purchase, weighing the pros and cons of the decision. Then she purchases that which is "right" out of the funds she has earned and saved. Here we see wise consideration and responsible buying. A godly wife must make sound, wise, well thought-through, responsible decisions; but not to the extent that she (and her family) stays stagnant and unwilling to expand her boundaries (see the prayer of Jabez). She must have the resources and be willing to work hard.

Verse 17 picks up then on how she must act once her boundaries are expanded by careful decision-making. She then doesn't look back but sets forth to work vigorously doing the task assigned to her within the family structure. She is prepared to do the work by having developed her strength and abilities, in order to succeed in her area of responsibility. Down the line, her earning will allow her to expand her influence and presence. We must act similarly in God's kingdom's work.

2003 — FELLOWSHIP

PITTSBURGH, PENNSYLVANIA

Dear Christine and Jeremy,

It has been a big, busy, and trying summer for you and An-nie as you move from a warm, loving community (residency) to more of a "real world" environment. I am utterly confident in your ability to get through it all but I want you to know that I recognize the challenge of the year, and I pray for all four (including the baby growing inside) of you daily. Annie is such a blessing. I so enjoyed being "Grandad" to her while she was recently in Illinois.

Proverbs 31

The rest of our study of Proverbs is a continuation of the writer's description of a "wife of noble character." Although it can describe a human person and certainly sets the mark for our choices and behavior, it also describes the characteristics of Christ's body (the church)–His bride, as He has envisioned it would act. Verse 18 encourages profitable business and transactions in the world, its marketplace, and with others. The interactions are to be of profit to the family, and to God the bridegroom. They are to be conducted with justice and compassion but diligently and without rest or lack of diligence. The time is short and we need to use it wisely and without waste—even working far into the night, or in spiritual terms, into the latter days and hours before the new dawn. Verse 19 is a picture of making cloth from wool and is intended to show the hard work, diligence, and energy of the woman for her appointed task. The church (bride) must be driven also by God's energy and by a deep love of Him, which results in efficient, effective, diligent, productive work.

It seems to be getting around, Christine, that you will be joining the Mahomet group next year. The patients all smile when they talk about it and tell me how wonderful it must be for me to have my daughter coming to work at the same clinic. Of course it is, but I do not presume more than is realistic and appropriate to your needs and entitlement for a professional life of your own.

Proverbs 31:20 and 21 continue the description both of a godly, responsible, competent woman, and the proper functioning of God's bride—we the church. Verse 20 talks about her care of the poor and needy. I feel it should be a proactive goal for all families to reach out and give to those who are less fortunate. I feel this is healthy and places our own prosperity in perspective while teaching generosity and compassion to the children of the family. Although we did this some in our family, I regret we didn't do this as a more "conscious" choice. It takes a parent who has such a heart and prioritizes the family's time and efforts to make this happen. Likewise the church must have the vision and compassion to reach out in a proactive manner to the poor and needy. Verse 21 tells us that the family (especially the woman) must see that proper clothing is available for all when the weather becomes hostile. Not just clothing, but scarlet cloth—indicating a prosperous family able to obtain high quality goods. Not just a mother of funds, but also of choice, priority, and responsibility. Likewise the church offers the royal blood of Christ that protects us from the harshness of the evil world and its destructive elements.

We received two pictures of Annie today. One of them has become my absolute favorite. It touches me and moves me to a spiritual level— honoring and thanking God for His creation and our granddaughter.

Proverbs 31:22 and 23 carry on the dual message of this section. Humanly it depicts the woman creating a home and a personal presence of honor, pride, security, and blessedness. "Coverings for the bed" and "dressed in linen and purple" depict an exalted, regal, honored, and high station in life. The husband is about the affairs of the world and is recognized as one of great wisdom, high judgment, honor, and power. Such roles and station in real life can only come as the couple dwell with and know intimately the true King and Creator–it can only happen (to whatever extent) as a result of a deepening spiritual walk. Looking deeper, we once again see Christ and His bride (the church). Christ now, and forever, will govern the world (along with the saints) in heaven (Isa. 53:13); He will be honored as great and govern with truth, justice, and authority. His bride the church will be seen as royal (bride of the King) and deeply blessed and secure, as she exists and thrives because of Christ, the bridegroom. This depicts the high and exalted status of Jesus and His church, now and forever. We are a "royal priesthood, sons and daughters of the King."

Although I love hearing about Annie and her developmental steps, it makes me grieve that I can't be there. I look forward to being a more present part of her life next year.

Proverbs 31:24-25 continues to allegorically describe Christ's body/His church. It also encourages high character traits for the wife and mother of a home. Verse 24 is interesting: linen is a cloth that symbolizes purity and dedication to a cause. Christ and His church are the source of true purity and strength of purpose and are the dispensers of this to the world. It is our job to provide to the world the means (belief in Christ as our personal Savior) to achieve purity and empowerment. The "sash" represents strength and power; here again Christ via His church provides this to the people of the world (merchants). Verse 25 tells us that the body of Christ is covered with His strength and dignity (self-respect and humble high regard for its station in the world) because He gives it such (out of His storehouse) when it seeks Him. The church can look with clarity to the future (revealed in the Scripture) and not be overwhelmed and distressed by it; it will be saved from its cutting edge and be blessed indeed.

This was the verse I used in my comments at my mother's funeral.

I hope your fall has been a good one in Pittsburgh. I bet you, Jeremy, have been very busy with the fall sports season. I miss Annie and wonder about her development and personality changes. I pray every day for all of you, including the new baby boy! It is hard for me to conceive of a baby boy in the family—I've come to associate babies and children only with females. I look forward to an opportunity to change this perspective.

Proverbs 31:26 tells us that the ideal wife/mother (and spiritually, Christ's church) should speak with wisdom and instruction. Wisdom is knowledge applied to life; it is truth derived from attuning oneself with God's perspective. Instruction is both by verbal disclosure and, more importantly, by example of one living a life pleasing to and productive for God. The church has the responsibility of giving its members, and the world in general, this wisdom and instruction. True wisdom only comes by means of God's Spirit that indwells us as we seek Him, love Him, and dwell with Him (Ps. 91). The women must (as must His church) seek Him in His Word, in prayer, and in experience.

Verse 27 encourages diligence, industry, and productiveness. The time is short and the windows of opportunity shut only after a brief time of being open. The family must be benefited by such a woman, and the kingdom of God by such a church. Matthew 16:19 relates how Jesus gave His true church the "key to the kingdom of heaven"—the delegated authority to see to His affairs here on earth in His absence. We dare not do this without fear and diligence or in any degree of idleness.

Soon you will be back to Illinois for Thanksgiving. I'm anxious to see you all and to be "Grandad" to Annie. It has been so rainy here the last four to five days. It needs to stop so your road can be created and your site cleared. I was so impressed again by how beautiful the home site is, overlooking the pond and surrounded by such beautiful trees.

Proverbs 31:28 tells of how both the husband and children of a woman of God recognize her godliness, righteousness, worthiness, and honorable character. She has won this esteem by her choices, actions, priorities, commitments, selflessness, and speech. She is a witness to her children and the pride of her husband. Likewise, the church is the pride of Christ and will act (if it allows Him to be the head) in such a way that future generations will see an example of godliness and righteousness. Despite the challenges to her, the church will persevere and proclaim truth. It will pour out compassion on the world and be viewed as "blessed."

Verse 29 compares this woman to other women, and concludes that she surpasses all others. Certainly the woman empowered and led by God will act differently and exhibit (continuously over time) superior, supernatural, godly qualities compared to the character and values of the worldly women. Likewise, the church of God will stand apart as an instrument of truth, caring, strength, and confident dependency. Comparing it to human, secular institutions, it will stand out and will attract the people of the world.

Well, here it is, the last letter in my writing on Proverbs. I would never have thought it would be eleven and a half years in the making (excluding summers and holidays). It has been a joy and a privilege to write you on the wisdom of God as presented in this unique and awesome part of Scripture. My one request is that you also instill this wisdom in your children as you relate to them over the years ahead. I will be a part of that process to the extent you desire and as God makes available.

Proverbs 31:30 is a beautiful verse. It tells us that true beauty in a woman (or a man for that matter) is not on the surface as the world tells us, or in human social charm as society defines it. Beauty is really in the "fearing" of the Lord. This brings us back to the beginning of our study eleven plus years ago. A woman who loves God and whose heart-throb is to know Him more deeply and to serve Him more fully is the ultimate blessing to her husband and children. She is to be praised and highly honored. Likewise, the church is to fear God—seek Him and depend on Him. Only in that is the church truly a thing of beauty and worthy of praise.

Verse 31 tells us to shout our praise for such a woman to the entire world–to acknowledge her godliness, honor her walk with God, and speak of her deep spiritual beauty. Do it at the "city gates"–the place that is public and official. Such a woman is rare and highly sought after. Christ, the bridegroom of the church, publicly proclaims her at the gates of heaven, at the right hand of the Father–continually and with His highest praise and honor.

I am planning to continue to write to you both if you so wish. I would like to continue looking at God's wisdom for living but turn to the New Testament. Let's look at Jesus' teaching on the subject through the Sermon on the Mount in Matthew. I will continue to move through Proverbs with your sisters.

Printed in the United States
201297BV00001B/19-108/A